CROSS-CULTURAL INTERPERSONAL COMMUNICATION

INTERNATIONAL AND INTERCULTURAL COMMUNICATION ANNUAL

Volume XV   **1991**

Editor
Stella Ting-Toomey
California State University, Fullerton

Coeditor	**Editorial Assistant**
Felipe Korzenny	Jon Bruschke
San Francisco State University	*University of Utah*

Consulting Editors for Volume XV

Michael Argyle	Young Yun Kim
University of Oxford, England	*University of Oklahoma*
Stephen Banks	Kwok Leung
University of Idaho	*Chinese University of Hong Kong, Hong Kong*
Mary Jane Collier	Tsukasa Nishida
Oregon State University	*Nihon University, Japan*
Steve Duck	Barnett Pearce
University of Iowa	*University of Massachusetts*
Howard Giles	Harry Triandis
University of California, Santa Barbara	*University of Illinois*
William Gudykunst	Alan Sillars
California State University, Fullerton	*University of Montana*
Geert Hofstede	John Wiemann
State University of Limburg, the Netherlands	*University of California, Santa Barbara*
C. Harry Hui	Richard Wiseman
University of Hong Kong, Hong Kong	*California State University, Fullerton*
Tamar Katriel	Myong Jin Won-Doornink
University of Haifa, Israel	*Washington State University*
	June Ock Yum
	Towson State University

INTERNATIONAL AND INTERCULTURAL COMMUNICATION ANNUAL
VOLUME XV   1991

CROSS-CULTURAL INTERPERSONAL COMMUNICATION

edited by

Stella TING·TOOMEY
Felipe KORZENNY

Published in Cooperation with
the Speech Communication Association
International and Intercultural Communication Division

SAGE PUBLICATIONS
The International Professional Publishers
Newbury Park   London   New Delhi

For information address:

 SAGE Publications, Inc.
2455 Teller Road
Newbury Park, California 91320

SAGE Publications Ltd.
6 Bonhill Street
London EC2A 4PU
United Kingdom

SAGE Publications India Pvt. Ltd.
M-32 Market
Greater Kailash I
New Delhi 110 048 India

Printed in the United States of America

Library of Congress Cataloging-in-Publication Data

ISBN 0-8039-4047-5
ISBN 0-8039-4048-3 (pbk)
ISSN 86-640884

FIRST PRINTING, 1991

Sage Production Editor: Astrid Virding

Contents

PART II: INTERCULTURAL-INTERPERSONAL COMMUNICATION

Preface

This is the fifteenth volume of the International and Intercultural Communication Annual. This series is sponsored by the Speech Communication Association's International and Intercultural Communication Division. The series presents theme-based publications that aim at promoting better understanding of the international and intercultural communication processes. The guiding principle in preparing for this volume was to bring together current theoretical and research studies that compare interpersonal communication across cultures. This volume includes both refereed chapters and invited chapters.

The volume is divided into two sections. Part I presents recent conceptualizations and research findings in comparative, cross-cultural interpersonal communication. Topics include interpersonal morality, Chinese interpersonal relationships, family nicknaming practices, acquaintance relationships, romantic relationships, self-disclosure reciprocity, conflict competence, evolution of intimacy, and translation-context dialectics. Part II emphasizes the different facets of the intercultural-interpersonal relationship development process. Major themes include the intercultural information-seeking process, cultural similarity versus attitudinal similarity, language and intercultural attraction, mutuality of involvement, and intercultural communication competence. This volume reflects the diverse conceptual perspectives and multiple methodological orientations in the study of cross-cultural interpersonal communication.

Many individuals contributed to the fruition of this book. First, I would like to extend my special appreciation to all the authors who donated their time and energy to this volume. Without their labor and creative ideas, this volume would not exist. Second, I would like to give special thanks to: Felipe Korzenny, my coeditor, for his continued support, hard work, and cheerful dedication throughout the editing of this volume; Jon Bruschke, my editorial assistant, for spending countless hours assisting on many "tedious" yet important editorial tasks; and to all the editorial board members for generously offering their time and expert service in reviewing the submitted manuscripts. Third, I would like to thank my colleagues in the Department of Speech Communication, California State University, Fullerton, for providing a pleasant, supportive environment in which to conduct my scholarly work.

Finally, I would like to express my special gratitude to Bill Gudykunst, Young Kim, and Richard Wiseman for their constant encouragement and professional "giving" throughout every phase of editing this volume. I would also like to acknowledge the continued support of Sara Miller McCune, Ann West, Marie Penchoen, and the staff of Sage Publications for their expert editorial help and advice on the volume. Last but not least, I want to thank my two special family members here—Charles and Adrian—for serving as continuous reminders of the pleasures of the "interpersonal aspects" of this book.

Stella Ting-Toomey
Fullerton, California

1

Cross-Cultural Interpersonal Communication
An Introduction

STELLA TING-TOOMEY ● *California State University, Fullerton*

The theme of the volume, "cross-cultural interpersonal communication," can be broadly defined as the comparative study of differences and similarities of relational communication patterns between two or more cultural communities. Although many excellent volumes have been compiled in intercultural communication and interpersonal communication (see, for example, Asante & Gudykunst, 1989; Duck, Hay, Hobfoll, Iches, & Montgomery, 1988; Kim & Gudykunst, 1988; Roloff & Miller, 1987) in recent years, this volume brings multiple theoretical and methodological orientations to the study of cross-cultural interpersonal communication.

This volume is meant to reflect the current conceptualizations and recent research findings in the area of interpersonal communication across cultures. The book is divided into two sections. Part I comprises nine chapters and addresses comparative, cross-cultural interpersonal communication issues. Part II includes four chapters and addresses intercultural-interpersonal communication issues. Whereas Part I emphasizes the encounter process between two culturally similar individuals within one culture in comparison with the interpersonal encounter process in another culture, Part II focuses on the analysis of the intercultural-interpersonal encounter process between two culturally dissimilar individuals who are interpersonally linked in a relationship.

Overall, five content themes can be identified in the volume. First, while some of the studies in this book uncover major differences in cross-cultural interpersonal relationship patterns, other studies reveal major similarities in relationship patterns across cultures. In particular, although salient, cultural differences are found in initial intercultural relationship stages, these differences are often diluted by interindividual and relational factors in the more established, intercultural relationship maintenance stages. Second, many authors acknowledge the importance of the influence of particular relationship stage or relation-ship type (e.g., acquaintance, friendship, or romantic relationship) and its impact on other communication variables such as relational open-ness, relational involvement, conflict competence, communication competence, language usage, attitudinal similarity, and cultural simi-larity. Third, almost all the authors acknowledge the complexity of con-ducting cross-cultural interpersonal communication research. Fourth, several authors emphasize the importance of examining the situational context in framing the intercultural-interpersonal communication pro-cess. Finally, all data-based studies provide results that support the interplay between the context of discovery and the context of verifica-tion (Kaplan, 1964). In the context of discovery, new interpersonal communication constructs and insights are introduced, and in the con-text of verification, findings are claimed to be compatible with previous studies in the intercultural-interpersonal relationship domain (for a review, see Gudykunst & Ting-Toomey, 1988).

THE STUDIES

The first three chapters provide a broad context for this book. Spe-cifically, Chapters 2, 3, and 4 address fundamental philosophical/theo-retical questions concerning context, personhood, and interpersonal communication across cultures. Chapters 5, 6, and 7 compare and contrast differences and similarities in acquaintanceship, friendship, and romantic relationships' interactions. Chapters 8, 9, and 10 provide different approaches (an ethnic cultural approach, a historical approach, and a theoretic-method approach) to the study of culture and interper-sonal communication. Chapters 11, 12, and 13 explore the critical motifs and themes that influence intercultural-interpersonal relation-ship development processes. Finally, Chapter 14, on intercultural com-munication competence, provides a fitting conclusion to this volume by probing the metatheoretical assumptions of the nature of communica-tion competence.

The chapters in Part 1 cover a wide range of cross-cultural interper-sonal communication topics. More specifically, Miller (Chapter 2) challenges the contemporary, Western perspective on the study of inter-personal morality. She argues that the study of interpersonal morality is grounded primarily upon Western philosophical/psychological mod-els. She advocates that the study of interpersonal morality should be grounded in the philosophical and psychological premises of the particular culture. Along a similar line of argument, Chang and Holt (Chapter 3) introduce the importance of the influence of Buddhism on interpersonal relationship development in the Chinese culture. They point out that, while the Western model of interpersonal communication relies heavily on the concepts of interpersonal control and "strategizing," the Eastern model of interpersonal communication places a heavy emphasis on the relational context in which the relationship originates. Blum-Kulka and Katriel (Chapter 4) examine nicknaming practices in Israeli and Jewish-American families. Based on audiotaped and videotaped dinner-table conversations and interviews, they theorize that nicknaming practices serve a variety of communication functions within these families across cultures.

Sanders, Wiseman, and Matz (Chapter 5) analyze uncertainty reduction in acquaintance interaction in Ghana and the United States. Results reveal both similarities and differences in uncertainty reduction communication patterns. While the findings support a cultural-general motive for uncertainty reduction in these two cultures, the communication modes in reducing uncertainty in these two cultures differ. Gao (Chapter 6) studies romantic relationship development in China and the United States. Based on dyadic interview data, dimensions of relational openness, involvement, shared nonverbal meanings, and relationship assessment emerge as critical themes that characterize stable romantic relationship interaction in both cultures. Won-Doornink (Chapter 7) conducts a replication study on self-disclosure reciprocity in male dyads in South Korea and the United States. Results indicate more cross-cultural similarities than differences in self-disclosure reciprocity at three interpersonal relationship stages.

Collier (Chapter 8) explores conflict competence in three ethnic groups in the United States. Her findings reveal that Anglo American respondents emphasize freedom in expressing conflict ideas, African Americans emphasize a problem-solving orientation in conflict, and Mexican Americans stress the importance of relational support in close friendship conflict. From a macro-evolutionary perspective, Adamopoulos (Chapter 9) argues that the analysis of interpersonal intimacy should be placed in both cross-cultural and historical contexts. He proposes a resource-exchange model with universal dimensions of exchange mode, interpersonal orientation, and resource type. Historical changes in the experience of intimacy are considered in the context of this framework. Moving beyond these data-based studies, Banks and Banks (Chapter 10) discuss the critical issues of translation in cross-cultural interpersonal communication research. They argue that translation poses a potential threat to the reliability and validity of the cross-cultural data interpretation process. They propose a conceptual scheme that emphasizes the importance of the relationship between translation and context in conducting cross-cultural communication work.

Part II comprises three data-based studies and one theoretical chapter on intercultural-interpersonal relationship development. Lee and Boster (Chapter 11) investigate the information-seeking process for initial uncertainty reduction in both intracultural and intercultural encounters. Their results show that social penetration is more difficult in intercultural initial interactions than intracultural initial interactions. In addition, the anticipation of future interaction is found to create no impact on information-seeking behavior in the initial interaction stage. In testing for language effect in intercultural attraction process, results in Kim's study (Chapter 12) reveal that, while a native person's perception of a nonnative partner's host language competence is related positively to the attraction process, the nonnative partner's perception of the native person's speech accommodation is not related to the attraction process. In addition, attitudinal similarity rather than cultural similarity emerges as the prime predictor of the intercultural attraction process.

From the interpretive theme analysis perspective, Gudykunst, Gao, Sudweeks, Ting-Toomey, and Nishida (Chapter 13) uncover the dimensions of relational typicality, communication competence, similarity, and relational involvement as the pancultural factors that influence Japanese-U.S. dyadic relationship development. The presence, form, and interconnection among the themes and subthemes in intercultural acquaintanceship, friendship, and romantic relationship are systematically assessed and discussed. Finally, Kim (Chapter 14) proposes that a systems-theoretic view should be used as the metatheoretic framework that guides the conceptual development of intercultural communication competence research. More specifically, intercultural communication competence is viewed as the overall internal capability of an individual to manage the key challenging features of intercultural communication, namely, cultural differences and unfamiliarity, intergroup posture, and the accompanying degree of stress. The macroholistic systems framework provides a fitting ending and, simultaneously, a beginning for further conceptualizing and reflecting about the intercultural-interpersonal communication process.

FUTURE DIRECTIONS

The chapters in this volume, as a whole, provide a sounding board for further theorizing and research in the area of cross-cultural interpersonal communication. Multiple theoretical perspectives, such as an interpretive theme perspective, cultural identity perspective, uncertainty reduction perspective, resource-exchange perspective, social penetration perspective, systems-theoretic perspective, and philosophical/religious perspective, are presented in this volume. In addition, diverse methodological approaches such as the participant observation method, ethnographic interview method, naturalistic and laboratory interaction methods, and survey method are used by various researchers in different studies. While some progress has been made in the area of cross-cultural interpersonal communication research, much more rigorous conceptualizations of interpersonal communication constructs in both cross-cultural and intercultural relationship domains need to be pursued.

The remainder of this chapter will highlight three directions for future research in the area of intercultural-interpersonal relationship development. The first direction concerns the study of the dynamics of change in intercultural-interpersonal relationship development process. While most work in this volume focuses on the initial and sustained interpersonal relationship stages, more work needs to be carried out in the maintenance, oscillation, and deescalation phases of intercultural relationship developmental process. While several authors have examined communication patterns in different interpersonal relationship types, the dynamics of change, especially in the intercultural-interpersonal relationship formation process, need to be closely scrutinized and described. Basic questions that can be addressed by researchers interested in examining the intercultural-interpersonal relationship transformation process may include the following: What are the conditions that propel the intercultural-interpersonal relationship to move forward, to stabilize (positively or negatively), or to regress and deescalate? What are the critical turning points that move the relationship from the intercultural-intergroup level to the interindividual-interpersonal level? How do changes in cultural and individual identity affect changes in relationship identity, and vice versa? How do members in different cultures resolve relational paradoxes and dilemmas in different relationship development stages?

As a side observation, while recent trends in interpersonal communication research have placed a heavy emphasis on the dialectical nature of interpersonal relationship development (see, for example, Baxter, 1990; Cissna, Cox, & Bochner, 1990), intercultural-interpersonal researchers may do well to pay close attention to the philosophical and religious roots of a culture in the framing of the "dialectics" concept. For example, the different philosophical assumptions in the East and the West may cause the East to view the dialectical pairs (such as autonomy-connection, openness-closedness, and predictability-novelty; Baxter, 1990) in interpersonal relationship development in complementary, harmonious terms, while the Western perspective may tend to view these dialectical pairs as contradictory, tension-filled, polar opposites. Thus the different interpretations of interpersonal dialectics may profoundly influence the movements of the intercultural-interpersonal relationship development process.

The second direction of research is concerned with the "relational" unit of analysis in conducting intercultural-interpersonal communication research. While several authors in this volume have begun to examine intercultural-interpersonal relationship development from a "relational" unit of analysis, more concerted effort is needed in adopting a relational viewpoint of analysis in understanding the intercultural-interpersonal relationship development process. The study of "interpersonal" communication is, at the baseline level, relational and dyadic in nature. While divergent stories and accounts may be obtained from the relational "couple," the different images and representations, nevertheless, represent the multiple "truths" of the relational history of the couple. In addition, more attention needs to be devoted to different spheres of the intercultural-interpersonal relationship development process such as the bicultural family socialization process, intercultural-interfaith marriage, intergenerational family interaction, multicultural social networks, children's friendship development, and elderly communication in different cultures.

Finally, I would like to reemphasize the importance of using a "process" approach to the study of intercultural-interpersonal relationship development. In particular, more longitudinal work needs to be done in the areas of (a) affective expressions of relational emotions at different relationship stages in different cultures; (b) the nonverbal rhythms and pacing of intercultural-interpersonal relationship development; (c) the use of metaphors, allusions, and everyday talk (Duck, 1990) in conceptualizing one's core versus secondary interpersonal relationships; (d) the boundary conditions that individuals create for different types of interpersonal relationship and the different communication activities that accompany such relationships in different cultures; and (e) the meanings and functions of situational context on the interpersonal relationship development process (Ting-Toomey, 1989a, 1989b, in press).

In sum, cross-cultural interpersonal communication research is a wide-open field with many promising directions for interpersonal communication researchers. On the conceptual level, the scope conditions of the theory are tested when one conducts cross-cultural interpersonal communication research. In addition, new concepts that cut across ethnocentric cultural biases may be uncovered. Finally, because most of the interpersonal communication theory-development concepts originate largely from individualistic, Western cultures, it is inevitable that terms that have been widely tested in the field reflect a Western-based ideology of intimacy. Concepts such as "relational intuition," "relational comfortableness," "relational acceptance," and "relational letting go" are much more difficult to conceptualize and measure and sound much too ambiguous and "soft" for rigorous scientific testing. This orientation, however, should not undercut the importance of studying such "fuzzy and ambiguous" concepts, as these concepts are deemed to play an important role in collectivistic, Eastern cultures (Ting-Toomey, 1989a). Methodologically, greater collaboration among researchers from multiple cultures, utilizing multiple methods, along a longitudinal time frame, and studying intercultural relationship dyads will definitely help to enhance the theory-development phase of explaining and interpreting the complexity and the richness of the evolutionary process of interpersonal relationship development across cultures.

If this volume stimulates more theoretical depth and rigor in the conceptualization of intercultural-interpersonal relationship development process in the next few years, it will have fulfilled its basic purpose.

REFERENCES

Asante, M., & Gudykunst, W. (Eds.). (1989). *Handbook of international and intercultural communication*. Newbury Park, CA: Sage.

Baxter, L. (1990). Dialectical contradictions in relationship development. *Journal of Social and Personal Relationships, 7*, 69-88.

Cissna, K., Cox, D., & Bochner, A. (1990). The dialectic of marital and parental relationships within the stepfamily. *Communication Monographs, 57*, 44-61.

Duck, S. (1990). Relationships as unfinished business: Out of the frying pan and into the 1990s. *Journal of Social and Personal Relationships, 7*, 5-28.

Duck, S., Hay, D., Hobfoll, S., Iches, W., & Montgomery, B. (Eds.). (1988). *Handbook of personal relationships*. London: John Wiley.

Gudykunst, W., & Ting-Toomey, S. (1988). *Culture and interpersonal communication*. Newbury Park, CA: Sage.

Kaplan, A. (1964). *The conduct of inquiry*. San Francisco: Chandler.

Kim, Y., & Gudykunst, W. (Eds.). (1988). *Theories in intercultural communication*. Newbury Park, CA: Sage.

Roloff, M., & Miller, G. (Eds.). (1987). *Interpersonal processes: New directions in communication research*. Newbury Park, CA: Sage.

Ting-Toomey, S. (1989a). Culture and interpersonal relationship development: Some conceptual issues. In J. Anderson (Ed.), *Communication yearbook 12* (pp. 371-382). Newbury Park, CA: Sage.

Ting-Toomey, S. (1989b). Identity and interpersonal bonding. In M. Asante & W. Gudykunst (Eds.), *Handbook of international and intercultural communication.* Newbury Park, CA: Sage.

Ting-Toomey, S. (in press). *Intercultural communication process: Patterns and variations.* New York: Guilford.

I

CROSS-CULTURAL INTERPERSONAL COMMUNICATION

2

A Cultural Perspective on the Morality of Beneficence and Interpersonal Responsibility

JOAN G. MILLER • *Yale University*

This chapter offers a cultural reinterpretation of claims that beneficence and interpersonal responsibility represent discretionary rather than fully moral obligations. The dominant philosophical and psychological approaches to morality, it is shown, accord beneficence and interpersonal responsibility discretionary moral status because of problems in limiting the scope of such obligations and/or because of the particularistic nature of such issues. Cross-cultural evidence is presented challenging this view and documenting that the moral status of beneficence and interpersonal responsibility is culturally grounded.

Psychological theories of morality (e.g., Gilligan, 1982; Kohlberg, 1981) have traditionally assumed that a sharp asymmetry exists between obligations that involve rights-based justice and those that involve beneficence or interpersonal responsibility. The term *interpersonal responsibility* is employed here to refer to expectations to meet another's wants or needs that are based, at least in part, on the agent's role relationship to the other. Interpersonal responsibility differs from beneficence in that beneficence is non-role based in character.

Obligations involving rights-based justice have generally been viewed in fully moral terms. In contrast, obligations involving beneficence or interpersonal responsibility have tended to be seen as discretionary in character. This dichotomy is assumed to derive from difference in the respective status of these obligations as negative versus positive injunctions or from their role-based and affective nature.

This chapter critically examines the basis for this distinction between justice as contrasted with beneficence and interpersonal responsibility. It is maintained that the distinction cannot be defended on purely logical grounds and cannot be assumed to be universal. Rather, it is argued that the sharp asymmetry between the prohibition-oriented morality of justice and the positive morality of beneficence and interpersonal responsibility is grounded, in large part, in certain individualistic premises specific to Western culture and is not present in cultures maintaining more relational cultural conceptions of the person.

The chapter is organized into three sections. The first section focuses on the philosophical arguments for distinguishing between justice as contrasted with beneficence and interpersonal responsibility as fully moral versus discretionary obligations and on ways these philosophical arguments are reflected in current psychological theory and research. Second, some cross-cultural research that challenges the universality of these distinctions is described and a cultural reinterpretation offered of the moral distinctions drawn between justice versus beneficence and interpersonal responsibility. Finally, implications of this reinterpretation for various philosophical and psychological theories of morality are considered.

CLAIMS REGARDING THE MORAL STATUS OF BENEFICENCE AND INTERPERSONAL RESPONSIBILITY

Philosophical Perspectives

Most Western philosophers define morality formally in terms of criteria such as impartiality, universality, priority, and legitimacy of social regulation (Gewirth, 1978; Kant, 1788/1949, 1797/1964; Rawls, 1971). As Gewirth (1978, p. 1) describes it:

> A morality is a set of categorically obligatory requirements for action that are addressed at least in part to every actual or prospective agent, and that are concerned with furthering the interests, especially the most important interests, of persons or recipients other than or in addition to the agent or the speaker. The requirements are categorically obligatory in that compliance with them is mandatory for the conduct of every person to whom they are addressed regardless of whether he [she] wants to accept them or their results, and regardless also of the requirements of any other institutions, such as law or etiquette, whose obligatoriness may itself be doubtful or variable. Thus, although one moral requirement may be overridden by another, it may not be overridden by any non-moral requirement, nor can its normative bindingness be escaped by shifting one's inclinations, opinions, or ideals.

In this view, moral rules are viewed as impartial in that they are based on more than just the personal preferences of individuals or groups. They are also regarded as universalizable or as applying to all other similar agents in similar circumstances. In addition, moral concerns are considered to take precedence over nonmoral concerns. Finally, moral rules are seen as public standards, legitimately subject to social enforcement. As Mill (1951, p. 60) argues: "It is part of the notion of Duty in every one of its forms, that a person may rightfully be compelled to fulfill it. Duty is a thing which may be *exacted* from a person, as one exacts a debt. Unless we think it may be exacted from him, we do not call it his duty."

Arguments tend to be made that, unlike justice obligations, beneficence obligations fail to satisfy all of the above definitional criteria distinctive of morality (Gert, 1988; Kant, 1797/1964; Urmson, 1958). These arguments are based on the differential success agents can expect to have in meeting each type of expectation. In particular, as negative injunctions, justice expectations are nontaxing to meet and bounded in scope. To fulfill a justice expectation merely requires refraining from particular types of actions. Justice expectations then can be met even if they are general in form (e.g., "do not harm others"). In contrast, to fulfill beneficence expectations always requires some form of positive action. This means that such expectations are inherently taxing to fulfill and that problems may arise in fully meeting them. For example, an agent who attempted to fulfill a general beneficence expectation (e.g., "help others") would quickly find that all of his or her resources were directed toward others and that he or she had no resources left to devote to his or her own needs.

Making the assumption that such extreme self-sacrifice is not a requirement of beneficence, philosophers have conceptualized the beneficence obligation in conditional terms—for example, as "the duty to help another when he is in need or jeopardy, provided that one can do so without excessive risk or loss to oneself" (Rawls, 1971, p. 114; see also Sidgwick, 1874/1962). Still, however, difficulties remain in fulfilling beneficence obligations completely. As Gert (1988) notes, an agent expected to help all needy others whom he or she could help without great sacrifice would find him- or herself unable to relax, in that there would always be some needy others whom he or she could be helping. It is also argued that it is difficult to identify when a given beneficence obligation has been fulfilled, because there are a wide range of positive acts that can be seen as fulfilling it.

Because of these problems associated with fulfilling beneficence obligations, theorists have concluded that beneficence needs to be relegated to a moral realm qualitatively distinct from that of justice. Specifically, beneficence has come to be considered as a superogatory obligation. As such, it is assumed to differ from justice in two key respects: First, beneficence is regarded as a sphere for personal decision making and not as legitimately sanctionable. This makes it possible to avoid the situation in which an agent is held accountable for meeting an expectation that he or she is unable to realize completely. Instead, compliance with beneficence expectations is considered discretionary—that is, violation of a beneficence obligation represents a nonsanctionable lack of virtue rather than a sanctionable vice. Second, beneficence is viewed as having lesser priority than justice. This ranking then reflects the status of the two types of obligations as "perfect" duties, which can be met in all nonconflictual cases, versus "imperfect" duties, which represent general guides to action that cannot be met in all such cases (Kant, 1797/1964).

It should be noted that role-based beneficence or interpersonal responsibility, such as that found in friendship, has also been assumed to differ from justice in similar ways. Blum (1980), for example, argues that the altruistic expectations entailed in friendship are characterized by a distinct type of morality that differs from the morality of justice. In particular, it is maintained that friendship is based on an agent's affective commitment to another individual. It is assumed that the expectations in friendship are not subject to social regulation in that they depend on the particular relationship involved rather than on abstract rules. Although this view places greater weight on emotional factors than does that of Kant, it, nonetheless, retains the Kantian premise that justice considerations are paramount and take precedence over friendship and other interpersonal commitments in cases of conflict.

In sum, work in Western philosophy has tended to relegate beneficence expectations and interpersonal responsibility to moral domains distinct from and subordinate to those of justice. The rationale for this classification differs somewhat in the two cases, with consideration of the difficulty of fulfilling them fully emphasized in the case of beneficence and with consideration of their root in affectively based relationships emphasized in the case of friendship expectations and other interpersonal responsibilities. In both cases, however, the claim is made that beneficence and interpersonal responsibility differ from justice in at least three key respects. In particular, beneficence expectations and interpersonal responsibilities (a) are assumed not to be legitimately subject to social regulation, (b) are assumed to be of lesser priority than justice obligations, and (c) are assumed to be more conditional in form than justice obligations, applying only to the extent that they do not impose a great hardship or sacrifice on the agent.

Psychological Perspectives

Major psychological theories of moral reasoning have tended to make the same types of assumptions about the moral status of beneficence and interpersonal responsibility as made in the philosophical views discussed. In particular, theorists such as Kohlberg (1981), Eisenberg (1986), Nunner-Winkler (1984), and others have tended to adopt the first position, viewing beneficence as a superogatory moral requirement. In contrast, Gilligan (1977, 1982) has tended to adopt the second position, emphasizing the affective nature of interpersonal responsibilities.

Beneficence as superogatory. Perhaps the dominant psychological view of beneficence portrays it as superogatory (Eisenberg, 1986; Higgins, Power, & Kohlberg, 1984; Kohlberg, Levine, & Hewer, 1983; Nunner-Winkler, 1984). It is assumed that beneficent actions are morally virtuous but beyond the realm of moral duty. This categorization of beneficence tends to be justified on the basis of the first philosophical position discussed—that is, on the basis of the inherent differences between duties of omission as compared with duties of commission.

In the Kohlbergian framework, for example, only matters involving justice and individual rights are seen as possessing all the characteristics of the moral (Higgins et al., 1984; Kohlberg et al., 1983). Although regarded as virtuous, helping another in distress is not considered a requirement of morality. The only exception to this view of beneficence appears in Kohlberg's description of the Heinz dilemma, in which it is argued that Heinz has a positive duty to steal drugs to save his wife's life. It should be noted, however, that Kohlberg justifies this duty in terms of individual rights—that is, the duty to protect the wife's right to life—and not in terms of beneficence per se.

Other psychological theorists have maintained that, even in such life and death situations, beneficence cannot be considered a moral duty. Nunner-Winkler (1984, p. 354), for example, raises concerns about scope in challenging the Kohlbergian position:

A universally accorded right to life implies the universal duty to save "all men whose lives can be saved regardless of personal ties," even if that would require violation of property rights. Thus we all are not only required to give away all the money we own but also justified—in fact, maybe even obligated—to rob all banks as well as all members of our society who own more than they need to feed themselves so as to be able to save the starving children in the third world, whose sad fate is well known to all of us.

Empirical research in this tradition has tended either not to focus on the question of the superogatory character of beneficence or to be limited to Western populations. For example, one of the most innovative programs of work on this topic has been conducted by Eisenberg and her colleagues in their investigations of prosocial moral dilemmas— that is, dilemmas in which "the individual must choose between satisfying his or her wants or needs and those of others in a context in which the role of laws, punishment, authorities, formal obligations, and other external prohibitions is irrelevant or de-emphasized" (Eisenberg, 1982, p. 230).

Among its contributions, this program of research has identified stages of prosocial moral reasoning that parallel those of justice reasoning (Eisenberg, 1982, 1986; Eisenberg-Berg, 1979). However, possibly because it is assumed that the dilemmas under consideration are superogatory, no data have been collected regarding whether subjects conceptualize them in discretionary as contrasted with mandatory terms. Smetana, Bridgeman, and Turiel's (1983) research, in contrast, does provide some empirical support for claims that beneficence is considered a discretionary obligation. It is shown that older children tend to maintain that helping issues should not be subject to social regulation. Limited to American subjects, this research, however, provides no information concerning the cross-cultural status of beneficence.

Interpersonal responsibility as a distinct form of morality. The argument that a distinct form of morality applies to interpersonal responsibility has been articulated most forcefully by Gilligan (1977, 1982) and her colleagues. In a position similar to that of Blum (1980), Gilligan describes some of the unique features of the morality of caring that differentiate it from the morality of justice. It is argued that the morality of caring has its roots in affectively based interpersonal commitments and is contextual rather than rule based in character.

In this view, interpersonal responsibility tends to be portrayed as discretionary. Such a perspective is evidenced, for example, in the following description of responsibility offered by an 11-year-old girl:

> If you have a responsibility with somebody else, then you should keep it to a certain extent, but to the extent that it is really going to hurt you or stop you from doing something that you really, really want, then I think maybe you should put yourself first. But if it is your responsibility to somebody really close to you, you've just got to decide in that situation which is more important, yourself or that person, and like I said, it really depends on what kind of person you are and how you feel about the other person or persons involved. (Gilligan, 1982, pp. 35-36)

As may be seen in this response, caring for another is treated as a personal consideration rather than as a mandatory duty.

The morality of interpersonal responsibility and caring is assumed, in this view, to be gender related. It is claimed that, through gender-linked socialization processes, women come to develop such an orientation more than do men.

Some empirical work supports claims that U.S. adults recognize a category of role-related and discretionary interpersonal responsibilities. Higgins, Power, and Kohlberg (1984), for example, demonstrate that U.S. adults' reasoning about caring dilemmas is influenced by their membership in different school-based communities, with a greater sense of moral obligation experienced in schools with more communal orientations. Some descriptive data are also cited to suggest that caring responsibilities are regarded in discretionary rather than mandatory terms. The work, however, concerns only U.S. adults and thus does not address the question of the cross-cultural status of interpersonal responsibility.

A CULTURAL PERSPECTIVE ON BENEFICENCE AND INTERPERSONAL RESPONSIBILITY

Some Cross-Cultural Evidence

Some recent research provides evidence that cultural differences may occur in reasoning about beneficence and interpersonal responsibility (for reviews, see Edwards, 1981, 1986; Eisenberg, 1986; Snarey, 1985). In particular, these investigations have documented the presence of culture-specific moral orientations, stressing collectivist and cooperative ideals rather than merely justice considerations. For example, such orientations have been reported in the egalitarian communalism of various small-scale communities, such as Israeli kibbutzim or villages of Kenya and Papua New Guinea (Edwards, 1975; Snarey, Reimer, & Kohlberg, 1985; Tietjen & Walker, 1985) as well as in the hierarchical collectivism of cultures such as China, with its stress on filial piety (Lei & Cheng, 1984). This past research, however, has tended not to focus explicitly on the question of whether the various prosocial orientations identified are conceptualized in as fully moral terms as are justice orientations.

Recent research that I have conducted in India and the United States addresses this question directly. This issue is first examined in a study comparing U.S. and Hindu Indian adults' moral evaluations of actual everyday incidents involving breaches either of (a) justice, such as plagiarism, cheating, or lying, or of (b) role-related interpersonal responsibilities, such as disloyalty to friends and colleagues, infidelity to spouses, or noncaring behavior toward family members (Miller & Luthar, 1989).

Results revealed that only U.S., and not Indian, respondents differentiated between the interpersonal and justice issues in the ways predicted by the philosophical and psychological claims. Consonant with these claims, U.S. respondents tended to categorize the interpersonal breaches in personal terms while categorizing the justice breaches as moral issues. In contrast, Indians tended to categorize both the interpersonal and the justice breaches as moral issues. No sex or socioeconomic differences occurred in subjects' reasoning.

The nature of the observed cross-cultural differences is illustrated below in interpretations of the same deviant behavior offered by both Hindu and U.S. respondents:

> This involved an individual whose parents brought him up very well. They gave him a good education, sacrificing things for themselves in order to give to him. But after his marriage and after he got a good position, this son did not treat his parents very well. The son's father had asthma, which naturally required some expenditure of money to treat. Also, moneywise and physical discomfortwise, the father was acting as an irritant to the son. So the son did not let his parents live in his house. Now the parents are staying with distant relatives in another state. I know that their physical needs are being looked after, but the son himself was in a position to look after them. I feel the son shouldn't have sent his parents away. (Miller & Luthar, 1989; p. 253)

The following justification was typical of those offered by Indian respondents for categorizing such behavior as a moral violation:

> Because it's a son's duty—birth duty—to take care of his parents. It's not only money that matters. It's being near your dear ones which counts more. So even though they were being looked after elsewhere, they were not with their own children. Secondly, even from the simple philosophy of give and take, the son has no business to ask his father to go away. Even if the parents had not exerted so much for the son, still he is expected to have a certain responsibility towards his parents. (Miller & Luthar, 1989, p. 253)

In contrast, the following justification exemplifies the arguments offered by U.S. respondents for categorizing such behavior in personal terms:

It's up to the individual to decide. It's duty to the parents versus one's own independence and, I guess, one's self interest. He's fulfilling the minimal obligations to his parents. It wasn't a life and death situation and their needs were being taken care of. Beyond that it's a personal choice. Whether he wants to live with them has more to do with their emotional and personal relationship. Gratitude is something that's either there or it's not. You can't look at the parent-child relationship as a contractual one—or as a tit for tat. (Miller & Luthar, 1989, p. 253)

The Indian respondent, it may be seen, conceptualized caring for elderly parents as a moral duty. Such a duty appeared to be based on more than reciprocity obligations and to extend beyond just extreme need situations. In contrast, the U.S. respondent judged that the demands of the situation were beyond the call of duty and that personal choice considerations applied.

In a second study examining the impact of need and role on views of social responsibilities (Miller, Bersoff, & Harwood, 1990), the scope of this cross-cultural difference in conceptualization of beneficence was assessed. U.S. and Hindu Indian children and adults were asked to evaluate incidents in which an agent failed to help another person who was dependent on the agent for having needs met. This need was described as extreme (e.g., a need for emergency resuscitation), moderate (e.g., a need for psychological support before surgery), or minor (e.g., a need for directions to an art sale). In a between-subject manipulation, the relationship between the agent and the dependent other was portrayed as that of (a) parent to their young child, (b) best friend, or (c) stranger.

Results revealed that Indians tended to conceptualize social responsibilities in fully moral terms under all three need and role conditions. In contrast, U.S. respondents tended to conceptualize social responsibilities as the agent's own business in all cases, except those involving life-and-death situations or the moderately serious needs of young children. Whereas virtually no role or need effects occurred in Indians' judgments, U.S. subjects' judgments varied along both dimensions. In particular, U.S. subjects' tendencies to consider a social responsibility as an objective obligation increased with the magnitude of the other's need and with the intimacy of the role relationship involved. These various effects showed no relationship to sex and only a weak relationship to socioeconomic status.

Other studies, nearing completion, address the two remaining philosophical claims identified in regard to the differential moral status of justice as contrasted with beneficence obligations. One study compares U.S. and Hindu Indian adults' and children's reasoning about conflicts between justice obligations and interpersonal responsibilities, matched in perceived importance (Miller & Bersoff, 1990). Contrasting U.S. and Hindu Indian adults' views of everyday family obligations, a second study examines cultural differences in role-based expectations. The results of these studies will be presented in depth elsewhere and thus will not be discussed here. It may be noted, however, that preliminary trends from this research challenge the universality of the latter two philosophical claims—suggesting that, in India, justice considerations tend not to be given priority over beneficence and that self-sacrifice to meet another's needs tends to be viewed as morally required and not merely as morally virtuous.

In sum, the studies described demonstrate that cultural differences exist in the moral status of beneficence and interpersonal responsibility. Consonant with philosophical assertions, North Americans tend to regard meeting the needs of dependent others as discretionary. In contrast, contrary to philosophical claims, Indians tend to accord full moral status of such issues.

A Cultural Interpretation

This finding that Indian, but not U.S., respondents reasoned about issues involving beneficence in a way contrary to the dominant Western philosophical views may be interpreted in at least two ways. One interpretation would hold that there is only one logical way of viewing beneficence and interpersonal responsibility and thus the Indians' judgments must be considered illogical. This interpretation, however, is called into question because the interviewees in the study consisted of middle-class Indian adults with high levels of education (including individuals with postgraduate degrees). The Indian adults interviewed can be presumed to have been capable of reasoning logically.

In contrast, an alternative interpretation would hold that the philosophical and psychological accounts offered for the discrepancy between justice obligations versus beneficence and interpersonal responsibility are incomplete in themselves. Rather than offering self-evident arguments for the unique moral status of beneficence and interpersonal responsibility, the philosophical and psychological positions offer arguments that are compelling only in the context of various Western cultural assumptions.

As reflected in social contract theory, Western cultural premises start with the view of persons as inherently autonomous and asocial

(Dumont, 1965). Such an assumption may be seen, for example, in Rawls's attempts to construct a morality from the position of the individual in a "veil of ignorance," who is stripped of identifying social and personality characteristics (Rawls, 1971). In this view, the individual is regarded as primary, with the social order considered a derivative, to which one voluntarily contracts in order to protect his or her individual rights.

Assumptions of this type lead to a minimal view of morality, with only justice, and not beneficence, regarded as legitimately regulated. In such a system, the paramount moral goal is protection of individual rights. Social regulation then is viewed as justifiable only to the extent it directly serves individual interests by providing protection from harm. As Mill (1951, p. 197) asserts:

> The sole end for which mankind [humankind] are warranted, individually or collectively, in interfering with the liberty of action of any of their number is self-protection. That the only purpose for which power can be rightfully exercised over any member of a civilized community, against his [her] will, is to prevent harm to others.

In such a cultural framework, beneficence is accorded a subordinate moral status. Although helping others is considered desirable, it is not seen as a fundamental right that can warrant constraining individual freedom of choice.

Cultural assumptions of this type also entail the view that the fundamental social unit is the autonomous individual and that role commitments are not in the realm of moral duty (Miller & Bersoff, 1988; Tufte & Myerhoff, 1979). As recent work on U.S. family law has documented, in such a system, relationships tend to be conceived as temporary associations designed to satisfy individual inclinations rather than as enduring commitments having intrinsic moral worth (Schneider, 1985). Social regulation of role relationships then is considered illegitimate in that it infringes on individual preferences.

In contrast, Hindu Indian culture tends to forward a more social and holistic view of the person (Dumont, 1970; Marriott, 1976; O'Flaherty & Derrett, 1978). Persons are regarded as inherently part of the social body, with relationships of hierarchical interdependence assumed to be both natural and normatively desirable. In this perspective, individual inclination and social requirements tend to be seen as congruent rather than as opposed. Duty tends to be experienced on the one hand as mandatory, rather than, as in the Western view, a matter of choice and consent, yet also as natural, rather than as an imposition. Such a stance is reflected, for example, in the Hindu concept of *dharma*—a concept that denotes simultaneously both individual nature and social duty and that applies to all living things, not merely to humans.

These cultural assumptions lead to the view that moral obligations are expansive, encompassing not merely prohibition-oriented issues but also beneficence toward others. Obligations to meet the needs of others tend to be treated as just as fundamental and relevant to self-interest as justice obligations. Although not altogether absent, the concept of individual rights is considered much less fundamental than in the West. With the cultural focus on the desirability and naturalness of mutual support, rather than on the undesirability of constraint, little ambivalence exists then that would preclude treating beneficence in fully moral terms.

In assuming that the dyad rather than the autonomous individual is the most basic social unit, Hindu cultural views also encompass a view of role-related obligations as fully moral (Dumont, 1970). Duties tend to be conceived as relative to one's role and stage of life. As Ramanujan (1980, p. 11) notes in contrasting traditional Hindu orientations with those of the West:

> The main tradition of Western/Christian ethics is based on a premise of universalization—Manu[1] will not understand such a premise. To be moral, for Manu, is to particularize—to ask who did what, to whom and when. . . . Each class (*jati*) of man [woman] has his [her] own laws, his [her] own proper ethic, not to be universalized.

In the Hindu Indian cultural view, the particularistic nature of role relationships then does not result in their being viewed as beyond the realm of moral regulation but rather as central to morality.

IMPLICATIONS OF CULTURAL PERSPECTIVE ON BENEFICENCE

Implications for Philosophical Perspectives

The cultural considerations reviewed highlight certain culture-specific premises that underlie the dominant Western philosophical accounts of beneficence. In particular, such considerations call into question the philosophical claim that problems with scope are inherent in beneficence and cannot be resolved. They also imply that the philosophical focus on scope as the key problem of beneficence may be misguided.

On the one hand, the finding that Indians categorized social responsibilities in fully moral terms implies that it is possible to introduce qualifications that sufficiently delimit the scope of beneficence obligations to make them realizable (Miller et al., 1990). Unlike general beneficence, social responsibilities are defined as applying only to cases in which a needy other is situationally dependent on the agent and not to all cases involving a needy other. The range of acts that satisfy social responsibilities then is relatively circumscribed. It may be argued that the failure of Western philosophical accounts to qualify beneficence obligations in ways such as this—which make them realizable— reflects the general Western cultural value placed on the universal as contrasted with the context sensitive. In such a system, the only qualifications accepted on beneficence are those, such as cost to the agent, that have the effect of promoting individual rights and freedom of choice.

On the other hand, the finding that North Americans did not consider social responsibilities in fully moral terms implies that, even if problems with scope are resolved, the moral status of beneficence remains unchanged for North Americans. In categorizing social responsibilities as matters of personal choice, North Americans did not appear to be responding to problems of scope—problems that should also have occurred to Indians. Rather, as argued earlier, North Americans' reasoning appeared to reflect the value they place on individual rights and freedom of choice. Such culturally specific values are central as well to the Western philosophical arguments for beneficence as a superogatory rather than a fully moral obligation.

Finally, the evidence reviewed suggests that the philosophical claim that particularistic role relationships are not legitimately subject to social regulation also may be grounded in culturally specific conceptual assumptions (Miller & Luthar, 1989). Such a perspective, the evidence suggests, is premised on the contractual and voluntaristic view of role relationships stressed in Western culture. In cultures such as India, which emphasize the obligatory character of role-based commitments and their consonance with individual nature, this view does not appear to be held.

In sum, it may be concluded that the philosophical arguments for an asymmetry in the moral status of beneficence as contrasted with justice do not rest merely on logical or self-evident considerations. Rather, it has been seen that such arguments are informed, at least in part, by culturally specific beliefs, values, and conceptual presuppositions.

Implications for Psychological Perspectives

The research reviewed implies that the theories of Kohlberg and Gilligan each capture aspects of North Americans' orientations toward beneficence but that neither adequately describes cross-cultural variation in prosocial moral judgment (Miller & Luthar, 1989; Miller et al., 1990). A strength of Kohlberg's position, for example, is its clear depiction of the emphasis on personal choice in North Americans' orientations toward beneficence—a claim supported by the findings that North Americans tend to categorize beneficence issues in personal choice terms. Kohlberg's views, however, fail to predict the current observation that both beneficence and interpersonal responsibility are seen in fully moral terms by Indians. In turn, a strength of Gilligan's position is its recognition of the relationship-dependent nature of moral judgments. This view is supported by this research, showing that even North Americans' judgments of social responsibilities—a form of beneficence—are role dependent. Gilligan's views, however, fail to predict the findings that attitudes toward interpersonal responsibility vary by culture and not by sex, with Indians treating such issues in more fully moral terms than do North Americans.

The failure of each theory to adequately depict cross-cultural variation, if not also gender-related variation (Gilligan, 1982), in prosocial moral reasoning highlights the need for each theoretical perspective to pay greater attention to cultural factors in its explanation of the processes through which moral understandings develop. Although differing from each other, each theory, it may be argued, underestimates the extent to which individuals' interpretations of their experiences is mediated by the values, beliefs, and presuppositions of their culture.

A neglect of cultural processes is perhaps most evident in the Kohlbergian viewpoint. Following Piaget, it is assumed that moral reasoning develops in a self-constructive rationally based process of role taking. As critics have argued (Shweder, Mahapatra, & Miller, 1987; Simpson, 1974), however, the theory confounds considerations of structure and content—at least in its depiction of postconventional reasoning. In particular, it fails to recognize that certain presuppositions—such as that the autonomous individual is the fundamental moral unit—are not formal self-evident presuppositions but are nonrational content assumptions, which depend, at least in part, on culturally based premises (Miller, 1984).

Although the theory of Gilligan allows for more subgroup variation than does that of Kohlberg, it still retains the assumption that a given set of experiences—such as experience in the nurturing role—leads to only one interpretation—such as the development of a caring moral perspective. It is not recognized that the meaning of objective experiences varies depending on the culturally constituted interpretation it is given. Thus, as the evidence reviewed suggests, individuals' attitudes toward relationships may more closely reflect their acquisition of a rights-versus duty-oriented cultural ideology than their direct experiences in particular roles.

In sum, it may be concluded that greater attention needs to be paid to the culturally variable precepts that individuals apply in moral judgment. The morality of the West cannot be assumed to be either universal or optimal. Rather, it must be recognized that any moral code presents its own priorities, with an expansion in the sphere of personal decision making and freedom of choice linked, at least in some cases, to a narrowing of the moral force of interpersonal commitments.

NOTE

1. Reference here is to a classical sacred Hindu text *The Laws of Manu* (in Buhler, 1964).

REFERENCES

Blum, L. A. (1980). *Friendship, altruism and morality.* London: Routledge & Kegan Paul.

Buhler, B. (Trans.). (1964). *The Sacred books of the East* (Vol. 14). Delhi, India: Motilal Banarsidass.

Dumont, L. (1965). The modern conception of the individual: Notes on its genesis. *Contributions to Indian Sociology, 66,* 429-436.

Dumont, L. (1970). *Homo hierarchicus.* Chicago: University of Chicago Press.

Edwards, C. (1975). Societal complexity and moral development. *Ethos, 3,* 505-527.

Edwards, C. (1981). The comparative study of the development of moral judgment and reasoning. In R. Munroe, R. Munroe, & B. Whiting (Eds.), *Handbook of cross-cultural human development* (pp. 501-527). New York: Garland.

Edwards, C. (1986). Cross-cultural research on Kohlberg's stages: The basis for consensus. In S. Modgil & C. Modgil (Eds.), *Lawrence Kohlberg: Consensus and controversy* (pp. 419-430). Sussex, England: Falmer.

Eisenberg, N. (1982). The development of reasoning regarding prosocial behavior. In N. Eisenberg (Ed.), *The development of prosocial behavior* (pp. 219-249). New York: Academic Press.

Eisenberg, N. (1986). *Altruistic emotion, cognition, and behavior.* Hillsdale, NJ: Lawrence Erlbaum.

Eisenberg-Berg, N. (1979). Development of children's prosocial moral judgment. *Developmental Psychology, 15*, 128-137.

Gert, B. (1988). *Morality: A new justification of the moral rules.* New York: Oxford University Press.

Gewirth, A. (1978). *Reason and morality.* Chicago: University of Chicago Press.

Gilligan, C. (1977). In a different voice: Women's conceptions of the self and morality. *Harvard Educational Review, 47*, 481-517.

Gilligan, C. (1982). *In a different voice: Psychological theory and women's development.* Cambridge, MA: Harvard University Press.

Higgins, A., Power, C., & Kohlberg, L. (1984). The relationship of moral atmosphere to judgments of responsibility. In W. M. Kurtines & J. L. Gewirtz (Eds.), *Morality, moral behavior and moral development* (pp. 74-106). New York: John Wiley.

Kant, I. (1949). *Critique of practical reasoning* (L. W. Beck, Trans.). Chicago: University of Chicago Press. (Original work published 1788)

Kant, I. (1964). *The doctrine of virtue.* New York: Harper & Row. (Original work published 1797)

Kohlberg, L. (1981). *The philosophy of moral development: Moral stages and the idea of justice: Vol. 1. Essays on moral development.* New York: Harper & Row.

Kohlberg, L., Levine, C., & Hewer, A. (1983). Moral stages: A current formulation and a response to critics. In J. A. Meacham (Ed.),*Contributions to human development* (Vol. 10). Basel, Switzerland: Karger.

Lei, T., & Cheng, S. W. (1984). *An empirical study of Kohlberg's theory and scoring system of moral judgment in Chinese society.* Unpublished manuscript, Harvard University, Center for Moral Education, Cambridge, MA.

Marriott, M. (1976). Hindu transactions: Diversity without dualism. In B. Kapferer (Ed.), *Transaction and meaning* (pp. 109-142). Philadelphia: Institute for the Study of Human Issues.

Mill, J. S. (1951). *Utilitarianism, liberty, and representative government.* New York: E. P. Dutton.

Miller, J. G. (1984). Culture and the development of everyday social explanation. *Journal of Personality and Social Psychology, 46*, 961-978.

Miller, J. G., & Bersoff, D. M. (1988). When do American children and adults reason in social conventional terms? *Developmental Psychology, 24*, 366-375.

Miller, J. G., & Bersoff, D. M. (1990). *Culture and moral judgment: How are conflicts between justice and friendship resolved?* Manuscript submitted for publication.

Miller, J. G., Bersoff, D. M., & Harwood, R. L. (1990). Perceptions of social responsibilities in India and the United States: Moral imperatives or personal decisions? *Journal of Personality and Social Psychology, 58*, 33-47.

Miller, J. G., & Luthar, S. (1989). Issues of interpersonal responsibility and accountability: A comparison of Indians' and Americans' moral judgments. *Social Cognition, 3*, 237-261.

Nunner-Winkler, G. (1984). Two moralities? A critical discussion of an ethic of care and responsibility versus an ethic of rights and justice. In W. M. Kurtines & J. L. Gewirtz (Eds.), *Morality, moral behavior and moral development* (pp. 348-361). New York: John Wiley.

O'Flaherty, W., & Derrett, J. (Eds.). (1978). *The concept of duty in South Asia.* Delhi, India: Vikas.

Ramanujan, A. K. (1980). *Is there an Indian way of thinking?* Paper presented at the ACLS-SSRC Joint Committee on the South Asia-sponsored "Person in South Asia" project, Chicago.

Rawls, J. (1971). *A theory of justice.* Cambridge, MA: Harvard University Press.

Schneider, C. E. (1985). Moral discourse and the transformation of American family law. *Michigan Law Review, 83,* 1803-1879.

Shweder, R. A., Mahapatra, M., & Miller, J. G. (1987). Culture and moral development in India and the United States. In J. Kagan & S. Lamb (Eds.), *The emergence of morality in young children* (pp. 1-89). Chicago: University of Chicago Press.

Sidgwick, H. (1962). *The methods of ethics* (7th ed.). Chicago: University of Chicago Press. (Original work published 1874)

Simpson, E. L. (1974). Moral development research: A case study of scientific cultural bias. *Human Development, 17,* 81-106.

Smetana, J. G., Bridgeman, D. L., & Turiel, E. (1983). Differentiation of domains and prosocial behavior. In D. L. Bridgeman (Ed.), *The nature of prosocial development* (pp. 163-183). New York: Academic Press.

Snarey, J. R. (1985). Cross-cultural universality of social-moral development: A critical review of Kohlbergian research. *Psychological Bulletin, 97,* 202-232.

Snarey, J. R., Reimer, J., & Kohlberg, L. (1985). Development of social-moral reasoning among kibbutz adolescents: A longitudinal cross-cultural study. *Developmental Psychology, 21,* 3-17.

Tietjen, A. M., & Walker, L. J. (1985). Moral reasoning and leadership among men in a Papua New Guinea society. *Developmental Psychology, 21,* 982-992.

Tufte, V., & Myerhoff, B. (1979). *Changing images of the family.* New Haven, CT: Yale University Press.

Urmson, J. C. (1958). Saints and heroes. In A. I. Melden (Ed.), *Essays in moral philosophy* (pp. 198-216). Seattle: University of Washington Press.

3

The Concept of *Yuan* and
Chinese Interpersonal Relationships

HUI-CHING CHANG ●
G. RICHARD HOLT ● *University of Louisville*

*We take exception to the general trend of regarding Chinese interpersonal
relationships as primarily influenced by Confucian philosophy. Instead, through
extended interviews with 10 Taiwanese graduate students studying in the United
States, together with a variety of cultural materials from Chinese literature and
the Mandarin Chinese language, it is shown that the Buddhist conception of
yuan (dependent origination) also plays a significant role in structuring how
Chinese think about their interpersonal relationships. Moreover, it is argued
that yuan is a considerably richer, and potentially more valuable, metaphor for
thinking about relationships, Chinese and otherwise. By emphasizing the role
of context, this study serves as a critique of Western conceptions of communication and relationship, thus further enhancing understanding of interpersonal
communication.*

Issues concerning interpersonal relationships have long played a significant role in Western studies of communication. Only recently, however, have interpersonal communication scholars taken cognizance of
the fact that any approach to interpersonal communication must necessarily reflect the underlying philosophical assumptions made by the
investigator. As Parks (1982, p. 80) notes, the value-laden nature of such
assumptions can present serious obstacles to the communication scholars: "The point at which observations meet value systems is inherently
problematic for the communication scientist."

This phenomenon is nowhere more noticeable than in comparisons
of interpersonal communication between Western and Eastern countries. In the West, communication scholars have held that the study of
interpersonal relationship is inextricably tied to the study of communication because relationship is seen to be manifested through communication (Parks, 1982; Sillars & Weisberg, 1987). The key to this
perspective is the widespread belief (especially among North Americans) that relationships can be "worked on" through training in communication competence. Many problems encountered in interpersonal

relationships typically are seen as "communication problems." As Katriel and Philipsen (1981, p. 315) point out, many North Americans feel that they need "communication" to make a relationship "work" and that " 'communication' is a culturally distinctive solution to the universal problem of fusing the personal with the communal. In the ideology in which 'communication' is a pivotal term, affirming oneself in and through a process of social interaction is the highest good."

It is not surprising that this prototypically Western conceptualization of interpersonal communication has proven largely untenable when applied to the study of predominantly Eastern patterns of relationship and communication (Kincaid, 1987; Yum, 1988). Westerners tend to view relational outcomes as primarily *dependent on* communication: "The interest in relationships is limited . . . to the extent to which two or more individuals share information with one another and the extent to which they move toward mutual understanding and agreement. *Other aspects of human relationships are not considered* [italics added]" (Kincaid, 1987, p. 339). This somewhat limited perspective on human relationships and interpersonal communication can be illuminated and enriched through a comparative investigation of the ways in which other cultures view interpersonal transactions, especially considering the views of Eastern people, who hold a considerably less instrumental view concerning the role of communication in relationships.

In line with the theme of this volume, we hold that there are many aspects of Asian relationship that Western philosophies, and their resultant models of communication, are ill-equipped to handle. The major overriding factor that contributes to cross-cultural misunderstanding is the differing views of *causation*. The Eastern view—that causation is multidirectional—will be difficult to understand by anyone who is aware only of Western traditions, which generally hold that causation is unidirectional (Maruyama, 1974; Redding & Martyn-Johns, 1979). This is why this study is necessary. Only through an awareness that the *underlying* views of causation in Asian countries are fundamentally different than those found in the West can cross-cultural dialogue about interpersonal communication be facilitated. These inherent differences lead to fundamentally different attributions about how interpersonal relationships are formed, maintained, and dissolved.

Recognizing the essential differences outlined above, we want to examine the role of context in Chinese interpersonal relationships in somewhat greater depth. In particular, we want to focus on how the concept of *yuan* is manifested in the interpersonal relationships of

Chinese on the island of Taiwan. *Yuan* (緣) is a concept derived from Buddhism, and it can be very briefly defined as "secondary causation." Yuan is thought to be the chief force that allows contextual factors to play a role in determining whether people will or will not be associated with each other. Chinese will often say, "I have yuan with another person," meaning conditions are right for them to be together. This concept plays a significant role in influencing present-day Chinese relationships.

To Chinese, the influence of yuan is of equal importance to that of other philosophies. In the past, studies of Asian interpersonal relationships have tended to focus on the role of Confucianism (see, for example, Yum's, 1988, analysis of East Asian interpersonal relationships). However, Confucianism explains only the *primary* causes of relationships, that is, those factors that are under the direct control of individuals; much of Confucianism, for example, is devoted to descriptions of how the *chun-tzu* (superior person) should behave in dealing with others and avoids the more abstract, less easily explicable, facets of relationships, such as the context in which they develop. Therefore, for a truly complete picture of Chinese relationships, one must also examine the principles of other Chinese cultural influences, such as Buddhism. By examining the influence of Buddhism, we are made more aware of the less noticeable, but equally important, influences of Chinese culture on interpersonal relationships.

In this chapter, we will provide a rich, descriptive portrait of Chinese interpersonal relationships through an interpretive analysis of the concept of yuan. Our analysis will be advanced in six stages. First, we will briefly describe the method we used to gather material for our study. Second, we will define in detail the concept of yuan, beginning with its origins in Buddhist theology. Third, we will provide a modern interpretation of yuan through an analysis of interviews with Chinese students. Fourth, we will relate the interview data with eight key Chinese expressions that explain different facets of yuan. Fifth, we will examine the significance of yuan for conceptualizing Chinese relationships. Finally, we will discuss the implications of yuan for the study of Chinese interpersonal communication. Throughout, we emphasize the contrast between the conceptualization of Chinese interpersonal communication under the impact of yuan as a perspective that accounts for contextual factors in relationships, as opposed to the individualistic and self-controlled viewpoint on interpersonal communication that drives much of Western thinking about relationships.

METHOD

The study of yuan, a subtle philosophical concept expressed in a variety of ways in very indirect and suggestive language, requires an interpretive approach toward cultural description. As Geertz (1973, p. 5) writes,

> The concept of culture I espouse ... is essentially a semiotic one. Believing, with Max Weber, that man [woman] is an animal suspended in webs of significance he [she] himself [herself] has spun, I take culture to be those webs, and the analysis of it to be therefore not an experimental science in search of law but an interpretive one in search of meaning. It is explication I am after, construing social expressions on their surface enigmatical.

Thus the meaning of a given culture begins with the interpretive voice of the natives of that culture. For this reason, certain methodological strategies (such as quantitative approaches like attitude measurement and statistical analyses or even detailed lists of questions such as those to be found in ethnography of speaking; Hymes, 1972; Saville-Troike, 1982) are inadequate for exploring the linguistic and philosophical richness of ideas like yuan. Such methodologies, even though they may appeal to some consensual idea about appropriateness shared by an intellectual community (Jackson, 1986), are not sensitive enough to elicit meanings enacted by the cultural Other.

The key to understanding this broader conceptualization of detecting the meanings of a given culture lies in the realization that *we can never get direct access to what is in the native's mind*. Rather, researchers must formulate an analysis according to their interpretations of the natives' interpretations of their own lives. As Geertz (1973, p. 6) puts it,

> From one point of view, that of the textbook, doing ethnography is establishing rapport, selecting informants, transcribing texts, taking genealogies, mapping fields, keeping a diary, and so on. But it is not these things, techniques and received procedures, that define the enterprise. What defines it is the kind of intellectual effort it is: an elaborate venture in, to borrow a notion from Gilbert Ryle, "thick description."

The concepts underlying such analysis are, of course, considerably divergent from those to standard experimental psychology or of so-called objective ethnographic designs. The approach we take in analyzing yuan is derived from Geertz's broader, more flexible interpretation of what constitutes cultural meanings. The richness and meaning of a given cultural concept such as yuan must rely primarily on the ways in which the natives of a culture interpret it. This is why a simple etymological analysis of the word *yuan* is insufficient to explain its richness. Rather, the study of such concepts is best accomplished through a qualitative analysis of a variety of cultural materials.

To elicit responses adequate to the richness of the topic, we conducted 10 in-depth interviews, ranging in length from one-half to one-and-a-half hours, in March and April 1989. The interviewees were graduate students from Taiwan, ranging in age from 22 to 30 years, attending a large midwestern university; residence times in the United States ranged from eight months to three years. All interviews were conducted in Mandarin Chinese and were audiotaped, in private areas, and later synopsized in English. Interviews followed a semistructured protocol that aimed at eliciting the respondents' views on the following related subjects: (a) their interpretation of yuan through various Chinese linguistic expressions, (b) their personal attitudes toward the development of relationships, and (c) their interpretation of the role of communication in regard to Chinese interpersonal relationships.

These interviews served as our basic source of data. We organized the interview material according to a schema consisting of eight Chinese linguistic terms that refer to yuan. To enhance, amplify, and enrich the basic interview data, as well as the eight linguistic expressions, we also examined other Chinese cultural artifacts, including newspapers, literature, written cultural accounts, electronic media (i.e., popular music and television), and the personal experiences of the principal author, a native Taiwanese. Fortunately, the idea of yuan is so pervasive in Chinese life that its expression is to be found in almost any situation in which Chinese talk or write about their personal relationships. The consideration of all of these sources of data—taken together—will provide a richer, "thicker" account of the concept of yuan.

THE CONCEPT OF *YUAN*

Because yuan is a concept with its origins in Buddhism, to understand it requires the grasp of at least some of the basic ideas behind Buddhism. Although yuan is an extremely complex notion, its exegesis can be made considerably more understandable if one attends to the meaning of two key Buddhist terms: (a) *karma* and (b) *dependent origination*. First, we will briefly define these two terms, and then, based on these definitions, we will provide a more complete definition of secondary causation (yuan).

The first important key to Buddhism is the concept of karma, a kind of blanket responsibility for an individual's acts on earth during a given lifetime. Karma accumulates throughout uncountable lifetimes spent on earth. "Any deed is invariably accompanied by a result. All that we are at the present moment is the result of the karma that we have produced in the past" (Niwano, 1980, p. 104). Causation, according to Buddhism, is a result of one's acts through various lifetimes and does not stem from some supernatural agency.

A second important aspect of Buddhism concerns its depiction of a universe of interdependent factors, that is *dependent* origination. Any event results from innumerable causes interacting and interpenetrating each other. It is no wonder, with so many contributing factors, that Buddhists regard the natural world as ephemeral and impermanent. Rather than a fixed, Aristotelian/Thomist view of identifiable causes leading to specified results, we are presented with a shifting tapestry of interdependent forces, the slightest change in any of which leads to far-reaching alterations in all the others. As Niwano (1980, p. 94) writes, "Our lives continue from the unlimited past to the endless future; 'today' does not exist in isolation but is like a deep pool or a shoal of the endless river of life."

This perspective can be traced to the Buddhist theology of Tian-Tai Zhi-yi. In an important and influential 20-section work, Tian-Tai Zhi-yi systematized the various teachings in the Buddha's *Lotus Sutra,* generally regarded by Buddhists as his most profound work (Chan, 1963; Fung, 1983). A central facet of Tian-Tai Zhi-yi's work is the Doctrine of the Ten Suchnesses. This consists of ten characteristics of context prefaced by the phrase "such a" or "such an." Of these ten, numbers six, seven, and eight are essential for an understanding of *yuan:* "such a primary cause," "such a secondary cause," and "such an effect." Niwano (1980, p. 111) notes,

> Even when there exists a cause, it does not produce its effect until it comes into contact with some occasion or condition. For instance, there is always vapor in the air as the primary cause of frost or dew. But if it has no secondary cause that brings it into contact with the ground or the leaves of a plant, it does not become frost or dew. Such an occasion or condition is called "such a secondary cause." When a primary cause meets with a secondary cause, a phenomenon (effect) is produced. This is called "such an effect."

Thus primary cause is equivalent to most Western ideas about causation, while secondary cause can be seen as the context that facilitates the achieving of an effect.

This complex account of causation is little known in the intellectual traditions of the West. Aristotle, for example, spoke of four causes—material, efficient, formal, and final—but this is a peculiarly linear notion. It certainly did not allow for the context (secondary causation, or yuan) to have any influence on the effect. Buddhism portrays causation as constrained by the other, secondary, factors. In this view, the cause does not produce an effect by itself but must have the proper conditions before the result will occur.

Keeping in mind these definitions, we are now in a position to define *yuan* as

> a co-operating cause, the concurrent occasion of an event as distinguished from its proximate cause. It is the circumstantial, conditioning, or secondary cause, in contrast with the direct or fundamental cause. . . . *The direct cause is the seed, and yuan is the soil, rain, and the sunshine.* [italics added] (Soothill & Hodous, 1968, p. 440)

To return to our original thesis, recall that we wanted to discuss yuan in terms of Chinese interpersonal relationships. The multiplicity of secondary conditioning factors (for "secondary conditioning factors," read "yuan") gives rise to an interpersonal realm whose complexity is only partially known to the social actor. Buddhists speak of an inability to see all causative or conditioning factors and of the limitation that results from this, namely, that things happen for which one has no explanation.

The principle of yuan has significant implications for interpersonal relationship. According to Buddhism, it is impossible to identify "the," or even "a," major cause of a given event. In this view, the Westerner's preoccupation with communication as a sole, or even as a major, factor in relationship is misdirected. In Chinese thought, any relationship has its roots in uncounted numbers of lifetimes and is situated in a complex web of interdependent causative factors that are outside the control, or even the comprehension, of the human mind. It is much more difficult for Chinese to try to provide a causal account for relationship, in contrast with the Westerner's insistence that communication is one of the factors that can account for relationship success or failure.

Influenced by Buddhism, many Chinese conceptualize relationships as taking place at the nexus of a multitude of causes that an individual accrues in this and other lifetimes. As Nakamura (1984, pp. 147-148) writes,

> In order to explain the true nature of differences in individual existences, aspects, forms and appearances, I must be able to accept or subscribe to a different context, a framework in which every individual, so to speak, receives influences from other individuals as well as from all other things. ... All of this must be attributed to countless conditions and causes imposed by an immeasurable past that brings forth unique personalities.

This leads us to what is perhaps the feature most characteristic of Chinese views of relationship: If one does not form a relationship with another, and cannot explain why, more often than not, that person *will not seek to identify a cause why the relationship did not blossom and grow.* He or she will simply say, "We probably did not have yuan." Rather than relying on their ability to identify causative factors in the relationship that can be "worked on" (such as communication), Chinese are more likely to accept the conditions imposed by the context, even if they do not fully understand those conditions.

It is against this backdrop, then, that we must view yuan. Yuan between individuals results from the causes that make up both individuals' lives: their karma, in other words. The results, the fruits, of these karmic decisions, when they encounter secondary causation (yuan), are seen as determining who you will be involved with, to what degree, the kind of relationship, and how long it will last. For example, one might want to make friends with someone else. the primary cause in this case is the subjective willingness or volition on the part of both parties to form some kind of relationship. However, the friendship, according to Chinese belief, will not grow unless conditions of secondary causation (yuan) are fulfilled.

It is worth noting that the notion of yuan exists on at least two distinct levels for the Chinese. The more abstract sense of the word relates (as we have shown) to the complexities of Buddhist theology and particularly to its depiction of a shifting, unstable world of innumerable causative factors. Yet, even though the concept of yuan began in theology, the Chinese have always preferred that which is most immediately useful to them (Chan, 1963). Chinese have appropriated the idea of yuan and find it useful as a means of conceptualizing relationships without having to bother with many of its philosophical subtleties. This second level relates to immediate experience and serves as a metaphor by means of which Chinese come to describe their relationships. This is the "common" usage of the word. To see how modern Chinese define this concept, let us now turn to an analysis of the interviews.

MODERN CHINESE INTERPRETATION OF *YUAN*

As must be the case with any concept that undergirds the philosophy of a given culture, we found a great deal of repetition among our respondents' references to yuan. The same explanations, and even, in some cases, the same metaphors, are used to express certain ideas about yuan. Therefore, it makes more sense to present our findings in terms of certain key ideas that are brought out by the respondents considered as a group rather than trying to describe each respondent's answers separately. As we examine the data from the interviews, there are two facts to keep in mind: First, there are minor but noticeable variations in the way our respondents talk about this topic, and, second, there is general agreement on the basic principles of yuan. We feel that the former fact is a testimony to the richness of yuan, while the latter is proof of its ubiquity in the Chinese culture.

Some of our respondents considered yuan to be, in the words of one, "a very precious chance" for people to meet. Chinese consider that, out of the many people you *may* come into contact with, conditions will only be right for you to form a relationship with a very few. Thus it is thought that people meet each other *not by accident* but because yuan facilitates the encounter (which is quite different from the Western approach, where the focus is more on relationship maintenance and less on the reasons why people meet each other). In the Buddhist theological language we alluded to earlier, it seems appropriate to refer to such fortuitous opportunities as *facilitative conditions.*

The people we interviewed generally agreed on the importance of yuan as a facilitative condition in which two seemingly unrelated people are brought together. As one female said, "If today I meet you, it is because we have yuan . . . when I say 'nice to meet you,' this 'nice' has the flavor of yuan." Later, this same respondent characterized yuan as "a kind of opportunity": when the proper conditions are satisfactory, one will be able to form a relationship with the other person.

The other side of this coin is that, when conditions are not satisfactory, no amount of effort will ensure one's having a relationship with the other. Thus, as one informant said, "If you can arrange something by yourself, this is not yuan, but if you try very hard and are still prevented from achieving success, we say this is due to a lack of yuan."

The above account illustrates that Chinese people see relationships in ways very differently than those in the West. In fact, to some extent, Chinese pay more attention to secondary causation (yuan) than to primary causation. Westerners tend to believe that personal and individual effort can overcome most obstacles in relationships and seldom if ever pay attention to appropriate conditions—not, at least, until a relationship gone wrong forces this realization upon them. Chinese, by paying attention to yuan at the outset, take a broader and more philosophical perspective toward their associations with other people.

Two common Chinese aphorisms show how pervasive this theme is in Chinese culture. The first expression is, *Ren suan bu ru tian suan* (human beings cannot count what God counts). (Note: All quoted Chinese expressions are Romanized according to the Pinyin system, Choy, 1981.) This can be taken to mean that humans can be aware only to a small degree of the contexts in which they function. Full knowledge of context is reserved only for the deity. In terms of relationships, unless the facilitative conditions are fulfilled, one cannot predict how the relationship will eventuate.

A second common Chinese expression is *tian shi, di li, ren he* (to be successful requires the timing, the place, and the human factors). An individual has a certain degree of control only over the third of these factors, the human factor. Again, this common saying points to the Chinese belief that only when all three conditions are fulfilled can there be a facilitative situation that allows events to transpire.

As we mentioned earlier, relationship is seen by Chinese as similar to a seed: Unless it encounters the right conditions of humidity, rain, temperature, soil nutrients, and so on, it cannot grow. This idea was illustrated in a recent story in a Taiwan newspaper (Song, 1988). In this story, a young man was about to be married. He said that someone had introduced him to his bride-to-be some two years previously. The young man said that, if he had known at that time that she would eventually become his wife, he would have married her then. However, the writer disagreed: She felt that it was only at the later point, when their yuan was right, that they could be together: "I always hear people say, 'If only I had known earlier, I would have . . . ,' " the writer commented, "but even if you had 'known earlier,' it would still have been useless." Because yuan possesses its own timing, one must wait until the environmental conditions allow an association to occur. In contrast to the Western approach (where timing would not have been considered nearly so important a factor), the modern Chinese allows unknown factors to play a significant role in forming a relationship. An individual's effort can succeed only when conditions facilitate it.

To this point, we have seen how modern Chinese people have interpreted the classical Buddhist concept of yuan to help them account for interpersonal relationships. But there is much more to yuan than this very basic definition. To elaborate these ideas more extensively, we now turn to eight key Chinese expressions related to the concept of yuan. In each instance, we will show not only that the interviewees share some definitions of the basic linguistic expression but also that there is considerable individual variation in how they choose to interpret the expression and actualize it in their own interpersonal relationships.

EIGHT KEY CHINESE LANGUAGE EXPRESSIONS RELATING TO *YUAN*

One of the ways that a culture's richness can be manifested is through its language. This is particularly true of the Chinese language, which assigns a large and diverse number of meanings to each individual character. In this section, we will examine eight key Chinese expressions that serve to define the concept of yuan. These eight expressions can be categorized on the basis of their relation to Western ideas of interpersonal activity, with two expressions illustrating each of the following categories: (a) presence or absence of association, (b) quality of relationship, (c) mutual attraction, and (d) attitude toward association.

Presence or absence of association. As we have seen, success or failure in relationships is often attributed by Chinese to whether or not two people "have" yuan. Two commonly used expressions to describe this situation are *you yuan* (有 緣), meaning "to have *yuan*," and *wu yuan* (無 緣), meaning "not to have *yuan*."

Let us examine *you yuan* first. Chinese do not see association as random; therefore, one expects to associate only with those with whom one has yuan. Moreover, the extent or degree of the relationship is also a factor controlled by yuan. One respondent felt very strongly about the destiny of association: "If two people are destined to have yuan, they will meet each other, even if they have never known each other before. When the time is right, all other factors will accumulate to bring about the chance for them to meet." As one common Chinese saying puts it, "If you have yuan with each other, though you are thousands of miles apart, you will still meet. If you don't have yuan, even if you are face-to-face, you will never know each other." Thus Chinese consider those with whom they do associate to be very special. Yuan itself is, on one sense, a reciprocal concept: those you associate with are considered to have yuan with you, and those who have yuan with you are those with whom you will likely have important relationships.

Because associations based on shared yuan are considered to be very special, Chinese may develop favorable feelings on the basis of intuitive judgments about whether or not they feel they are likely to have yuan. Such a feeling can vary in degree according to how much yuan one actually has with another. Most female respondents said that they know intuitively who they have yuan with from the very first encounter (that is, those with whom they expect to have subsequent encounters). As one woman pointed out, the feeling of yuan must exist "before I have decided to make friends with someone." Nevertheless, none of these female respondents stated that her decision on whether she has yuan is based on the attractiveness of the other person's personality; rather, it is thought to be some kind of unexplainable feeling. According to one respondent, one can have yuan with another and yet be different in temperament from that person (that is, the yuan may exist, but the attraction on the basis of personality may not). She went on to say, "Most of the time my [initial] judgment is correct" but also that she still reserved her final judgment for later in the relationship.

Because you yuan is considered to represent likelihood of association, it is in romantic relationships that Chinese most strongly hope that they share yuan with the other. Moreover, they usually also hope that they have a great deal of yuan, so much so that they will be able to associate with the other for an entire lifetime. One informant stated that she has a foreign boyfriend (Canadian) and that, even though their relationship is stable at the current time, she sometimes is unsure about how long they will be together. Nevertheless, she says that, if they have a lot of yuan, they will be "together forever." Not knowing how long the relationship will last, this woman leaves the unknown factors to take their own course. Perhaps this is a form of resignation, based on the fact that the informant has had several, largely unsuccessful, romantic relationships in the past.

Next, let us consider *wu yuan*. This means that there is *no* chance for association or interaction with another person. One respondent offered several examples of how this can occur:

Suppose you live in the same building as some other person for three years, and yet in all that time you have not been able to connect that person's name and face. You don't have yuan with this person: you might look at him or her without really seeing. Suppose a person is in front of you and still cannot attract your attention: with this person you don't have yuan either. Another person and I might admire each other (in terms of a romantic relationship), but somehow I might also know we will never be together: the other person may have some commitment to someone else, or else there is no match between our personalities. With such people, I will say that we have no yuan.

Another respondent put the matter this way: "There are some people," she stated, "that I feel I have less yuan with, either from the first encounter or after several meetings. I feel that we won't have much chance to interact with each other, or even if I have such a chance, I would not like to interact with them." *Wu yuan,* then, carries a double meaning: People either don't have the *opportunity* to associate with each other or else they have the opportunity but *do not want* to associate. As this respondent told the interviewer, "I always use wu yuan to fend away unwanted suitors." Because they are not rejected outright, "that makes them feel much more comfortable."

Wu yuan is considered to be the saddest condition to have in a romantic relationship. If either romantic partner has the inclination to continue associating with the other, but there is wu yuan between them, then conditions will not allow their romance, regardless of how much one person may want it to occur. A common saying reflects this yearning: "If we do not have yuan in this life, then let us have yuan in a next life." Many Chinese romantic novels revolve around this theme. It is interesting that most of the references our respondents made to wu yuan occurred after we questioned them about reincarnation; though most said they either cannot verify, or do not believe in, a subsequent life, they still consider continuing yuan in a next life to be a very romantic concept. As one female respondent put it, "We think of the next life so that we will not feel so sad in this one." Here one gets a sense of the deep sadness that accompanies the loss of yuan: There is still some emotion, but the *conditions* do not allow the association to continue. Thus there is still something remaining (the emotion), but something has been lost (the facilitative conditions). This is why it is hoped that the emotion will carry on into another lifetime, where perhaps the context *will* allow association. While Chinese acknowledge the importance of personal effort in maintaining a given relationship, they also believe that, to a certain extent at least, failure or success of the relationship depends on the contextual factors.

Wu yuan can also occur between parent and child. In one example known to the principal author, a Taiwanese couple adopted a child and, as is the custom with Chinese parents, went to a fortune-teller for a prediction of the child's life. Without knowing that the child was adopted, the fortune-teller stated simply, "This child will not have yuan ["wu yuan"] with his parents." The parents took this to mean that the child and his natural parents would not be associated to any significant degree. Regardless of whether one grants the prediction any validity, the usage of the term *wu yuan* reveals its inextricable association with Chinese ideas concerning ability, or inability, to associate.

Quality of Relationship

Not only is yuan something that either does or does not exist between people, the term can also serve to describe the *quality* of a relationship. In general, yuan is described as *yuan fen* (緣份), an expression that denotes a "good" relationship (*good,* in this sense, meaning that one "has yuan" with another). In common Chinese usage, as confirmed by our informants, to have yuan is considered to be good, something very special, to be cherished in and of itself.

One important reason that yuan is nearly always considered to be good is that Chinese consider the chance to associate with another to be a very precious opportunity. Because only those who have yuan are destined to be associated, and because the fortuitous combination of secondary causes happens only rarely (depending not only on oneself but on many uncontrollable factors), Chinese respect and make the best use of this opportunity when it presents itself. So important is this feeling that, even if you associate with someone you do not like very much, you will try to cherish the chance to interact with that person.

This seemingly contradictory prescription is perhaps one of the clearest reflections of the collective nature of Chinese society. Many Chinese feel that even stressful relationships have come about as a result of the combination of many different types of primary and secondary causative factors, as these relationships are brought about by the individuals' karmic decisions. Suppose, for example, that one is involved in an unhappy marriage. Even though one may be unhappy, one may yet continue the relationship and comfort oneself with the knowledge that it is not easy to have yuan with the other person. Moreover, because it is brought about by the accumulations of one's own deeds through countless lifetimes, yuan cannot be avoided. Or, in the case of obstreperous in-laws, Chinese may say, "It is not easy to become an in-law; many factors had to combine to cause our families to associate with each other."

Yuan is held in such high regard that disturbance of yuan is considered by most Chinese to be an extremely grave matter. For example, if two people are interested in each other, and one of them asks a third person to offer an opinion about whether or not their association will be good, the third person can only serve to *assist* the two people to associate, never to hinder them from doing so. As one common Chinese expression says it, "When you advise people in their relationship, advise them to associate rather than to dissociate." Older people in Chinese society believe that interference in a couple's relationship will be punished. Once again, we can see how important relationship is to the Chinese cultural fabric: Any relationship is to be cherished and tolerated, and one must not purposefully interfere with any chance of association.

These examples of respect for yuan may reflect not only the high esteem in which Chinese hold interpersonal relationships but also the Buddhist origins of this concept. Buddhists hold that yuan is accumulated over many thousands of existences. Thus to tamper in the current lifetime with what has been perfected slowly and painstakingly in past lives is to generate extremely negative karma.

This is not to say that Chinese interpersonal relationships are always good. Chinese reserve the expression nie yuan (孽 緣) to describe a "bad relationship." The linguistic background of this distinction is very interesting: notice that yuan fen is simply the description of yuan, with no evaluative adjective coupled with it (*fen* simply means "share"). Thus, when Chinese want to distinguish unfavorable relationships, they are forced to couple the word *yuan* with the word *nie,* an extremely derogatory term that means simply "very bad." The description itself can be extremely repugnant to Chinese; as one respondent put it, "This term [*nie yuan*] very seldom comes to my mind. The word 'nie' sounds extremely bad to me, *so I do not even want to look at it* [italics added]." She said that she would rather interpret the phrase as "mistakenly arranged yuan" in order to banish the expression from consideration. "Yuan could not be so bad," she protested, "it could only be a mistake." This is a very clear echo of the point we made previously: Chinese hold human relationship above nearly every other aspect of their culture. It takes a great deal for them ever to give up on a relationship.

Nevertheless, there are many instances of nie yuan, some of which were pointed out by our respondents. One of the most common is the ill-fated romantic affair. One respondent offered the example of two people, each married to someone else, associating and deciding that they have met each other too late. This arrangement must be a "mistake," because social rules (which Chinese hold in high regard) condemn such association. If the two people never associated with each other, everything would be fine. Therefore, the informant explained, "I even use moral standards to make judgment—I would describe this case as being "immoral.' "

Another respondent suggested that nie yuan sometimes occurs in the case of two people who get married, find out later that they do not love each other, and then get divorced. The hapless spouse in such a relationship may be seen as a victim of nie yuan: A relationship between the two partners should never have happened, but the relationship came about anyway, so the result is guaranteed to be bad. However, another respondent claimed that, if one partner decides to remain faithful to his or her spouse, this could constitute a betrayal of the heart, which is also a kind of nie yuan.

The determination of nie yuan in romantic relationships can become quite complex, however. As one respondent noted, by *nie yuan,* Chinese mean that one has already tried hard to avoid the relationship but has been unsuccessful "because the yuan between the two of you is too strong." According to her, simply falling in love with someone you should not fall in love with is not nie yuan. Nie yuan is reserved for instances of uncontrollable associations that are seemingly compelled by fate.

Moreover, it should not be surprising to find that a person in the throes of a nie yuan-type relationship is often unaware of that fact. Indeed, one respondent said that nie yuan is used to describe a relationship *only after* it turns out to be bad. Another informant said: "You cannot know the result in advance. . . . After the event is over and you reflect on it, you conclude that, 'This relationship should never have happened, but it did, so it is a true nie yuan.' "

Mutual Attraction

As shown previously, the meaning of yuan relates to facilitative conditions and can thus serve as a basis for Chinese to be associated with one another. To Chinese, such persons are noteworthy in a very specific sense: the relationship is held to be interdependent, because yuan has dictated the association not simply for one but for both. Yuan thus becomes a quality that each person possesses and serves as a way for people to decide to associate with each other: In other words, they associate if they "match yuan." Because of this special feeling, yuan becomes a quality to describe the relationship between people rather than simply a statement of conditions of secondary causation.

One example of this idea among Chinese linguistic expressions is *tou yuan* (投緣), which denotes a matching of yuan. One male respondent explained this by means of an unusual metaphor:

Before I knew my girlfriend, I didn't feel tou yuan with any girl. I knew a lot of girls and some of them were either very pretty or very well off, but I didn't feel that I wanted to marry them. You may want to take a picture with a beautiful girl or with a marvelous building to show your friends, but you wouldn't want to live in that building. But the feeling of "matched yuan" is different. When I am with my girlfriend, I want to marry her. I feel comfortable with her and want to live in the building.

Tou yuan is considered by our respondents to be a very comfortable feeling, a sense that "everything is all right" with the other person. This respondent went on to say that tou yuan refers to the feeling you have when a person comes along who fits exactly into your idea of an ideal mate: "The other person 'shoots into' your definition" (in the Chinese language, *tou* means not only "to match" but also "to shoot into").

To Chinese, "matched yuan" is a deeply mysterious feeling, unexplainable by reference to ordinary personality similarities or differences (as compared with the standard Western social psychological account of the role of personality or attitude similarity in forming and maintaining relationships). One female respondent explained, "Matched yuan does not occur because of time, or because of interactions between participants that make them familiar with each other." Our respondents believe that even those with vastly different, even dissonant, personalities can still have "matched yuan" with each other.

However, there can also be a feeling of *bu tou yuan* (不投緣), or "not matching yuan." In such relationships, one is uncomfortable with the other person not because there is a problem in terms of personality incompatibilities, or with communication, but because of a feeling that association with the other is "just not right." One needn't hate such people, or have open conflict with them. It is simply that one knows that relationship with them is impossible. This is different from *wu yuan* (no yuan). In that case, the proper environmental (secondary causation) conditions make relationship impossible. In "nonmatched yuan," the environmental conditions may permit a relationship, but there is always a sense that the relationship is "going nowhere."

Earlier we cited our informants' opinion that yuan is desirable in and of itself. Therefore, if yuan is not matched, this is considered to be undesirable. As one female informant said, "If it is 'not matched yuan,' I would not even use the term 'yuan' to describe it." *Bu tou yuan* (unmatched yuan) is not held to be a problem of communication; it is simply a feeling that "things are not right."

Another expression used to denote mutual attraction is *ren yuan* (人緣), or "human yuan." Persons who are, in general, liked by many other people are said to have ren yuan. Ren yuan is unique among Chinese descriptors of yuan in that it is the only expression that specifies a relationship between an individual *and a group*. As one female informant said, "When I say 'human yuan,' I refer to the relation between a person and a group of people, whereas other kinds of yuan denote a relationship between two people who, together, form an interaction system . . . the meaning of [this term] is different from the other kinds of yuan we have been discussing."

Unlike *tou yuan* and *bu tou yuan*, however, *ren yuan* refers to a condition in which personality does play a large (though by no means the only) part. As one informant said, such a person "is easy to get along with, is nice to others, and others like him." In a famous Chinese novel, *Where There Is Water in the River, There Is Reflected a Moon* (Xiao, 1990), a mother is praised for giving her daughter ren yuan instead of giving her a beautiful face. The reason personality plays such a large role in ren yuan is that those so designated learn to deal with people and situations in a positive and constructive way. However, people who are simply "nice" or "popular" may not have "human yuan." To Chinese, popularity often simply means that one is sociable, in the sense of having social skills; however, this sort of skillfulness, often manifested through communication, is seldom considered a virtue by Chinese (Becker, 1988).

There was a great deal of controversy about ren yuan among our informants. Some argued that people who have ren yuan know "how to deal with things," that is, they are more socially mature and hence have stronger personalities. As one respondent said, "Those with 'human yuan' need to know a lot to behave appropriately." Some people, according to this informant, may be nice but cannot please everyone because they do not know how to do things in the right way.

However, other respondents claimed that those who have ren yuan are simply *more naive* than those around them. One informant stated flatly that ren yuan means that one finds it easy to please others, so that "others are happy about you." Such individuals, this informant argued, have *no* strong personality and, therefore, find it easy to survive. For this reason, the informant said, the term ren yuan is more often used to describe children than adults.

Perhaps it is for this reason that another of our female informants refused to consider the term *ren yuan* as complimentary. In her interview, she stated, "Usually, such people [those with ren yuan] have less individual personality to claim for their own. They have no guiding spirit and therefore they are easily accepted by others. It is not a very complimentary term."

Generally, our informants believe that one can judge whether another has ren yuan without really knowing the other person very well. However, some informants reserve their judgment until it is verified or rejected by subsequent interactions. One informant claimed that it is necessary for one to have more interactions with someone before judging whether that person has ren yuan. "When you are in a group," this respondent explained, "your judgment is very easily influenced by the judgments of others. If everybody says, 'That person has no human yuan,' I probably will take this as an explanation of his behaviors and keep my distance. If in fact I do have yuan with him, it will take a longer time to know him."

Attitude toward yuan. Even though the preceding discussion has shed some light on the complexities of yuan as a descriptor of Chinese relationships, we have had little to say about how Chinese respond to the influence of yuan in their interpersonal spheres of activity. Two terms reveal the Chinese attitude toward *yuan*: (a) *sui yuan* (隨緣), which means "follow yuan", and (b) *xi yuan* (惜緣), which means to "cherish yuan."

First, let us consider *sui yuan,* or "follow yuan." A great deal of Chinese philosophy and culture is based on the idea that wisdom and happiness are achieved when one discovers the ways of the natural world and acts in harmony with them (Haas, 1956). Thus, because yuan is in fact a metaphor that stands for the sum total of all conditions in the natural world, it is to be expected that Chinese would place a great deal of importance on acting in accord with yuan. As one informant stated, "Sui yuan is a feeling of *not forcing* contact between yourself and others in your life. Rather, you naturally meet and interact with people . . . but [on the other hand] you do not *purposefully avoid* chances to meet people." Or, as a male respondent put it, "If there is a relationship, it is OK; if there is no relationship, that is OK, too."

Following yuan is important to our respondents because it is a symbol of respect for the other person. One informant said, "Forcing others to do something they don't want to do is useless. You cannot change his heart. He is here but his heart is not here." Another said, "Even if you can force someone to do something through your personal power, this is not beautiful, and for that reason it cannot be yuan."

The novel *Where There Is Water in the River, There Is Reflected a Moon* (Xiao, 1990) illustrates the depth and beauty of the notion of "follow yuan." In this novel, a young woman attributes her relationships with her family, friends, and lover to yuan. She describes all the love, concern, and care among people as they meet each other. She especially emphasizes the relationship she has with her lover. At the novel's conclusion, after she has quarreled with her lover, she tries to contact him to tell him how much she loves him. She walks over to his house but hesitates to go upstairs to see him. She sees the light on in her boyfriend's room; after staying there for three hours, she suddenly realizes that their yuan has gone and she leaves without seeing him. As the heroine of the novel says, "Perhaps it is better not to see you. What can I say if you have already made up your mind, if you do not suffer in your heart? To be able to stand like this is fortunate enough for me. Knowing you in this life has already fulfilled my life" (Xiao, 1990, p. 336).

In this complex and moving narrative, one can see what appeals to some people about yuan and also what repels them. Many Easterners would probably like to believe that the heroine of this story is destined somehow to be associated with her boyfriend. This is a very romantic notion, tied to the oldest myth about love, that somewhere there is a "special someone" for each of us and that, when we find this person, we will be truly happy.

Nevertheless, some people (Westerners in particular) might look on the heroine's behavior as too fainthearted and timid. Why does she wait below, instead of "talking things over" with her boyfriend? Between the two of them, they might have been able to change things and get back on the road to recovering their relationship ("get things back on track"). Above all, why does she wait *for three hours,* at the end of which time she "suddenly" decides that the yuan may have vanished? It seems as if she is looking at the concept of yuan to justify her own sense of cowardice, rejecting the one opportunity she has to make things different. Some might say that she has simply given up to fate and not even a fate that has been thrust upon her but one that she clearly chooses herself.

But Chinese see this situation entirely differently. First of all, Chinese see human relationship as something that cannot be forced. The problem is not just that the woman in the novel does not want to talk to her boyfriend, she instead wonders whether the conditions (the yuan) allow her to do so. Chinese do not see relationships as primarily affected by the individual actions of a single person (particularly communicative actions, such as "talking things over") but as the responsibility of both parties (as one respondent said, "you need to respect the other person"). For the heroine to have taken it upon herself to go to her boyfriend, to have forced the issue, would have been useless, because the boyfriend could not have been forced to do something that he did not want to do.

Second, even if she does force the relationship, such a course would not be natural and hence would not be beautiful. For Chinese, nature sets the model for human beings to follow (Haas, 1956). In this regard, Chinese can be said to have a more "spontaneous" romantic view of relationships: If they do not work out, Chinese would prefer to let them die, beautifully, rather than desperately attempting to keep them alive by extraordinary means. Only when the love story dies beautifully inside the lovers' hearts can the story be kept forever, regardless of how much outward bitterness lovers must suffer. For the Chinese, it is useless to use strategies to achieve relational outcomes; even if the goal is achieved, it is still not beautiful. This can be contrasted with the Western strategic approach to interpersonal communication, which sees relationship as an outcome of communication. To Westerners, communication is often viewed as a *strategy* that produces relational outcomes (O'Keefe & Delia, 1982).

Implicit in the novel is the heroine's realization of her own responsibility in bringing about these results and of the Buddhist doctrine of *sui yuan*. She realizes that sui yuan is not the passive acceptance of an all-powerful fate (Buddhism admits of no such "first causes"), but that any intention she has to act against nature (to try to sustain the relationship by artificial means) is merely a reflection of her own desire, and that this desire will lead her to more suffering. As the heroine of this novel implies, the transcendent experience of realizing the truth of yuan is far to be preferred. It is only through the bitterly difficult process of giving up one's own desire that a spiritual realization can be achieved and one's life can be elevated to a higher sphere.

One of the respondents agreed with this idea but thought it would be difficult to try in practice. "If yuan is not according to your wish," she explained, "of course you will still try hard to change the situation. You won't follow the natural development and surrender quietly: after all, you are only human." This respondent felt that "follow yuan" is more something you say when an association has come to an end and you look back. "You have these feelings only when you have experienced life, and have passed through several other stages. It is not an imaginary feeling; rather, it is a very high spiritual achievement. Understanding is comparatively easy, but to achieve a spiritual awareness is very difficult."

This is not to say, however, that all respondents agreed that these lofty spiritual assessments are to be preferred. Some respondents, in fact would agree with most Westerners that "follow yuan" is entirely too passive. For example, one respondent thought that people sometimes say "follow yuan" as an excuse to avoid action: "If you say 'follow yuan' without doing anything, of course the result will be less than satisfactory. There is still a lot that can be done by human beings; you can do a lot to get the best out of your situation."

Whether "follow yuan" is active or passive is primarily a matter of individual judgment. Sui yuan can have many other implications, as the informants pointed out. As one said, "Such a feeling depends on an individual's attitude." Another respondent concurred, stating that "follow yuan" depends on individual response: If bitten by a dog, one person may say "How unlucky I am!" while another may feel fortunate not to have been hit by a car. Nevertheless, another informant disagreed with this relativistic viewpoint, likening yuan to "a moving force." In "following yuan," she said, one is doing something very active. "You do not falter, but rather you keep going. Thus, to follow yuan is not passive at all."

As important as the concept "follow yuan" is to our informants, however, there is one remaining idea that is even more significant: *xi yuan* (惜 緣), or "cherish yuan." In fact, a common Chinese proverb states, *sui yuan bu ru xi yuan* (it is better to cherish yuan than just to follow it). The reason for this distinction is that "cherish yuan" is considered more active and hence more appropriate given the importance of yuan to Chinese culture. *Xi yuan* means that two people do their best to maintain their relationship because the felicitous combination of external causes and internal feeling does not occur very often. Therefore, it is important to treasure the relationship, here and now.

Most of our respondents agree with the elevation of *xi yuan*, believing that "follow yuan" is too passive. One male respondent pointed out that xi yuan puts more emphasis on individual action: "Personally, I think this is a good attitude . . . if you work harder your life will be better. Human beings are limited, but beyond human beings, the *world* is unlimited. I attribute all of this to yuan because I have a need to feel a sense of certainty." One female respondent explained, "Xi yuan represents a sensitivity toward yuan. Those who cherish yuan are more idealistic and sentimental. Only those who are affectionate will feel strongly about yuan. When you see that the relationship is important to you, you cherish it while it lasts, and when it has gone, you hope you will be able to continue it in a future life."

Our informants especially felt the need to "cherish yuan" when a relationship with another was uncertain, such as when there was a danger of the relationship ending. "If we are here," said one respondent, "and our parents are far away, we won't have much time to spend with them. Since human beings are mortal, we will feel strongly about cherishing yuan with them." For Chinese, the chance to have a relationship is so precious that it must be cherished and not strategically manipulated.

SIGNIFICANCE OF *YUAN* FOR CONCEPTUALIZING CHINESE RELATIONSHIPS

From the foregoing, it should be evident that yuan is not equivalent to relationship but that it serves to reveal how Chinese *think* about their relationships as well as being a means for Chinese to shape their interactional activities. Such knowledge is vital if we are to avoid the pitfalls of trying unreflectingly to apply Western models of communication to Eastern interpersonal relationships (Kincaid, 1987).

As a central organizing metaphor, yuan obviously has a wide range of rich and variable meanings. Nevertheless, these meanings can be summed up in three basic principles: (1) *yuan* is typically used to describe initial interaction conditions; (2) *yuan* is typically used to account for more important relationships; and (3) *yuan* cannot be forced.

First, *yuan is used to describe initial interaction conditions.* Because of the influence of secondary causation, Chinese feel that the initial contact between two people is an extremely significant event. The most important aspect for our discussion is that such occasions for initial interaction do not come about all that easily. In fact, to Chinese, *all initial encounters* share the same quality of specialness. Several informants said that there are millions of people in the world, so that you do not meet any one of them by chance.

Though some people say that the amount of yuan is what sustains the relationship past its initial stages, many Chinese contend that the function of yuan is simply to bring people together. Later on, they argue, the relationship depends upon one's own personal effort. Thus it is possible for Chinese to attribute the success of a relationship to individual effort while at the same time acknowledging that the conditions governing initial interaction remain largely beyond one's personal control. This accords perfectly with the Chinese attitude that one should try one's best and leave the rest to the unknown.

A second overarching characteristic revealed by the interview data is that *yuan is used to account for important relationships.* As discussed before, if people are associated in any way at all, then they are considered to have at least some yuan with each other. Moreover, the amount of yuan will vary in degree according to the relationship. Chinese believe that a relationship will become significant only if people have *a great deal of yuan* with each other; thus the concept of yuan is reserved in common parlance primarily to describe those individuals with whom one shares important relationships.

One female informant expressed the idea explicitly: "I have three circles of friends. One is simply acquaintances, one is friends, and the most inner one is close friends. I will only use *yuan* to describe close friends and friends. I won't feel I particularly have yuan with those who are merely acquaintances." Or, as another informant put it, "If you break up with a boyfriend who you do not like very much, you won't use *wu yuan* ["no yuan"] to describe the situation. You will only use yuan to describe a relationship which is very important to you. Although you still have yuan with him to some degree, who cares about yuan with him?"

It is clear that, because our respondents see relationships as something very special and precious, their feeling becomes particularly strong toward those with whom they have the deepest relationships. A sense of "having yuan with," then, becomes very strong when another is associated with you to a significant degree. As one male informant put it, "We always use *yuan* to describe a potential spouse, because you are going to marry that person and will have a lot of involvement with her."

Another important kind of relationship that Chinese view as a manifestation of yuan is that of *kinship*. One informant said that the most difficult thing in the world is to be someone's child or to be someone's sister or brother. The kinship relationship is considered to be very important, primarily because (according to Buddhist theology, at least) the linkages of association among members of a family require a great deal of yuan.

A third metatheme revealed in the interviews is that Chinese view *yuan as something that cannot be forced.* This idea may reflect the very important Taoist influence upon Chinese culture: nature says nothing, the Taoists tell us, yet it paves the way for all things to occur (Chan, 1963). Thus, for the Chinese, the best path for humans is to imitate nature (Haas, 1956). Under the guiding principle of yuan, relationship is not something that can be manipulated but something that must follow its own development, extending beyond human control. By not forcing a final solution to relational problems, Chinese apparently lack the strategic view of "relationshipping," which is the most significant difference between East and West concerning interpersonal relationship development.

THE IMPLICATIONS OF *YUAN* FOR CHINESE INTERPERSONAL COMMUNICATION

The above-mentioned three basic principles of yuan shed light on the way Chinese view their relationships, as contrasted with the Western focus on interpersonal communication in relationships. Basically, the idea of yuan makes it possible to avoid three possible sources of confusion in applying Western communication models to Eastern interpersonal communication: (a) the role of the individual, (b) the likelihood of future involvement, and (c) the use of interpersonal communication as a means of comforting.

First, the notion of yuan can regulate how cross-cultural researchers view the role of the individual in interpersonal communication and the individual's instrumental approach toward communication. In the Western approach, communicators are seen as separate: "Each communicator is perceived to be a separate individual engaging in diverse communicative activities to maximize his/her own self-interest, usually by means of some form of persuasion" (Yum, 1988, p. 376). According to this Western mode of reasoning, the role of communication thus bears directly on the relational outcome. For example, note Burleson's (1986) review of research confirming that children's peer status can be enhanced through development of communicative competence. Duck (1985) contends that the chief contribution interpersonal communication scholars can make to the study of interpersonal relationships is to investigate the role communication plays in "relationshipping." Berger and his associates, in their theory of uncertainty reduction (Berger & Bradac, 1982; Berger & Calabrese, 1975), argue that close relationships are built upon the extent to which one partner has information about the other—information that is gained, of course, through communication.

According to this Western view, communication is seen to serve primarily functional and practical purposes in the creation and maintenance of interpersonal relationships. A clue to the pervasiveness of this general model can be seen in what Parks (1982) calls the "ideology of intimacy," that is, the belief that, so long as relational partners disclose to each other, the *resultant* relationship will be better (deeper, more intimate). This viewpoint, confirmed by the Katriel and Philipsen (1981) study of how North Americans view communication, holds that such intimacy, achieved through communication, assumes predominance over all other factors in the relationship. For Chinese, however, communication is not seen as having a direct relational outcome: Such an idea is subsumed and absorbed by, and must be mediated by, the overarching themes surrounding the concept of yuan, which focuses upon contextual, not individual, factors.

A second issue raised by the awareness of yuan has to do with speculations about future involvement trajectories. The concept of yuan can serve as a cognitive guide to real situations, because it has to do not just simply with how we talk about the relationship but also with the evolution of *chances* to interact with the other person in the future. As one of the respondents noted, when people associate with each other, some may attribute it to *you yuan* from the very beginning, a factor that can lead to having more chances for subsequent encounters. It is important to realize that Chinese, because they have access to the idea of yuan, possess a relationship-shaping tool that remains inaccessible to most Westerners. In a similar vein, Chinese may retrospectively attribute a relationship to yuan only after several encounters. Whether the remark about yuan is made in the initial encounter or in a subsequent meeting, the result is the same: Yuan paves the way for future encounters.

In this view, the objective facilitating conditions are taken as a subjective force in engaging or disengaging a relationship. Chinese relationships, thus conceived, are not seen as problems of communication or an issue of complementarity between relational partners (Duck, 1985) but as the degree to which one is *willing* to engage a relationship within the allowance of the conditioning factors, as determined by the interactant's personal judgment. Such an approach toward the mysterious feeling about one's relational partner, and its consequent result of increasing chances for interaction, is at odds with earlier Western views that center on the theme of personality, holding that mutual attraction occurs when people's personalities complement one another or when they hold similar attitudes toward one another. This position is also at odds with the Western model because it questions whether relationship is manifested through communication.

Third, the cross-cultural investigator should be alert to the differences in how comforting is perceived by those who know about yuan. For Chinese, the concept of yuan can serve as a means for comforting another in a relationship. While North Americans often try to invoke communication as a means of relational repair, Chinese are more resigned to relational difficulties because they can attribute them to, and explain them by means of, yuan. Rather than going to an intermediary, such as a marriage counselor, to resolve communication problems in conflict resolution, Chinese do not perceive communication as something that can be strategically employed as a means to an end: that is, to rescue the relationship. One informant (who had served as a social worker, a profession developed in the West) recalled:

> A lot of problems which confuse our clients are more practical issues than relational issues. People who have troubles in their relationships, when they finally decide to come to ask our help, do not perceive their problems as communicative problems. It was not until we told them that they had problems in their communication that they became aware of it.

The cross-cultural researcher who knows about yuan knows that, outside the West, there are considerably greater restraints on how much a relationship can be "worked on." As we have pointed out, the concept of yuan denotes the natural development of a relationship according to its facilitating conditions, conditions that cannot be forced. By resigning themselves to unknown factors that bring association as well as dissociation between people, Chinese feel no need to develop specifically communicative strategies to maintain their relationships. By cherishing the chance of association, and by allowing the relationship to develop according to its own course, Chinese are more willing to tolerate a bad relationship or to disengage a relationship without using communicative strategies to do so. Moreover, even though communication is not perceived as a tool to affect an outcome, Chinese nevertheless realize the importance of communication. Yet, even in this realization, communication is not seen as the chief factor determining whether people are allowed to associate with one another. For if yuan does not allow the association, there is no way one could rescue a relationship, whether good or bad. Relationship is not perceived as an activity to be actively pursued by the actors through communication training but as an activity that develops in its own way and in its own time.

From the above analysis, three conclusions can be drawn. First, acceptance of yuan does not mean that Chinese are fatalistic, giving up on relationships and letting them die. Second, even though Chinese do acknowledge that they can work on relationships, they do not consider communication as the only means of doing so. Third, and finally, granting that Chinese are able to work on relationships through means other than communication, they are willing to leave certain aspects of the relationship to contextual factors, which they regard as largely unknown and unknowable.

In this chapter, we have tried to offer a richer and more philosophical account of Chinese relationships than that proposed by consideration of Confucianism alone. While there is no question that Confucianism, with its specification of roles and its ordering of society, is the most obvious and identifiable aspect of Chinese culture, it is also true that Confucianism's very obviousness precludes its use as a complete account of Chinese interpersonal relationships, with implications for Chinese interpersonal communication. Chinese are subtle and indirect in many respects but in none more so than their interactions with other people. We feel that a consideration of the subtleties of Buddhist thought enables us to apprehend Chinese thinking about relationship more completely.

In fact, much of what our respondents told us about their relationships would (at least from a Western viewpoint) seem to be quite illogical were it not for the organizing principle of yuan. When we place Confucian social prescriptions in the field of yuan, or secondary causation, we are provided with a powerful metaphor for explaining how Chinese come to view relationship and the extent to which relationship is, or is not, an outcome of communicative competence. Such a realization aids us in approaching the goal articulated by Kincaid (1987), that is, to challenge and expand the scope of our own thinking about human communication through an investigation of the similarities and the differences between the Western and Eastern philosophical models.

For Chinese, the concept of yuan is not only an abstract philosophy of interpersonal relationship but also an attitude toward life. From our earlier example of the newspaper story (Song, 1988) about the young couple getting married, we can extract a quotation that simultaneously sums up this attitude and at the same time provides a fitting conclusion to this chapter:

> Don't regret that you meet each other too late, but do be precious about your yuan, because in this life, any yuan is not easy to get. Only those who know enough to cherish yuan will realize that even a small encounter might have been prepared for thousands of years. When yuan is mature, try your best to make it flower with the most beautiful blossoms. Whether the flower blossoms or dies, if you try your best, you will have no regrets.

REFERENCES

Becker, C. M. (1988). Reasons for the lack of argumentation and debate in the Far East. In L. A. Samovar & R. E. Porter (Eds.), *Intercultural communication: A reader* (pp. 243-252). Belmont, CA: Wadsworth.

Berger, C. R., & Bradac, J. J. (1982). *Language and social knowledge: Uncertainty in interpersonal relations.* London: Edward Arnold.

Berger, C. R., & Calabrese, R. J. (1975). Some explorations in initial interaction and beyond: Toward a developmental theory of interpersonal communication. *Human Communication Research, 1*, 99-112.

Burleson, B. R. (1986). Communication skills and childhood peer relationships: An overview. In M. L. McLaughlin (Ed.), *Communication yearbook 9* (pp. 143-180). Beverly Hills, CA: Sage.

Chan, W. (1963). *A sourcebook in Chinese philosophy.* Princeton, NJ: Princeton University Press.

Choy, R. (1981). *Read and write Chinese: A simplified guide to the Chinese characters* (4th ed.). San Francisco: China West.

Duck, S. (1985). Social and personal relationships. In M. L. Knapp & G. R. Miller (Eds.), *Handbook of interpersonal communication* (pp. 655-685). Beverly Hills, Ca: Sage.

Fung, Y. (1983). *A history of Chinese philosophy* (Derke Bodde, Trans.) (2 vols.). Princeton, NJ: Princeton University Press.

Geertz, C. (1973). *The interpretation of cultures.* New York: Basic Books.

Haas, W. (1956). *Destiny of the mind, East and West.* New York: Macmillan.

Hymes, D. H. (1972). The ethnography of speaking. In J. A. Fishman (Ed.), *Readings in the sociology of language* (pp. 99-138). The Hague, the Netherlands: Mouton.

Jackson, S. (1986). Building a case for claims about discourse structure. In D. G. Ellis & W. A. Donohue (Eds.), *Contemporary issues in language and discourse processes* (pp. 129-148). Hillsdale, NJ: Lawrence Erlbaum.

Katriel, T., & Philipsen, G. (1981). "What we need is communication": "Communication" as a cultural category in some American speech. *Communication Monographs, 48,* 301-317.

Kincaid, D. L. (1987). *Communication theory: Eastern and Western perspectives.* San Diego, CA: Academic Press.

Maruyama, M. (1974). Paradigmatology and its application to cross-disciplinary, cross-professional and cross-cultural communication. *Dialectica, 28*(3), 135-196.

Nakamura, H. (1984). Interrelational existence. In K. K. Inada & N. P. Jacobson (Eds.), *Buddhism and American thinkers* (pp. 143-152). Albany: State University of New York Press.

Niwano, N. (1980). *Buddhism for today.* New York: John Weatherhill.

O'Keefe, B. J., & Delia, J. G. (1982). Impression formation and message production. In M. E. Roloff & C. R. Berger (Eds.), *Social cognition and communication* (pp. 33-72). Beverly Hills, CA: Sage.

Parks, M. R. (1982). Ideology of interpersonal communication: Off the couch and into the world. In M. Burgoon (Ed.), *Communication yearbook 5* (pp. 79-108). New Brunswick, NJ: Transaction.

Redding, S. G., & Martyn-Johns, T. A. (1979). Paradigm differences and their relation to management, with reference to south-east Asia. In G. W. England, A. R. Neghandi, & B. Wilpert (Eds.), *Organizational functioning in a cross-cultural perspective* (pp. 103-125). Kent, OH: Kent State University Press.

Saville-Troike, M. (1982). *The ethnography of communication.* London: Basil Blackwell.

Sillars, A. L., & Weisberg, J. (1987). Conflict as a social skill. In M. E. Roloff & G. R. Miller (Eds.), *Interpersonal processes: New directions in communication research* (pp. 140-171). Newbury Park, CA: Sage.

Song, Y. (1988, April 12). *Yuan-shou* [Maturation of yuan]. *Central Daily News* [Overseas edition].

Soothill, W. E., & Hodous, L. (Comps.). (1968). *The dictionary of Chinese Buddhist terms.* London: Kegan Paul, Trench, Trubner.

Xiao, L. (1990). *Qian-jiang-you-shui-qian-jiang-yue* [Where there is water in the river, there is reflected a moon] (22nd ed.). Taipei, Taiwan (ROC): United Newspaper.

Yum, J. O. (1988). The impact of Confucianism on interpersonal relationships and communication in East Asia. *Communication Monographs, 55,* 374-388.

4

Nicknaming Practices in Families
A Cross-Cultural Perspective

SHOSHANA BLUM-KULKA ● *Hebrew University of Jerusalem*

TAMAR KATRIEL ● *University of Haifa*

This chapter analyzes the role played by nicknaming practices in the interactions of family members from a cross-cultural perspective. The analysis is based on observed instances of nickname use as derived from audio and videotaped dinners in Israeli and Jewish American families and on self-report data derived from open-structured interviews. Considerable cultural variability has been found with respect to the traffic of nicknames within and across family boundaries. A typology of the functions of nicknames as used in familial contexts is presented, and the sociocultural implications of differences in patterns of nickname use and in attitudes toward nicknames among the Israeli families as compared with the American Jewish families are discussed.

"From the day I sat down beside him at school, I was unaware that he had any other name. The crab—that was his name, and that was the nickname he had carried with him, he claimed, from the village. Not so his parents. They said that it was actually in the city that the nickname had been pinned on him. The truth is that childhood nicknames are like jokes, nobody knows their source, or who invented them. And they stick. It was more my own anxiety than his worry. I was following the phenomenon with great interest. . . .

"At first I thought that the nickname "crab" was given to him because of his appearance. His manner of walking was strange, the right leg pointing to the right and the left leg to the left, like the needle of a compass. Add to this his slimness, tallness and long neck—and you will need no more information about the source of his nickname.

"But that was not the case. When I became enamored with fishing, and came to know the characteristics of the sea-crab intimately, as intimately as a man knows his own secret, I was reminded of my friend

AUTHORS' NOTE: An earlier version of this chapter was presented at the Culture and Communication Conference in Philadelphia (October 1985). We are especially grateful to Hadas Sheffer, who has carried out subsequent analyses of data from dinner-table conversations, partly incorporated here (Sheffer, 1989). The research reported was supported by Israeli Science Binational Foundation grant no. 87-00167/1.

Hariz Ibn-Makitz, may his soul rest in peace, and realized that I had been wrong after all. Only then did I grasp that nicknames are related to the person's inner essence and not to his external appearance.

"There is something utterly mysterious about nicknames.

"And he, may his memory be blessed, resembled the sea-crab in his naivete and goodness of heart. An unmatched naivete. If the Arabs were a people of the beaches, they would probably have used the crab in their fables in place of the ostrich." (E. Habibi, "The Crab's Lament," 1988)[1]

The fascination with nicknaming practices, and the curiosity about the roles they play in social life, is shared by many users of language, and students of verbal behavior have provided considerable systematic insights into the forms and uses of nicknames. The study of nicknames has, indeed, attracted researchers from a range of scholarly disciplines, each of whom has tried to dispel some of the "mystery" associated with this linguistic practice. Sociolinguists have considered nicknames as part of the study of systems of personal address (see Philipsen & Huspek, 1985, for an extensive bibliography). Anthropologists have traditionally been interested in nicknaming practices as part of the study of the kinship terminologies and the social organization of the communities in which they have situated their inquiries (e.g., Antoun, 1968; Barrett, 1978; Brandes, 1975; Gilmore, 1982; Glazier, 1987; Manning, 1974). Folklorists have similarly explored the nature of nicknames as folk expressions (e.g., McDowell, 1981), and social psychologists have attended to their uses as observable mechanisms of group life (e.g., Morgan, O'Neill, & Harre, 1979). All these studies bring out the essentially group-related nature of the use of nicknames in everyday interaction, especially their grounding in small face-to-face primary group relations.

Moreover, as Glazier (1987) points out, in a study of an American Jewish community in the Midwest, cultural changes in social organization and kinship relations in modern urban settings can be reflected in shifting patterns of nickname use. Indeed, nicknames can be seen as symbols of both relationship and community, and their study can, therefore, offer insights both into patterns of cultural practice and into processes of cultural change.

Thus, drawing on the insights offered by these various studies, this chapter will add to the growing fund of research on nicknaming patterns by investigating their functions in the context of nuclear families in two modern, complex societies (Israel and the United States). We hope that both the focus on the modern, middle-class nuclear family as a social unit vis-à-vis nickname use and the attempt to develop a comparative, cross-cultural perspective for exploring this widespread and intriguing sociolinguistic mechanism will contribute to the understanding of nicknaming practices as an instance of the interaction of language and social life.

In his semiotically oriented analysis of nickname use, McDowell (1981, p. 5) has identified three questions that need to be asked with regard to each appellation unit:

(1) What is the scope of name use?
(2) What, if any, is the sense of the names employed in this unit?
(3) How do these names become associated with their name bearers?

THE NICKNAMING QUESTIONS

(1) What is the scope of name use? An answer to this would sketch the name's sociological boundaries, delineating the social categories, or persons, favorable to it and those that constrain it. We have restricted our attention to nicknaming practices within nuclear families. Whether the family group is the proper scope for nicknames, evincing patterns of use that are distinctive to it, is an empirical question that a study such as ours should address rather than presuppose. The answer, as we shall see, is not a simple one.

While nicknames do indeed tend to proliferate in some of the nuclear families in our study, and are perceived as restricted to them, they are uncommon in other cases or take the wider social network as their scope. At the same time, there is considerable evidence of internal differentiation in family groups with respect to nickname use, which may be constrained rather than facilitated by the presence of some family members. Examples of family coalitions sociolinguistically marked by the use of nicknames can serve both integrating and differentiating functions within nuclear families. Thus family coalitions, which are sociolinguistically marked by the use of nicknames, can serve as linguistic mechanisms of social demarcation, integrating the family both by preventing the spread of certain nicknames outside the family group and by keeping other nicknames from penetrating into the family circle.

(2) What, if any, is the sense of the names employed in this unit? Because a nickname does not only refer, as all names do, but also conveys a great deal of information, an answer to this question would address the degree of descriptive backing the nickname makes manifest and the character of the information it conveys. When the descriptive

backing is central to a nickname (which is not always the case, as in nicknames formed by morphological inflections on the official name), its sense must still be inferred. As McDowell (1981, p. 7) puts it: "The special province of the nickname is to make manifest an unorthodox descriptive backing." Because nicknames tend to convey their descriptive backing through indirect, metaphorical means—whether a person's nickname refers, for example, to some aspect of his or her external appearance, or to some character trait, or harks back to some childhood incident—its meaning is often left open to conjecture and may, indeed, change over the years for some of its users (as is indicated in the case of "the crab" in our epigraph).

Getting the "sense" of a nickname of this kind is very much like understanding a metaphor: the process involves establishing a cognitive link between the nickname bearer and some extraneous semantic domain in such a way as to highlight the properties of both. The nicknames that proliferate within the families we studied quite often lack such descriptive backing, as they are formed by morphological inflections on the official name. Yet, when they do carry information, it is of the kind that is deeply embedded in family history, and the retelling of the particular incident or trait that triggered the nickname reinforces part of a family's shared and bonding canonical repertoire.

(3) How do these names become associated with their name bearers? An answer to this question involves attention to the inventive, metaphorical powers of language as it performs the function of nomination. Nicknames, unlike official names, are not associated with institutionalized moments and conditions of performative nomination. That is, with a speech act that establishes a naming convention predicated on the power of language to transform, not merely depict, reality. Given the absence of an institutional procedure for accomplishing performative nomination in the case of nicknames, they earn their way into general usage by virtue of a combination of semantic appropriateness and aesthetic appeal. Nicknames are often tied to narrative anecdotes that rationalize, even legitimize, particular names. These tales, as McDowell (1981, p. 10) suggests, "substitute, in some acts of didactic nomination, for the missing act of performative nomination." It is because of this informal manner of nickname emergence that a particular nickname may be associated with conflicting "miniature etiological tales" concerning their source, as seems to have been the case with "the crab" mentioned above.

We must note, however, that formulating our task as the investigation of the uses of nicknames in families seems more straightforward than it actually is. Although the definition of a nickname as consisting of a name other than the "official name" is generally accepted, it implies an overly simplified dichotomy between the official name and the nickname. The dichotomy blurs the fact that nicknames are not all of a piece, and their uses reflect various degrees of institutionalization and routinization that underlie the degree of linguistic "markedness" that the various forms are felt to have in different contexts. Naming practices should, therefore, be placed along a continuum rather than be described in polar terms. Nicknames conventionally derived from given names (e.g., Debra from Deborah) turn within families into institutionalized replacements. These are usually the only appellations used, so much so that they are no longer perceived as falling under the category of "nicknames." In these cases, the official name is used so rarely as to make its utterance a sociolinguistically marked occasion.

Attention to these processes of gradual and differential institutionalization of nicknames—from "fresh," creative nicknames to routinized, standardized ones—is essential. Its merit lies in that it forces us away from the easier (and less interesting) task of considering nicknames as linguistic "products" to the more difficult (but more rewarding) task of exploring their uses with reference to the ongoing transactional web that makes for their gradual, differential adoption.

The comparative account of nicknaming practices within Israeli Jewish families and Jewish American ones undertaken here offers a functional analysis of nickname use in family discourse, whether the nicknames are used to perform a vocative or a referential semantic function (i.e., whether they are used in address or in mention). Within this context, we shall address the issue of scope, sense, nomination, and institutionalization in nickname usage. We thus hope to show that nicknaming practices constitute a significant component of cultural style for members of the two speech communities in question. Also a better understanding of the ways they are deployed can lead to a better grasp of conceptions of the family as a sociocultural unit in the two groups.

We now turn to a description of our data collection procedures and briefly address the question of the salience and scope of nickname use in both cultural groups. We then move on to develop a typology of nicknaming functions, which will incorporate a consideration of their semantics as vocatives and referential signs. Finally, we will discuss the sociocultural implications of our comparative findings, particularly in terms of what they tell us about families in the cultural groups studied.

NICKNAMING PRACTICES IN ISRAELI AND
JEWISH AMERICAN FAMILIES

Our data are derived from an examination of naming practices in family discourse in the dinner-table conversations of Israeli families, Jewish American families, and American Israeli immigrant families in Israel (12 in the United States and 23 in Israel). The families studied are all middle- to upper-middle-class Jewish families, with two to three school-age children. Three dinner-table conversations were recorded (one by video and two by audio) for each family, with an observer present at each dinner. Transcripts were coded for all instances of children being addressed by the parents, yielding a corpus of 887 vocatives. These were classified as follows: (a) the use of a name or an institutionalized nickname ("Stephen" or "Steve"), (b) the use of an innovative, individuated nickname (including morphological and phonological variations on the name, and (c) an endearment ("honey," "darling"; Sheffer, 1989). These data are complemented by insights gained during semistructured interviews with all the families in the project, in the course of which we asked family members to chart a "nicknaming map" (who addressed and refers to whom by which name or nickname) and discussed in depth the attitudes and narratives connected with specific naming practices.

In these conversations, it is Israeli parents who indulge in an extremely rich repertoire of nicknaming toward their children. Given the choices between using a name (or its institutionalized abbreviated version), a nickname, or a term of endearment, Israeli parents prefer nicknames in more than a third of the cases, while both Jewish American and immigrant parents revert to nicknames in fewer than 10% of the cases (Table 4.1). In the overwhelming majority of cases, Jewish American or immigrant parents address children by name or by terms of endearment, nicknaming being used in only 15% of all explicit instances of address.

Israeli parents use a wide variety of innovative nicknames, yielding a rich repertoire of emotively colored terms of address per child at every meal. Parents indulge in an extremely rich repertoire of nicknaming toward children of all ages (the use of eight to nine such appellations during dinner is not unusual). Linguistically, these nicknames usually take the form of morphological play on the child's official name (e.g., Dan/Danny/Danile/Danilus/Dudu, and so on). For example, a child named Jonathan, who was 10 at the time of the recordings, was variously addressed by his parents as [jonatanj]/[joni]/[onton]/[jonti], and [ontik]. Such effusive nicknaming practices are rare in our Jewish

TABLE 4.1 Parents' Terms of Address to Children in Three Family Groups

	Israeli (percentage)	Immigrant (percentage)	Jewish American (percentage)
Name	55	88	85
Nickname	37	10	7.5
Endearment	8	2	7.5
N	(436)	(188)	(263)

American and immigrant samples: At the dinner table, children are usually addressed by their names or by their institutionalized nicknames, occasionally interchanged with a conventional form of endearment. Thus a girl named Jennifer, aged 8, is addressed either as "Jennifer," "Jenny," or "darling." Clearly, the Israeli nicknaming pattern in this context differs considerably from the Jewish American one.

Is the effusive use of nicknaming in the Israeli families related to children's age? Do younger children in these families receive more nicknames than older ones? As can be seen in Table 4.2, the younger the Israeli child, the lower are his or her chances of being addressed by his or her official name. In this group, the use of nicknames decreases with age. We found no such trend in the Jewish American and immigrant families: The relatively small number of nicknaming vocatives (20 cases for each group compared with 163 for the Israeli families) are equally distributed by age in the Jewish American families and tend to be reserved for preschoolers and teens in the immigrant families.

The two cultural nicknaming patterns that emerge differ both in practice (from abundant use of nicknames to an almost complete avoidance of them) as well as in attitude toward the practice (from highly positive to highly critical). The attitudinal range was clearly verbalized during the interviews with the families. In the Israeli families, questions regarding nicknames were met with general, positive excitement, with all members of the family joining in to provide the full list and intercept with stories. In the Jewish American and immigrant families, nicknames were far from being considered a positive family asset. On the contrary, they were sometimes frowned upon and considered a practice that undermines a person's claim to individuality ("Actually I don't like nicknames and I always call the kids by their regular names, you know, their given names"). Yet, institutionalized nicknames (Jenny for Jennifer, Bobbie for Robert) are just as common in use in the Jewish American and immigrant families as in the Israeli ones, and narrative

TABLE 4.2 Proportion of Nicknames in Parents' Address to Children According to Age

	Israeli (percentage)	Immigrant (percentage)	Jewish American (percentage)
Preschoolers	100	20	33
School aged	88	8	33
Teens	50	25	29
N	(163)	(20)	(20)

anecdotes associated with familial nicknames were provided by family members in both groups. Hence, before we can explore the meaning of the sociocultural variation found in use and attitude, we need to delineate the functions nicknames can serve in the familial setting.

A FUNCTIONAL ANALYSIS OF NICKNAMES

In this section, we delineate the major communicative functions served by the nicknaming practices we have studied among middle-class Israeli and Jewish American families. Notably, the use of a particular nickname often serves more than one function in a given context—indeed, some of them are interdependent—but the various functions we specify can, nevertheless, be analytically distinguished. The advantage of distinguishing between the functions of nicknames in a systematic and schematic fashion is that this enables us to identify dominant functions of nicknames in given contexts and compare them across contexts and cultures. Some of the functions of nicknames we discuss are relevant to the analysis of nicknames in the aforementioned traditional anthropological studies.

The fact that comparable functions of nicknames within nuclear families in urban settings can be demonstrated is not self-evident, given the view that "in the relatively impersonal milieu of the large city, nicknames can have no significant impact; the anonymity of urban life prevents nicknames from operating as a check on behavior" (Brandes 1975, p. 146). Glazier (1987, p. 85) questions Brandes's conclusion and argues that "nicknames occur in cities and manifest characteristics deviating from what they are in European or Latin American villages," offering an intriguing analysis of the functions of nicknames as the vehicles of nostalgia and as emblems of a vanished community.

However, even in confirming the contemporary interest in nicknames as a phenomenon associated with urban life, and adding an identity-related function that is relevant to the sociocultural condition of the group he has studied, Glazier considers nickname use in public, and in male rather than domestic and familial contexts. In fact, he describes the antagonism middle-aged women feel toward the men's continued cultivation of their youthful nicknaming practices. As we consider familial exchanges, we will attend to the particularized ways that familiar functions of nicknames are used in this context.

Nicknames Can Perform an Individuating Function

Nicknames were found to serve the purpose of ready identification in communities whose naming repertoires consisted of a small number of surnames and rigid naming requirements that led to the frequent replication of names among kin or even nonkin (e.g., Antoun, 1968; Dorian, 1970; Brandes, 1975). In families, the individuating function of nicknames is more subtle and is not motivated by the requirement for simple identification. It may, however, be a token of attention to individual characteristics at a certain age, or to personalized occasions or circumstances.

In one of the Jewish American families, the younger boy was referred to for years as "Dan the wrecker," an appellation obviously recalling certain types of sanctioned behavior. In another, a girl (called Ruth, officially) acquired "Zelda" as a nickname due to a part she played in a school performance, an occasion cherished and remembered only by her family. It is interesting that it is members' joint awareness of the tale connected with the nickname, rather than the nickname itself, that generates a sense of solidarity.

Nicknames Can Perform a Social Demarcation Function

In this respect, they function like slang, as linguistic mechanisms of social demarcation. Because the descriptive backing of the nicknames generally refers to personal characteristics made manifest in face-to-face communication, such descriptors of personal appearance, social behavior, and personal habits of various kinds are the stuff of which nicknames are made. Their crystallization as part of the familial code both reflects and reinforces the existence and the continued cultivation of a shared family history, sketching the boundaries of the family as a social unit and enhancing a sense of solidarity among its members.

The same is true for the use of nicknames constructed through morphological play with the official name by means of addition or deletion of suffixes or infixes of various sorts. The nickname's integrative function is particularly pronounced when members consciously prevent their spread outside the scope of the family. As we were told by a girl called Noa, aged 18 at the time of the interview, the addition of the suffix "le" to her name (Noale) made it a nickname only her family had the right to use: "If my friends tried to call me [Noale] I wouldn't let them, I would say it's a reserved name [shem shamur]."

Another, perhaps subtler way in which nicknames are used to demarcate the family unit is through a process of abstention. For example, a child may obtain a nickname in a peer group, and his or her family may be quite aware of this nickname, yet they will never use it in addressing the child. Thus, for reasons long forgotten, a boy called Ilan has acquired the nickname of Benson; he is both Benson and Ilan to his friends but never Benson to his family. The mirror image of this process is gleaned from the words of the parents who said they abstained from addressing a child with many familial nicknames by anything other than his or her official name in front of the child's friends. Such parental abstention testifies to the symbolic role nicknames play in demarcating social boundaries.

Another example of the demarcation of nicknames along generational lines involves the differential use of nicknames by members of different generations. For example, in one of our Israeli Jewish families, a 15-year-old boy, whose name is Avraham, is addressed by everyone except his grandmother as Rami. His grandmother calls him "Avremele," a choice of nickname that testifies to a loyalty to the Jewish origins of the name, with the diminutive "le" pointing more specifically to an Eastern European, Yiddish-speaking tradition. The institutionalized nickname Rami does not bear clear traces of the original but assimilates in its sound pattern to other popular Israeli nicknames (Tami for Tamar; Gabi for Gabriel; Nati for Netanel, and so on). In this case, the generation gap reflected through the choice of nicknames is also a gap between two subcultures that coexist in contemporary Israel: The Jewish, Yiddish-colored culture of the East European heritage and the native, Hebrew-based culture of modern Israel.

It is interesting that, to hear the voice of the Eastern European Yiddish-colored cultural style (the background of all our families) in the Jewish American families, interviewees had to go back one generational step. It was the father in the family, not a child, who recalled his grandmother calling him by the Yiddish variation of his Hebrew name in his childhood: "She used to call me 'Gershi', you know, from 'Gershon.'" Another parent recalled the Russian sounding nicknames her grandmother used in addressing her: "She said things like [glansh]/

[glanchik]/[glanshuk]/, I can't even pronounce it anymore." For their own children, though, these parents sometimes revert to the child's Hebrew name (Shalva for a child called Jessica) and use that as a nickname, drawing on Jewish heritage for demarcating the family unit.

Generally speaking, then, the Israeli Jewish families seem to rely most heavily on nicknaming practices for demarcating the family unit, for drawing the boundaries between the inner, private familial circle and society at large, between the private and the public. This integrative function of nicknames in Israeli society was stressed by interviewees who specified the constraints related to the use of nicknames outside the family boundaries, "when strangers are around." Especially outspoken on this issue were (it is not surprising) the teenagers who used the interviews to voice a complaint against their parents' occasional lapse into nicknaming in the presence of "others." Yet most parents are aware of the necessity to draw the lines: A child named Dan is called Dan at school because his parents made a special point of keeping the official version of the name (not reverting to the usual "dani"). But at home his mother addresses him alternatively as [dudi]/[benush] (from "ben" meaning "son") and [dedi]; yet not in front of others: "I am aware it is embarassing for him. In front of friends I always call him 'Dan.' "

In the talk of the North American families, the naming practices employed are in greater accord with wider societal usage, primarily signifying membership in the community at large and not in the family circle as such. Thus the private/public distinction of the Israeli families is replaced by an informal/formal distinction in the North American families: "I am not crazy about being called around the house Rebecca—if it's a wedding, a dinner-party, yeah, but around the house I prefer Becky from family and friends." But note that both appellations are drawn from the general societal repertoire; their use is distinguished by the degree of situational formality: One type of appellation is appropriate for formal occasions at home (dinner parties) as well as elsewhere (weddings), the other for informal talks with family and friends.

Nicknames Can Perform a Social Control Function

In the broadest sense, the function of social control performed by the use of a nickname is not different in essence from the social power encoded in choice of address terms in general. Though the emphasis in the literature traditionally has been on the ways in which choice of address terms maps onto social relations of power and solidarity in the society at large (e.g., Brown & Gilman, 1960; Ervin-Tripp, 1972), sociolinguists have also been aware of the power potential embedded in address systems, which can be exploited in dynamic ways at any given discoursal instance. A convincing illustration of this is found in Ervin-Tripp's (1972) account of the Black physician who felt stripped of rank, position, and age by a White policeman addressing him as "boy." In tracing the social control function of nicknames within the family, we focus on this second, dynamic aspect of nickname use. Our interest here is in showing that alternations in naming practices can serve as important indexes in the language of social control—the use of an appellation sometimes being the sole carrier of both a mood and an elocutionary intent. Of particular interest is the double function of nicknames as both "aggravators" (intensifiers) and "mitigators" (softeners) of utterances meant to direct children's behavior.

In both the Israeli Jewish and the Jewish American dinner-table conversations we have recorded, the official name as well as the institutionalized nickname, spoken with a raised voice and an emphatic intonation, were occasionally used to perform a social control function in calling the child to order, telling him or her to stop whatever he or she was doing ("Hagit!"), or, when it is the child who is asking for attention, granting him or her permission ("Yes, David"). In most cases, though, naming practices do not stand isolated but combine with other linguistic means in the performance of social control acts. Thus, when the action is specified ("Nadavi, go wash your hands"), the use of the name or nickname preceding the utterance serves as a first signal for the control act to come. In trying to speed up compliance, the parent may further switch appellations, aggravating and intensifying a request by changing from name to nickname and vice versa, a sequence culminated in uttering either one as the sole carrier of the control act. In the following example, a father is talking to Dan (age 9), while fixing the son's bicycle:[2]

—Danny, I have not finished yet.

—Dan, stop!

—Danny!

In some cases, nicknames per se are used as aggravators or intensifiers. For example, in an Israeli family, Noga (age 4) is admonished by her mother: "Dai, dai, Nogi, ani otsi otax haxutsa! [Enough, enough, Nogi, I'll take you outside]" and Yonathan (age 8) is reprimanded: "Uton! Ma ata ose?! [Uton, what are you doing?]." In one of the Jewish

American families, repeated attempts to get Suzannah (age 4) to sit down, all addressing her as "Suzannah," culminate in "Sit down, Sue!" Another example is Jesse (age 9), who is always called Jesse except once, when his father says "Jess, that's enough!"

Yet far more common is the use of nicknames as mitigators, meant to soften the coercive impact of a directive. When a nickname prefaces or is appended to a directive, it usually serves a softening function, neutralizing the potential threat to face that attends directive use (Brown & Levinson, 1987). This mitigation mechanism is particularly salient when the obligation to comply with a request is lower—because it is unusual, or when the child it is addressed to is smaller. For this purpose, family members in Israel often revert to nonconventional morphological variations of the given name. In an example from our Israeli data, Hagit, a 5-year-old girl, is helping her mother set the table. The mother, apparently appreciative of her daughter's cooperation, instructs her to put spoons on the table, saying: "Hagitush, kapot, Havitush." The elliptical request for spoons (*kapot*) is embedded in between two free variations on the girl's name, Hagit, both of which are highly affectionate.

The used of nicknames as mitigators is particularly salient in Israeli families. This trend is evident in general preferences shown by Jewish American and Israeli parents in ways of marking for politeness when performing social control acts addressed to children. Israeli parents make extensive use of mitigated direct strategies, relying heavily on nicknames to serve the sweetening function, while Jewish American and American immigrant parents prefer to attend to the child's face needs by relying on conventional, indirect strategies.[3]

The interviews with the Israeli families further confirmed the salience of nicknames as mitigators in this culture. Asked in the course of an interview to "soften" a bald-on-record directive to a child, Israeli informants invariably responded by a shift in tone of voice and a questioning intonation, combined with an endearment suffix added to a name or nickname, so that [sivan] becomes [sivani] or [sivanush]. Jewish American respondents, on the other hand, marked the command for politeness by a shift in strategy from the direct to the conventionally indirect, typically using forms such as "could you" or "would you." Yet awareness of the power of nicknames as softeners is well established in both cultures. As we were told by a 10-year-old in one of the Jewish American families: "I call him 'Dad' on a normal basis, but if I am begging for something then I'll say 'Oh, please, Daddy, Daddy, Daddy.'" This last example brings forth the manipulative potential embedded in naming practices; both children and adults, across all groups, are aware of such uses. As one child put it: "When Mom says Danush I know she wants me to do something she needs." In these last cases, as in the cases to be discussed in the next section, the expressive function of nicknaming becomes salient as well.[4]

Nicknames Can Perform an Expressive Function

The use of a nickname may be indicative of the speaker's attitude toward the addressee. Affective nicknames are separately labeled as "terms of endearment" (*shmot hiba*) and are generally considered significant mechanisms for sustaining the family's relational web. As noted, there may be a discrepancy between the "sense" of the nickname and its intended function. Thus, even when the nickname is essentially derogatory, signifying a departure from some ideal norm (e.g., "Fatsy"), it may be used affectionately, as it often is within families. The close association between affect and the social boundaries of the family as a unit in the Israeli Jewish context has already been discussed. The use of the official name may signal the withdrawal of the affective connotations associated with the nickname (as in the Danny/Dan/Danny example mentioned earlier).

Another expressive function of nicknames relates to their role in articulating a person's mood. Informants were quite explicit about the fact that they interpreted the use of their nickname as a signal of the user's current mood. Thus the addition of affective diminutives to the name [jaroncik] for [jaron] is something an Israeli mother told us she engages in "in moments I feel like demonstrating a surplus of affection, when there is this special warmth; of course, it all depends on the mood." Children are well aware of the way the choice reflects the user's mood. In deliberation on the constraints on the choice between "Stephen" and "Steve," it is the son who supplies the rule for his father—"It is Stephen when you are angry."

A further expressive function of nicknames is the purely poetic one. During the interviews, both Jewish American and Israeli informants recalled several rhymed collocations they sometimes use in addressing their children. It is the sound play and the rhyme that binds these appellations rather than the meaning (e.g., [Yaron axbaron]/[Ofer blofer]/ [Dan the Man]). In one case, the nickname evoked for its sound play (Pumpkin-Pie) was grounded in an actual "poetic" text: "I used to read the kids this poem which had the line 'Pumpkin pie—a little boy that did not cry,' so I called them both 'Pumpkin Pie.' "

Nicknames Can Perform a Framing Function

Given their association with participants' moods, nicknames are sometimes used to frame or reframe the interaction either as playful (in the case of affectionate nicknames) or as combative (in the case of derogatory ones). An example of the use of nicknames as playful framing devices, which comes from our Israeli data, is the following leave-taking exchange:

Ram (at the door):	"OK, bye."
Mother:	Bye, Rami.
Grandmother:	Bye, Avremele.
Ram (to his brother and sister):	OK, so bye monkeys.
Mother, sister and brother (together):	Bye, Rami.
Sister to Rami:	Bye, Doctor Famous.

We do not know whether Rami, the oldest son in the family, is in the habit of addressing his younger siblings as "monkeys," but we know that his sister has coined the nickname "Doctor Famous" in reference to a specific event that got her brother mentioned in the newspaper. Her use of this name sustained the playful frame already introduced by her brother through nickname use. In fact, more often than not, nicknames are used for humorous effect, introducing a playful, creative element into the routinized rounds of family interaction.

Nicknames can thus perform a variety of communicative functions, often simultaneously. These functions relate to the constitution of the family as a social group, to power relations within it, to the affective dimensions of family interaction, and to the metacommunicative task of defining the interactional situation.

IMPLICATIONS FOR CROSS-CULTURAL ANALYSIS

The proliferation of nicknames around the dinner tables of the middle-class Israeli families participating in this study, and their relative scarcity in the dinner-table conversations of the Jewish American families seems, indeed, an interesting finding. We interpret this finding as manifesting differences in cultural styles grounded in cultural differences in processes of individuation, in assumptions concerning independence, and in rules for the display of involvement. For the Jewish American families, it is the official name that serves the individuating function. Even babies should know who they are in terms of the social identity encapsulated in their official name. Jewish American mothers pointed out that they insisted on calling the newborn baby by his or her name from the very first day ("Asher is Asher and I want him to know he is Asher," a mother said with reference to her 3-week-old infant). Nicknaming by other members of the family is discouraged. The Jewish American cultural emphasis on the "development of self-sufficient individuals" (Bellah, Madsen, Sullivan, & Swiddler, 1985, p. 57) is enacted by this insistence on a child acquiring a sense of selfhood through identification with his or her official name or its institutionalized variation, as used in parental address. In Israeli society at large, individuation often takes the form of a nickname. Many public figures in this society are known publicly by their nicknames only. The present mayor of Tel Aviv is "Chich," that of Jerusalem is "Teddy." In the family, it is not a specific nickname that marks the child as different but the particular set of nicknames, all associated with the child's name of his or her person.

Yet, while the two patterns may each contribute to establishing a sense of selfhood, they convey different messages in regard to the relation of self to others. In Bateson's (1972) terms, as interpreted by Tannen (1986), parents are constantly struggling with the dilemma of how to balance a need to show respect for a child's independence with the need to express affect. Anything said as a sign of affective involvement is interpretable as showing a lack of respect for individual space, while insistence on the dictum of nonimposition is amenable to being decoded as a lack of caring. Insistence on official names tips the balance in favor of nonimposition; thus, in the Jewish American families, it is the imposition-avoiding principles of deference-politeness (Brown & Levinson, 1987) that are expressed through naming practices.

On the other hand, nicknames as such connote a feeling of closeness because their origin is always within a close-knit group of family or friends, so they carry an aura of intimacy even when used publicly. When the mayor is called "Chich," social distance between him and the public is suspended in favor of a rhetoric of camaraderie. The distance-minimizing function of nicknames, in the well-documented tradition of Israeli "solidarity politeness" (Blum-Kulka, Danet, & Gerson, 1985; Katriel, 1986), begins in the family.

By tipping the balance in favor of a display of involvement over respect for independence, Israeli parents are stressing both affect and intimacy. Hence, nicknames in this context index simultaneously the uniqueness of the child and familial bonding. Yet effusive nicknaming of children in the family involves a double message: Because the right to nickname other family members is not equally distributed (children do not usually nickname parents), such affective coloring of address is also an expression of the asymmetrical power structure within the family.

These findings are particularly surprising if we consider the cultural affinity between the two groups in the sample: All are descendants of East European Jews and might be expected to share basic sociolinguistic patterns. And yet, in the course of one generation, acculturation processes have been strong enough to distinguish the groups from each other. For the Jewish Americans, it is the values of the American culture that predominate. For American immigrants in Israel, the picture is more complex: In some domains, like nicknaming patterns, the same values are preserved, while in others, such as the style of control, they develop an intercultural pattern of their own (Blum-Kulka, in press). Thus the difference between the groups testifies to the possibility of cultural change within a relatively short time span.

We were, indeed, surprised to discover that Israeli nicknames carried so many linguistic markers designating the Diaspora origin of their users, especially in the form of affixes. Both Russian and Yiddish influences are detected in the phonetic pattern of the Israeli nicknames. The Yiddish /-le/ or /-ile/ suffix: /asaf/ → /asafile/, /noa/ → /noale/. The Russian /-ik/ and /-ika/ suffix: /jaron/ → /jaronik/, /gali/ → /galika/, as well as the /sh/ and /tsh/ sounds embedded in the name, usually followed by one of the suffixes: /sivan/ → /sivantshik/ or /sivutsh/; /talja/ /tulish/; /mikal/ → /mushkale/; /jaron/ → /jarontshuk/. This category yields some highly creative "nonce nicknames" (i.e., created on the spur of the moment, perhaps never to be repeated) such as /tshapishaika/, /tushik/ and /tsahpuka/; /jonata/ → /onton/ and /ontik/. These last patterns are typical of address to very young children.

We found no equivalents in use in the immigrant American and Jewish American families, except for an occasional reference of a parent evoking a childhood memory of a Russian- or Yiddish-sounding nickname addressed to him or her by a grandparent. The reason for our surprise is the fact known to many Israelis, and documented in the onomastic literature (Weitman, 1988), that Israelis have tended deliberately to distance themselves from names that evoke their past Diaspora life and to choose names for their children that reflect a native Israeli identification. It appears, then, that, while care is taken to assume and project a native Israeli identity through the use of a native-sounding official Hebrew name, the East European, mainly Yiddish roots of these same speakers are allowed to thrive in the domestic domain and even become emblematic of a "sense of family." It is not that nicknames are not part of the sociolinguistic repertoire of Native Israeli (Sabra) culture. In fact, they are very common, and many of the old-time Israelis, the sung and unsung heroes of the prestate, nation-building days, still carry the nicknames pinned on them at the time as something of a badge of honor.

These nicknames, however, originated in and were strongly associated with the friendship network, which was the most important moving force in these people's lives (rather than the family, if it existed). We believe that the emergence of nicknaming practices as a central signifying mechanism in Israeli families, and the particular linguistic markers adopted in this process, are indicators of a more general re-emergence of familism in Israeli society (Katriel, in press) as well as a newfound affirmation of Israelis' Diaspora roots (Cohen, 1983).

The nicknaming patterns in Jewish American families seem to be more North American than Jewish. When a suffix is added to a name, or a name shortened, the sound patterns are not restricted to family use or to the Jewish community; transformation of the Jewish name Deborah is equivalent to that of the non-Jewish one: Deborah becomes Debbie and Deb, but also, Jennifer becomes Jen. Even terms of endearment follow conventional patterns: Darling, Dear, Honey, Sweetie, Kid, Fella, Son, and Sonny (no equivalent for girls) are the only ones used by the North American parents, while Israeli parents add to the conventional ones (/xamud/xamudi/motek) some innovative phonetic play of their own (/pitsputs/ and /puski/). It is interesting that the immigrant Jewish American parents continue the North American tradition in this respect; they use even fewer nicknames than the Jewish American families and scarcely ever use terms of endearment. Children in these families often have two variations of their name: one Hebrew (Yael) and another English (Jennifer). In other cases, the name is phonetically "translated" from Hebrew to English and vice versa, to accommodate the constant code-switching between the two languages common in these families (Olshtain & Blum-Kulka, 1989). Obviously, one must remember that dinner-table conversations may just not be the context in which nicknames find their natural place in this group, but the interview materials suggest that the pattern we have observed can be generalized to other familial contexts as well.

One question to be asked, of course, is whether the communicative functions performed by nicknames can be attributed to other sociolinguistic mechanisms in family interaction: How is social control affected? How is family solidarity signaled? How is mitigation accomplished? Another question relates to the sociocultural implications that spring from the presence or absence of particular communicative functions in family interaction: How can we describe and conceptualize the affiliative bonds of individuals (children, adults) within the family given the particular patterns of appellation we observe? What is the role of the wider cultural context as compared with the more immediate situational context in the emergence of naming patterns? What can this tell us about the place of the family in the lives of cultural members?

Clearly, we can only begin to answer these and other questions that suggest themselves in reflecting upon the findings of this study. We hope we have shown the richness that lies in this seemingly simple, intriguing device whose mystery is still borne out by members of urbanized, complex societies.

NOTES

1. This story appears in a translated collection of Arab liberature; the translation into English is our own.

2. Such examples run contrary to Brown and Ford's (1961) observation that usually it is the official, given name that is used by parents "manding" disobedient children and to Gumperz's (1970) account of parents switching from nickname to official name by way of intensification. It seems that the general belief in the power of official names to index control is subject to contextual variation and that, when more than one term of address is used in sequence, it is the ordering rather than the choice that determines the function of each.

3. These preferences emerge from the distribution of directive strategies in parent-child interaction across the three groups between (a) direct (nonmitigated), (b) direct and mitigated, and (c) indirect. Parents in all three groups address direct, nonmitigated requests to their children 40% of the time. But, while the next choice for Israeli parents are mitigated-direct forms (40%), for the American parents, it is the indirect mode that prevails here (40%). The American immigrant parents' preferences are equally divided between the three options (Blum-Kulka, in press).

4. Nicknames can be openly pejorative and function as sanctioning devices. This usage is widespread in Mediterranean countries as well as among Arabs (see Antoun, 1968; Griefat, 1986; Griefat & Katriel, 1989). Interview data we have collected from Israeli speakers of Arabic suggest that, although many derogatory nicknames are reported to have been coined within the family circle, usually by adults or older siblings addressing younger children, they are frequently adopted by others and sometimes accompany a person through life. We have been told of incidents in which children went to great lengths to prevent their siblings from spreading their derogatory home-based nicknames among their peers at school. The use of such nicknames among adults is strictly guarded and confined to contexts of mention (never address), even though familiarity with community members' nicknames is widespread. Some of the Arab informants we have interviewed stressed the fact that, in the Koran, there is an explicit injunction against the use of nicknames, but most admitted to using them at least in addressing young children.

REFERENCES

Antoun, R. (1968). On the significance of names in an Arab village. *Ethnology, 7,* 158-170.

Barrett, R. (1978). Village modernization and changing nicknaming practices in Northern Spain. *Journal of Anthropological Research, 34*, 92-108.

Bateson, G. (1972). *Steps to an ecology of mind.* New York: Ballantine.

Bellah, R., Madsen, R., Sullivan, W., & Swiddler, A. (1985). *Habits of the heart.* New York: Harper & Row.

Blum-Kulka, S. (in press). You don't touch lettuce with your fingers: Parental politeness in family discourse. *Journal of Pragmatics.*

Blum-Kulka, S., Danet, B., & Gerson, R. (1985). The language of requesting in Israeli society. In J. Forgas (Ed.), *Language and social situation* (pp. 113-141). New York: Springer Verlag.

Brandes, S. H. (1975). The social and demographic implications of nicknames in Navanogal, Spain. *American Ethnologist, 2*, 139-148.

Brown, P., & Levinson, S. (1987). *Politeness: Some universals in language usage.* Cambridge: Cambridge University Press.

Brown, R., & Ford, M. (1961). Address in American English. *Journal of Abnormal and Social Psychology, 62*, 375-385.

Brown, R., & Gilman, A. (1960). The pronouns of power and solidarity. In T. A. Sebeok (Ed.), *Style in language.* Cambridge: MIT Press.

Cohen, E. (1983). Ethnicity and legitimation in contemporary Israel. *Jerusalem Quarterly, 28*, 111-124.

Dorian, N. C. (1970). A substitute name system in the Scottish Highlands. *American Anthropologist, 72*(2), 303-319.

Ervin-Tripp, S. (1972). Sociolinguistic rules of address. In J. Pride, & J. Holmes, (Eds.), *Sociolinguistics* (pp. 225-241). London: Penguin.

Gilmore, D. D. (1982). Some notes on community nicknaming in Spain. *Man, 17*, 686-700.

Glazier, J. (1987). Nicknames and the transformation of an American Jewish community: Notes on the anthropology of emotion in the urban Midwest. *Ethnology, 26*(2), 73-85.

Griefat, Y. (1986). *"Almusayara" as a communicative style in Arab-Bedouin culture.* Unpublished master's thesis, University of Haifa, School of Education.

Griefat, Y., & Katriel, T. (1989). "Life demands musayara": Communication and culture among Arabs in Israel. In S. Ting-Toomey, & F. Korzenny, (Eds.), *Language, communication and culture: New directions* (pp. 121-138). London: Sage.

Gumperz, J. (1970). Verbal strategies in multilingual communication. In *Monograph on language and linguistics* (no. 23; 21st annual round-table). Washington, DC: Georgetown University.

Habibi, E. (1988). The crab's lament. In A. Nir & M. Peri (Eds.), *Water soldiers.* Tel-Aviv: Ma'ariv.

Katriel, T. (1986). *Talking straight: "Dugri" speech in Israeli Sabra culture.* Cambridge: Cambridge University Press.

Katriel, T. (in press). *Communal webs: Communication, culture and acculturation in contemporary Israel.* Albany: State University of New York Press.

Manning, F. (1974). Nicknames and number plates in the British West Indies. *Journal of American Folklore, 87*, 123-132.

McDowell, J. (1981). Toward a semiotics of nicknaming: The Kamsa example. *Journal of American Folklore, 94*, 1-18.

Morgan, J., O'Neill, C., & Harre, R. (1979). *Nicknames.* London: Routledge & Kegan Paul.

Olshtain, E., & Blum-Kulka, S. (1989). Happy Hebrish: Mixing and switching in American-Israeli family interactions. In S. Gass, C. Madden, D. Preston, & L. Selinker

(Eds.), *Variations in second language acquisition: Vol. 1. Discourse and pragmatics* (pp. 39-57). Philadelphia: Multilingual Matters.

Philipsen, G., & Huspek, M. (1985). A bibliography of sociolinguistic studies of personal address. *Anthropological Linguistics, 27,* 94-101.

Sheffer, H. (1989). *Nicknames in Israeli and American families.* Unpublished paper, Hebrew University, Jerusalem.

Tannen, D. (1986). *That's not what I meant.* New York: Ballantine.

Weitman, S. (1988). Personal names as cultural indicators: Trends in the national identity of Israelis 1882-1980. In N. Gertz (Ed.), *Perspectives on culture and society in Israel* (pp. 141-151). Tel-Aviv: Open University. (in Hebrew)

5

Uncertainty Reduction in Acquaintance Relationships in Ghana and the United States

JUDITH A. SANDERS • *California State Polytechnic University, Pomona*

RICHARD L. WISEMAN •

S. IRENE MATZ • *California State University, Fullerton*

The study examines cultural differences in the use of interactive uncertainty reduction communication—self-disclosure, interrogation, nonverbal immediacy, and other's self-disclosure—and their interrelationships with uncertainty reduction in intra- and interethnic acquaintance relationships in Ghana and the United States. Cultural differences were noted in how these forms of communication are used to reduce uncertainty. Implications for extant theory and future research are discussed.

Communication is the foundation of interpersonal relationships. Yet, for years, communication scholars have struggled with various theories that attempt to explain the relationships but not necessarily the communication creating those relationships. One approach that does focus on the communication forming relationships is uncertainty reduction theory. The theory has generated substantial intracultural and intercultural research. Unfortunately, current research has primarily been limited to studying uncertainty reduction communication in the United States (or other Western cultures) and in Asian cultures. This research seeks to broaden our understanding of uncertainty reduction theory by examining the interactive uncertainty reduction process in intra- and interethnic acquaintance relationships in the United States and the West African nation of Ghana.

AUTHORS' NOTE: This project was partially funded by a Faculty Research Grant from California State University, Fullerton. All authors wish to gratefully acknowledge the invaluable assistance of Stuart P. Matz in the study's data collection and William Gudykunst in the chapter's revision.

UNCERTAINTY REDUCTION THEORY

Uncertainty reduction theory is aimed at explaining both the motivation and the methods for communication in interpersonal relationships. As detailed by Berger and Calabrese (1975), the theory proposes that, as relationships develop, communicators have a high need to understand both the self and the other in an interaction situation. Communication generates that understanding (or a reduction of uncertainty) and thus serves as the basis of relationship development. The desire for uncertainty reduction is particularly strong in the early stages of relationships when the parties know little about one another. To choose appropriate behaviors for interacting with one another, communicators must be able to predict each other's behavior. Specifically, the theory posits that communicators are motivated to reduce uncertainty about another when (a) they see the relationship as potentially rewarding, (b) the other engages in deviant behavior, or (c) future interaction with the other is probable (Berger, 1979). Further, as uncertainty is reduced, the parties feel more comfortable with each other and thus like each other more, resulting in more intimacy.

Considerable empirical research supports the basic uncertainty thesis. For example, Clatterbuck (1979) found that knowing more about relationship partners (i.e., reducing uncertainty) increased attraction to those partners. Further, Gudykunst, Yang, and Nishida (1985) found that uncertainty reduction motive operative across acquaintance, friend, and dating relationships in the United States, Korea, and Japan. If, as it appears, uncertainty stimulates communication between interactants, what kinds of communication behaviors are generated?

Interactive communication is one of the primary ways communicators reduce uncertainty about other people (Berger, 1979). Interaction allows the soliciting of information directly from the other person. Among the interactive methods are interrogation (asking questions of the other) and self-disclosure (Berger, 1979). Self-disclosure results in uncertainty reduction at least in part because of its reciprocity effect. In addition, the use of nonverbal expressive affiliativeness (or immediacy) also results in a reduction of uncertainty by increasing the parties' levels of comfort with each other (Berger, 1987). Research confirms the use of these types of communication in uncertainty reduction. For example, Berger and Kellerman (1983) found that communicators use question asking, disclosure, and target relaxation to obtain information in face-to-face interactions. Subsequently, they found that information seekers used more positive nonverbal behaviors than persons not seeking to reduce uncertainty (Kellerman & Berger, 1984).

Uncertainty is reduced when people are able to understand what is occurring in the interaction (retroactive confidence) and feel more confident about their behavioral choices in interacting with another (proactive confidence). As Clatterbuck (1979, p. 148) notes, "For the individual, reducing uncertainty and increasing attributional confidence become synonymous." *Attributional confidence* is defined as the perceived adequacy of information with which to explain behavior that is occurring and to predict appropriate future behaviors—that is, the converse of uncertainty. Clatterbuck's (1979) research indicated that attributional confidence is an appropriate measure of uncertainty reduction. Because proactive confidence and retroactive confidence are highly correlated, either may accurately serve as a measure of reduced uncertainty.

Interactive communication and attributional confidence seem logically related. One method of learning more about another is asking that person questions (interrogation). Because disclosure is highly reciprocal, self-disclosure results in other's disclosure. By increasing the comfort levels of the communicators, nonverbal immediacy creates more open interaction. Thus interrogation, self-disclosure, other's disclosure, and nonverbal immediacy should increase attributional confidence. Research supports this supposition. For example, Gudykunst (1985b) found that the use of self-disclosure and interrogation increased attributional confidence. Likewise, Gudykunst, Yang, and Nishida (1985), examining data from three cultures, found that the use of self-disclosure, other's disclosure, and interrogation had positive effects on attributional confidence. Further, Gudykunst and Hammer (1987) found that increased nonverbal immediacy increased attributional confidence.

Uncertainty Reduction in Other Cultures

In examining the validity of any theory, it is important to test that theory in a variety of conditions to find its generalizability and/or limitations. As Gudykunst (1983b, pp. 49-50) notes,

> Examining the use of selected strategies and attributional confidence in other cultures will not only help advance the formulation of theory in intercultural communication, but it will also begin to test the generalizability of theories developed to explain communication behavior in the United States.

Why would culture affect the use of uncertainty reduction strategies? Thirty years ago, Edward Hall (1959) recognized that communication and culture are inseparable. Communication is the means for transmission of cultural ways and culture shapes our ways and means of communication. "Culture is a script or schema shared by a large group of people" (Gudykunst & Ting-Toomey, 1988, p. 30) that shapes their patterns of living. Consequently, different cultures produce different methods of communication and thus different ways of relationship formation, maintenance, and disintegration.

If relationship development does vary across cultures, is uncertainty reduction theory a valid perspective for examining relationships in other cultures? For the theory to be applicable cross-culturally, the desire to avoid uncertainty must be cultural general. As noted above, Gudykunst, Yang, and Nishida (1985) found the principle operative in Korea and Japan (in addition to the United States). Significantly, research by Hofstede (1983) found uncertainty avoidance to be a basic cultural orientation in his study of 50 countries and three regions across the world. Thus the motive for uncertainty reduction appears to have broad cross-cultural applicability.

Although research to test the validity of uncertainty reduction theory might proceed entirely on a culture-by-culture basis, such a methodology is clearly inefficient. Broad patterns of cultural variation should be examined to determine if they can be used to predict differences in the application of uncertainty reduction theory. Two such schemas have been widely used in this context: Hall's theory of context and Hofstede's four-dimension model of cultural variation.

Hall (1977) proposes that cultures vary in the extent to which communication is influenced by context along a continuum from high- to low-context systems. In high-context communication, much of the meaning is embedded in the setting or internalized in the person. In low-context communication, the meaning is derived from the coded explicit part of the message. He explains:

> HC [high-context] transactions feature preprogrammed information that is in the receiver and in the setting, with only minimal information in the transmitted message. LC [low-context] transactions are the reverse. Most of the information must be in the transmitted message in order to make up for what is missing in the context (both internal and external). (Hall, 1977, p. 101)

While no culture is entirely at one end of the continuum, the United States is near the low end and most Asian cultures are near the high end. Thus it might be reasonable to expect that context influences the uncertainty reduction process. Indeed, research indicates that this is so.

Gudykunst (1983b) found that members of high-context cultures appear to be more cautious, make more assumptions about strangers based on their cultural background, and engage in less nonverbal behavior than members of low-context cultures. Further, members of high-context cultures rely more on assumptions about strangers' backgrounds to increase attributional confidence than do members of low-context cultures.

Another theory of cultural variability is provided by Hofstede's four-dimension model of cultures (1983, 1984). Surveying 116,000 respondents in 50 countries and three regions, Hofstede found that cultures vary along four dimensions: power distance, uncertainty avoidance, masculinity, and individualism. *Power distance* is the extent to which power/status differences are regarded as inherent. *Uncertainty avoidance* refers to the ability to tolerate uncertain or ambiguous situations. *Masculinity* refers to the extent to which clear and traditional sex role distinctions predominate within a culture. *Individualism* (versus collectivism) is the extent to which the self is seen as central to activity. Countries high in individualism (such as the United States) view individuals as primarily responsible for their destiny and as the shapers of their own lives. Countries low in individualism (and thus high in collectivism) view individuals' lives as integrally tied to the groups to which they belong; they have a "we" consciousness. The nature of these differences ought to influence communication and thus uncertainty reduction behavior.

Research indicates that all four of Hofstede's dimensions interact with the stage of a relationship to influence the uncertainty reduction process but that, as the relationship becomes more intimate, cultural variability has less effect on the uncertainty reduction process (Gudykunst, Chua, & Gray, 1986). Further, Gudykunst and Ting-Toomey (1988) argue that the individualism-collectivism dimension of Hofstede's theory is a particularly strong cultural distinction because it is isomorphic with Hall's conception of distinguishing cultures as high or low context. That is, the predominant form of communication in individualistic cultures is low context; the predominant form of communication in collectivistic cultures is high context. Gudykunst, Yoon, and Nishida (1987) note that the individualism/collectivism distinction has been employed by numerous theorists across a variety of disciplines. Thus, in acquaintance relationships, we would expect to see differences in uncertainty reduction communication between individualistic and collectivistic cultures.

Intracultural Versus Intercultural Communication

If uncertainty reduction is a motive for communication in relationships, it seems logical that the theory would be particularly applicable where the members of the relationship were especially dissimilar, such as intercultural encounters. In essence, culturally dissimilar encounters might stimulate greater use of uncertainty reduction communication than culturally similar encounters. The research, however, has not confirmed such a simple relationship.

Culturally dissimilar encounters have been found to involve more interrogation than culturally similar encounters (Gudykunst, 1983a; Imahori, 1987a, 1987b). Further, Gudykunst and Nishida (1984) found that cultural dissimilarity resulted in higher levels of intent to interrogate, intent to self-disclose, and nonverbal immediacy than cultural similarity for both U.S. and Japanese respondents. However, Gudykunst (1983a) found no difference between the intent to display nonverbal immediacy in intracultural or intercultural encounters among U.S. Whites. Moreover, Gudykunst, Nishida, Koike, and Shiino (1985) did not find a significant effect for cultural similarity/dissimilarity on intent to self-disclose, intent to interrogate, or intent to display nonverbal immediacy for Japanese subjects. Consequently, the effects of cultural similarity are unclear.

Even though there are many forms of cultural dissimilarity, interethnic communication is a particularly important form because, in ethnically diverse cultures (such as the United States and many African nations), the opportunities for such communication are great. The interethnic encounter is one in which high levels of uncertainty are probable and the parties must negotiate the methods they use to reduce that uncertainty. Thus methods of uncertainty reduction might vary between intraethnic and interethnic acquaintances. Indeed, studying U.S. White and Black respondents, Gudykunst (1986) found that mean scores for self-disclosure and attributional confidence were higher in intraethnic than in interethnic encounters. This is somewhat inconsistent with the idea that culturally dissimilar encounters should produce higher levels of uncertainty reduction communication. It may be, however, that other methods of uncertainty reduction (such as interrogation or immediacy) are more prominent in interethnic encounters.

One reason differences between intra- and interethnic uncertainty reduction might occur in individualistic and collectivistic cultures is provided by the role of in-groups and out-groups. Triandis, Bontempo, Villa-real, Asai, and Lucca (1988) note that, in collective cultures, as opposed to individualistic cultures, people see greater differences between members of their in-groups than their out-groups. Consequently, in collective cultures, behavior toward in-group members is much more different than behavior toward out-group members. On the other hand, in individualistic cultures, little difference occurs. Gudykunst et al. (in press) argue that patterns of uncertainty reduction should vary between in-groups and out-groups in collective but not individualistic cultures.

Indeed, Gudykunst, Nishida, and Schmidt (1988) found that, among the Japanese (a collective culture), there was a tendency for more interrogation and display of nonverbal immediacy with members of in-groups than members of out-groups. However, more self-disclosure was found with members of out-groups. No such differences emerged from their U.S. sample. Likewise, Gudykunst et al. (in press) found that members of collective cultures (Japan and Hong Kong) had different patterns of communication for in-group and out-group members; however, members of individualistic cultures (the United States and Australia) did not. Because ethnicity is one basis on which in-groups and out-groups are formed in both collective and individualistic cultures (Gudykunst & Ting-Toomey, 1988; Triandis et al., 1988), we might expect to find greater differences between intraethnic and interethnic communication in collective cultures.

This review of the literature suggests that culture affects uncertainty reduction communication. Further, the intra- or interethnic nature of a relationship may also have an effect on uncertainty reduction communication. However, current research has been limited primarily to comparing U.S. (or other Western) cultures with Asian cultures. To make a broad test of the theory, Gudykunst (1983a, p. 64) argues,

> One final area for future research lies in the development of a data bank on cross-cultural comparisons of relationships and their development. Similar research protocols need to be applied in a variety of cultures so that theorists can begin to make predictions with respect to what might happen when people from two specific cultures come together. . . . This research should focus on how people in the culture define uncertainty, how they reduce uncertainty, what role they perceive similarity to play in the development of relationships, and what they consider to be an intimate relationship.

Before we assume that patterns found in technologically advanced cultures such as Korea, Japan, and Hong Kong are representative of all collectivist, high-context countries, consideration must be given to developing societies.

Focus of this Research

While Africa represents nearly one-fifth of the world's land mass, and a substantial percentage of the world's natural resources, much of the continent remains underdeveloped. Nonetheless, the future economic potential of the African nations, alone and as trading partners, make this an area of the world that cannot be ignored. Unfortunately, it is an area that has been understudied in social science research. If we are to develop international ties with Africa, we must come to understand its peoples. To assess the generalizability of uncertainty reduction theory and to provide additional insight into the communication behavior of members of underresearched Africa, we sought a developing, collectivist African nation in which to conduct our study. One such country is the Western African nation of Ghana. In 1957, Ghana became the first independent nation in Black colonial Africa. While it is rich in natural resources, those resources are underdeveloped. Recent governmental changes have resulted in an economic upturn that make it a model for the balance of Africa, but it is still a less developed nation (Noviki, 1987).

Ghana is a highly collectivist country (Hofstede, 1983), substantially more so than Japan but about the same as Korea. Both the ethnic group (tribe) and the family are the primary groups to which Ghanaians belong. Because the mass media are relatively limited in the country, much information received by Ghanaians comes from one of these primary groups. Ghana is also a country with a rich oral tradition. In fact, written communication was unknown in Ghana until contact with Eastern and Western societies occurred (Doob, 1961). Even today, oral social interaction is highly prized. For example, Earley (1984) found that Ghanaian workers used and valued oral social interaction more than U.S. or British workers.

Consistent with Gudykunst and Ting-Toomey's (1988) observation that collectivist countries are high context, Ghana is a high-context culture (e.g., Middleton, 1983). Even though verbal interaction is highly regarded, much of the meaning in a given interaction is based on nonverbal and situational cues (Doob, 1961). Thus we might expect that, while verbal strategies are used among Ghanaians, they are not a primary means of uncertainty reduction. Rather, as in other high-context cultures, we would expect more emphasis to be placed on gaining background information about the individual.

Because we were interested in comparing self-disclosure, other's disclosure, interrogation, and nonverbal immediacy as modes of communication for uncertainty reduction among culturally similar and dissimilar acquaintances, we formulated the following research hypotheses:

(1) Communicators in the United States and Ghana use self-disclosure, other's disclosure, interrogation, and nonverbal immediacy differently in intraethnic and interethnic acquaintance interactions.

(2) Attributional confidence is influenced differently by self-disclosure, other's disclosure, interrogation, and nonverbal immediacy for intraethnic and interethnic acquaintances in the United States and Ghana.

METHODS

Sample

A total of 1,386 college students volunteered to participate in the study. Of these, 1,189 were from three western universities in the United States. In terms of the U.S. sample's demography, the average age was 22.2 (SD = 5.1), 57.6% were female, and 64.1% were Caucasian. The remaining subsample consisted of 197 students from a university in northern Ghana, Africa. The Ghanaian sample's demographic information includes the following: the average age was 21.5 (SD = 4.5), 83.8% were male, and 66.5% were from the Gur ethnic group (with the others distributed among eight major ethnic groups). The larger proportion of males in the African sample is due to the fact that it is primarily males who are encouraged to obtain a university education. Because English is the official language in Ghana, all of the U.S. and Ghanaian respondents were fluent in the English language. Because the multivariate statistics employed in this study are influenced by differences in sample sizes, it was decided to create comparable sample sizes between the U.S. and Ghanaian data by randomly sampling 17% of the U.S. data through the SPSS sampling routine. This resulted in a sample of 203 cases, where the average age was 22.1 (SD = 5.1), 54.9% were female, and 52.1% were Caucasian (with the others primarily distributed among Asian and Hispanic ethnic groups).

Questionnaire

The first step in the construction of the questionnaire was to determine the characteristics of the person whom the respondents would be considering in making their responses to the items measuring uncertainty reduction strategies. Research on uncertainty reduction indicates a number of demographic influences on the process, namely, the other's gender (Gudykunst & Hammer, 1987), the level of intimacy in the relationship (Gudykunst, Chua, & Gray, 1986; Gudykunst, Sodetani, & Sonoda, 1987), and the status differences between the two communicators (Berger, 1979). In light of these influences, we attempted to control for these factors by specifying that the persons that the respondent would be thinking of when responding to the questionnaire items be (a) the same sex, (b) an acquaintance (defined in the questionnaire as "someone you are just getting to know"), and (c) an equal-status individual, that is, a fellow student. Because a primary research interest of this study was an examination of uncertainty reduction among intra- versus interethnic acquaintances, we asked the respondent to think of two persons with the above three characteristics—an acquaintance of the same ethnicity (in-group) and an acquaintance of a different ethnicity (out-group). To commit the respondents to thinking about specific persons having these characteristics, we asked them to write the first name of the persons they had in mind. The questionnaire referred to these persons as "Person A" and "Person B." To control for order effects, two forms of the questionnaire were created; one with the intraethnic questions first, and the other with the interethnic questions first. The two forms of the questionnaire were randomly distributed to the respondents.

The next stages in questionnaire construction were the operational-ization of the uncertainty reduction strategies. Four operationaliza-tions were required: (a) self-disclosure strategies, (b) interrogation strategies, (c) nonverbal immediacy, and (d) others' disclosure strate-gies. Based upon a review of relevant uncertainty reduction research (Gudykunst, 1985a, 1985b), a 12-item scale was chosen to operationa-lize self-disclosure strategies. Two examples of these items follow: "What I think and feel about religion; my personal religious views" and "What it takes to hurt my feelings." The 12 self-disclosure items were rated on a three-point scale: $0 = I$ have *not* talked about this information, $1 = I$ have talked about this information in general terms, and $2 = I$ have talked about this information in specific and detailed terms. The interitem reliability for these 12 items was fairly high (Cronbach's alpha for the intraethnic items = .83 and for the interethnic items = .83; Cronbach, 1951).

Interrogation strategies were operationalized via a modified version of Gudykunst and Hammer's (1987) intent to interrogate scale. These items were originally drawn from Gudykunst and Nishida's (1984) disclosure scale. The scale was modified to reflect actual behavior rather than intentions. This six-item scale consisted of content areas that the respondent inquired about of the other person. The six content areas were family, school major, hobbies and crafts, religious back-ground, political attitude, and ideas toward marriage. These items were rated on a three-point scale: 0 = I have never asked about this, 1 = I have sometimes asked about this, and 2 = I have frequently asked about this. The interitem reliability for these six items was only moderate (Cronbach's alpha for intraethnic = .68 and for intraethnic = .67), owing possibly to the variety of the content areas and the fewer number of items.

Nonverbal immediacy was operationalized as a four-point scale based upon the research of Gudykunst and Nishida (1984; see also, Gudykunst, 1983a). The scale items asked the respondents how often they engaged in four nonverbal immediacy behaviors: smiling at the other, looking at the other's eyes, standing close to the other, and shaking hands or touching the other in some way. These items were rated on a three-point scale: 0 = I have never done this, 1 = I have sometimes done this, and 2 = I have frequently done this. Interitem reliability for these four items was again only moderate (Cronbach's alpha for intraethnic = .65 and for interethnic = .68).

The last uncertainty reduction strategy to be operationalized was other's self-disclosure. To maintain consistency with the self-disclosure items noted above, the 12-item scale used to operationalize the respondent's own self-disclosure was adapted to measure other's self-disclosure. The converted response scale consisted of three points: 0 = Person A/B has told me nothing about this aspect of him- or herself, 1 = Person A/B has talked about this item in general terms with me, and 2 = Person A/B has talked about this item in detail with me. Interitem reliability for these 12 items was fairly high (Cronbach's alpha for intraethnic = .83 and for interethnic = .84).

The last step in questionnaire construction was the operationalization of the perceived level of uncertainty in the relationship between the respondent and the other person. This construct was measured via Clatterbuck's (1979) Attributional Confidence Scale. The scale consists of seven items designed to assess the degree to which respondents are confident in predicting the behavior, attitudes, feelings, and emotions of the other person. Clatterbuck (1979) presents evidence for the unidimensionality, internal reliability, and validity of the scale. All of the items were measured on a three-point scale: 0 = I am *not* at all certain about this aspect of Person A/B, 1 = I am somewhat certain about this aspect of Person A/B, and 2 = I am very certain about this aspect of Person A/B. The interitem reliability for this scale in this study was fairly high (Cronbach's alpha for interethnic = .84 and for interethnic = .85).

RESULTS

Two statistical analyses of the data were performed. First, to determine whether there were differences in uses of uncertainty reduction strategies between intra- and interethnic groups, multivariate analyses of variance (MANOVA) were computed for the U.S. and the Ghanaian samples. This analysis would ascertain whether there are intra- versus interethnic differences in the amount of use of uncertainty reduction strategies. Second, to determine whether there were differences among the interrelationships of the uncertainty reduction variables, multiple regressions were computed for the intra- and interethnic data from the U.S. and Ghanaian samples.

Multivariate Analysis of Variance

Before computing MANOVA for the U.S. data, the two major assumptions for MANOVA were tested. First, the Bartlett's test of sphericity for the U.S. data indicated that the covariance matrices had sufficient intercorrelations among the dependent variables for analysis, that is, they were not identity matrices (sphericity coefficient = 1419.0, df = 10, $p < .00001$). Second, the test to determine whether the variance-covariance matrices for the intraethnic and interethnic scales were homogeneous indicated that they were comparable, and thus multivariate analysis was warranted (Box's $M = 8.9$, $F = .6$, n.s.). Given the appropriateness for analysis, a MANOVA was computed on the data as presented in Table 5.1. The multivariate analysis of variance indicated that there was no significant effect for group, that is, no intra- versus interethnic differences for the amounts of self-disclosure, other's disclosure, nonverbal immediacy, interrogation strategies, and attributional confidence in the U.S. data (Wilk's lambda = .98, $F = 1.6$, n.s.).

As with the U.S. data, we tested the assumptions underlying the use of MANOVA for the Ghanaian data. First, the Bartlett's test of sphericity for the Ghanaian data indicated that the covariance matrices had sufficient intercorrelations among the dependent variables to warrant analysis, that is, they were not identity matrices (sphericity coefficient = 551.8, df = 10, $p < .0001$). Second, the test to determine whether the variance-covariance matrices for the intraethnic and interethnic scales were homogeneous indicated that they were comparable, and thus multivariate analysis was warranted (Box's $M = 5.9$, $F = .4$, n.s.). Given the appropriateness for analysis, a MANOVA was computed on the Ghanaian data as presented in Table 5.1. The multivariate analysis of variance found that there was no significant difference in the usages of

TABLE 5.1 Descriptive Statistics for Uncertainty Variables

		Intraethnic		*Interethnic*
	Mean	*Standard Deviation*	*Mean*	*Standard Deviation*
United States:				
self-disclosure	0.80	.42	.73	.41
interrogation	0.91	.42	.78	.41
nonverbal immediacy	1.47	.45	1.44	.45
other's disclosure	0.81	.42	.76	.41
attitudinal confidence	1.05	.48	1.00	.46
Ghana:				
self-disclosure	1.16	.32	1.16	.32
interrogation	1.11	.40	1.11	.40
nonverbal immediacy	1.42	.44	1.42	.44
other's disclosure	1.15	.34	1.52	.34
attitudinal confidence	1.26	.40	1.26	.40

the uncertainty reduction strategies between the intraethnic and interethnic groups of Ghana (Wilk's lambda = .99, F = .5, n.s.).

Regression Analyses

The above MANOVA analyses provide some insight into the use of uncertainty reduction strategies, however, they do not inform us as to the interrelationships among the strategies. Multiple regressions should ameliorate this need. More specifically, regression equations for the U.S. and Ghanaian data were computed in terms of intraethnic and interethnic attributional confidence and for intraethnic and interethnic other's level of disclosure.

The first set of regression analyses were computed for the intraethnic bases of uncertainty reduction. The multiple regressions of intraethnic attributional confidence included other's level of disclosure, level of self-disclosure, use of interrogation strategies, and nonverbal immediacy. The regression equations for intraethnic attributional confidence differed for the data from U.S. and from Ghanaian respondents. For the U.S. respondents, four significant beta coefficients were found (see Table 5.2): other's disclosure (beta = .44, F = 107.6, $p < .0001$, b = .50, se_b = .04), self-disclosure (beta = .22, F = 21.2, $p < .001$, b = .21, se_b = .03), use of interrogative strategies (beta = .18, F = 19.3, $p < .001$, b = .17, se_b = .03), and nonverbal immediacy (beta = .14, F = 11.7, $p < .01$, b = .13, se_b = .04). The amount of variation accounted for in the American regression equation for attributional confidence was 58% (R^2).

TABLE 5.2 Regression Statistics Predicting Attributional Confidence

	Beta	F	p	b	se_b	Tolerance
U.S. intraethic:						
self-disclosure	.22	21.2	.001	.21	.03	.37
interrogation	.18	19.3	.001	.17	.03	.40
nonverbal immediacy	.14	11.7	.01	.13	.04	.72
other's disclosure	.44	107.6	.0001	.50	.04	.35
U.S. interethnic:						
self-disclosure	.17	29.5	.001	.22	.03	.32
interrogation	X*	X	X	X	X	.25
nonverbal immediacy	.12	27.4	.001	.12	.02	.81
other's disclosure	.56	140.6	.0001	.53	.04	.34
Ghana intraethnic:						
self-disclosure	X	X	X	X	X	.44
interrogation	.17	8.0	.01	.17	.05	.73
nonverbal immediacy	.17	9.1	.008	.16	.06	.91
other's disclosure	.21	14.6	.003	.26	.08	.70
Ghana interethnic:						
self-disclosure	X	X	X	X	X	.44
interrogation	X	X	X	X	X	.73
nonverbal immediacy	.21	9.8	.002	.18	.05	.91
other's disclosure	.21	5.1	.02	.27	.10	.70

NOTE: An X indicates the variable did not enter the regression equation.

As noted in Table 5.2, the analysis of the Ghanaian data revealed only three significant beta coefficients: other's disclosure (beta = .21, F = 14.6, $p < .003$, b = .26, se_b = .08), nonverbal immediacy (beta = .17, F = 9.1, $p < .008$, b = .16, se_b = .06), and use of interrogation strategies (beta = .17, F = 8.0, $p < .01$, b = .17, se_b = .05). The amount of variance in attributional confidence accounted for in the Ghanaian data was 25% (R^2). For the Ghanaian respondents, level of self-disclosure did not add a significant amount of explained variance in the stepwise regression equation of attributional confidence. Further, the smaller unstandardized regression coefficient (b) for other's self-disclosure and the smaller coefficient of determination (R^2) suggests that Ghanaians place less stress on verbal information in understanding others than do North Americans.

The second set of regression analyses were computed for the interethnic bases of uncertainty reduction. The multiple regressions of interethnic attributional confidence included other's level of disclosure, level of self-disclosure, use of interrogation strategies, and nonverbal immediacy. The regression equations for interethnic attributional confidence differed for the data from U.S. and from Ghanaian respondents. As noted in Table 5.2, for the U.S. respondents, three significant beta coefficients were found: other's disclosure (beta = .56, F = 140.6, $p < .0001$, $b = .53$, $se_b = .04$), self-disclosure (beta = .17, F = 29.5, $p < .001$, $b = .22$, $se_b = .03$), and nonverbal immediacy (beta = .12, F = 27.4, $p < .001$, $b = .12$, $se_b = .02$). The amount of variation accounted for in the American regression equation for interethnic attributional confidence was 53% (R^2).

For the Ghanaian respondents, only two significant beta coefficients were found (see Table 5.2): other's disclosure (beta = .21, F = 5.1, $p < .02$, $b = .27$, $se_b = .10$) and nonverbal immediacy (beta = .21, F = 9.8, $p < .002$, $b = .18$, $se_b = .05$). The amount of variance in attributional confidence accounted for in the Ghanaian data was 25% (R^2).

DISCUSSION

The results of this research support a culture-general uncertainty reduction motive. Other culture-general similarities in uncertainty reduction were also isolated. However, we did not find support for differences in in-group and out-group communication for intraethnic and interethnic acquaintances in collectivistic and individualistic cultures. Cultural differences were found that were consistent with prior research findings on broad patterns of communication in collective and individualistic cultures.

The MANOVA analyses did not find mean differences between intraethnic or interethnic acquaintances in the amounts of self-disclosure, other's disclosure, nonverbal immediacy, interrogation, or attributional confidence in either the U.S. or the Ghanaian data. This suggests that the frequency of use of these behaviors does not vary between intra- and interethnic acquaintance relationships in either culture. This finding was somewhat surprising because of its inconsistency with the theory about the roles of in-groups and out-groups in collective and individualistic cultures and its inconsistency with prior research on both intercultural and interethnic communication.

A number of reasons could explain the failure to find such differences. First, it may be that ethnicity (tribe) is less of a factor in determining in-groups and out-groups for Ghanaian college students. We do not believe this to be the case. Because none of the Ghanaian respondents had any difficulty identifying the ethnic (tribal) identification of their interethnic acquaintance, obviously then, they are aware of differences. Further, ethnic identification has historically played an important role in Ghanaian culture and remains a strong factor today. We think that it is more likely that such differences did not emerge because of the limited role of verbal interaction in uncertainty reduction in high-context cultures.

The inconsistency with past research on intercultural-interpersonal communication may be due to a number of factors. First, there may be a difference in uncertainty reduction between macro-cultural variance and micro-cultural variance (see Gudykunst, 1986). Cultural differences are greatest when the communicators come from different countries. Second, the results may be explained by variant methodologies. Imahori (1987a, 1987b) content analyzed actual communication encounters. Our participants may have remembered fewer differences than actually occurred. Third, Imahori (1987a), Gudykunst (1983a), and Gudykunst and Nishida (1984) all examined initial interactions, while we focused on more developed acquaintance relationships. Our failure to find differences then would be more consistent with Gudykunst, Yang, and Nishida (1985) finding that, as relationships become more intimate, cultural differences play a lesser role.

The failure to find differences in the amount of use of uncertainty reduction communication does not necessarily mean that there are no differences between intra- and interethnic communication in either culture. In fact, the regression analyses indicate that, when the interrelationships of the variables are considered, differences indeed emerge. For the U.S. participants, 58% of the variance in attributional confidence was explained by self-disclosure, interrogation, nonverbal immediacy, and other's disclosure for intraethnic acquaintances. On the other hand, for interethnic acquaintances, only self-disclosure, nonverbal immediacy, and other's disclosure contributed to explaining the variance in attributional confidence (53%). This suggests that, although interrogation is used in interethnic acquaintance relationships, it does not independently contribute to the reduction of uncertainty. It may be that, when U.S. respondents develop acquaintances with ethnically similar others, they tend to follow traditional low-context communication patterns. That is, they use especially direct methods to reduce uncertainty, and thus interrogation plays an important role. However, when others are ethnically dissimilar, such direct strategies may be perceived as ineffective or inappropriate for reducing uncertainty, resulting in the use of more indirect means.

For the Ghanaian participants, 25% of the variance in attributional confidence was explained by interrogation, nonverbal immediacy, and other's disclosure in intraethnic acquaintance relationships. Self-disclosure did not independently contribute to uncertainty reduction. For interethnic acquaintances, only nonverbal immediacy and other's disclosure contributed to the explanation of attributional confidence (25%). Neither self-disclosure nor interrogation entered the equation. These results point to two significant patterns. First, self-disclosure is not perceived as a means of reducing uncertainty for Ghanaians. It may be that they do not recognize a reciprocity effect of disclosure. Thus disclosing about oneself is not seen as a means to learn about another. Second, as with the U.S. data, interrogation did contribute to attributional confidence for intraethnic acquaintances but did not for interethnic acquaintances. Again, such direct verbal strategies may be perceived as ineffective or inappropriate for ethnically dissimilar acquaintances.

Comparing the interrelationships of the uncertainty reduction variables across the cultures does support past research on the differences between collective, high-context and individualistic, low-context cultures. The first, and most obvious, difference is that, for both intra- and interethnic acquaintances, more than twice the amount of variance in attributional confidence was explained in the U.S. data than in the Ghanaian data. This is consistent with Gudykunst's (1983b) research, which found that members of high-context cultures tend to rely more on background information to reduce uncertainty. In such cultures, it is knowledge of one's background (and the groups to which one belongs) that allows reliable predictions about one's behavior. Direct verbal interaction is often mistrusted (Levine, 1985). Thus interactive communication may not be a primary means for the reduction of uncertainty.

The limited role that direct verbal communication plays in the reduction of uncertainty in high-context cultures is further evidenced by the role of disclosure. Not only did self-disclosure not help to increase attributional confidence in the Ghanaian participants, but the role of other's disclosure (in both intra- and interethnic acquaintances) was nearly twice as powerful in the U.S. data as in the Ghanaian data. Even though other's disclosure does help to reduce uncertainty for those from collective cultures, it does so much less so than for individualistic cultures. This is consistent with broad cultural patterns because, in individualistic cultures, one must come to know a specific individual to predict or explain his or her behavior because it is assumed that all individuals are different. Conversely, in collective cultures, one is assumed to be similar to the other members of the groups to which one belongs, so specific interaction is less important in predicting or explaining another's behavior. This is also consistent with past research, which found that individualistic cultures rely on more direct methods to reduce uncertainty than collectivistic cultures (Gudykunst & Nishida, 1984; Gudykunst, Yang, & Nishida, 1985).

Finally, the relative importance of nonverbal cues in high-context cultures was supported by our data (Gudykunst & Nishida, 1986). In achieving attributional confidence about different ethnic others, nonverbal immediacy played a more important role for Ghanaian participants than it did for U.S. participants. This supports Hall's distinction that, in low-context cultures, direct verbal cues are necessary to supply meaning to interaction while, in high-context cultures, nonverbal cues are more trusted.

CONCLUSION

This research found both similarities and differences in intraethnic and interethnic acquaintance relationships in the United States and Ghana. Uncertainty does appear to motivate communication, and interactive communication appears to reduce uncertainty in both cultures in intraethnic and interethnic acquaintance relationships. Further, in both cultures, interrogation appears not to play a significant role in the reduction of uncertainty for interethnic acquaintances.

Differences between the cultures supported broad patterns of cultural distinction based on collectivism/individualism and high/low context. In collective, high-context cultures, less stress is placed on direct interactive verbal communication to reduce uncertainty than in individualistic low-context cultures. On the other hand, nonverbal cues play a greater role in the reduction of uncertainty in high-context cultures than in low-context cultures. Thus this research provides additional support for the conclusion that there are distinctive patterns of uncertainty reduction communication between high-context, collectivist cultures and low-context, individualistic cultures.

REFERENCES

Berger, C. R. (1979). Beyond initial interaction: Uncertainty, understanding, and the development of interpersonal relationships. In H. Giles & R. St. Clair (Eds.), *Language and social psychology* (pp. 122-124). Baltimore: University Park Press.

Berger, C. R. (1987). Communicating under uncertainty. In M. E. Roloff & G. R. Miller (Eds.), *Interpersonal processes: New directions in communication research* (pp. 39-62). Newbury Park, CA: Sage.

Berger, C. R., & Calabrese, R. J. (1975). Some explorations in initial interaction and beyond: Toward a developmental theory of interpersonal communication. *Human Communication Research, 1,* 99-112.

Berger, C. R., & Kellerman, K. A. (1983). To ask or not to ask: Is that a question? In R. N. Bostrom (Ed.), *Communication yearbook 7* (pp. 342-368). Newbury Park, CA: Sage.

Clatterbuck, G. W. (1979). Attributional confidence and uncertainty in initial interactions. *Human Communication Research, 5,* 147-157.

Cronbach, L. (1951). Coefficient alpha and the internal structure of tests. *Psychometrika, 16,* 297-334.

Doob, L. W. (1961). *Communication in Africa: A search for boundaries.* New Haven, CT: Yale University Press.

Earley, P. C. (1984). Social interaction: The frequency of use and valuation in the United States, England, and Ghana. *Journal of Cross-Cultural Psychology, 15,* 477-485.

Gudykunst, W. B. (1983a). Similarities and differences in perceptions of initial intracultural and intercultural encounters: An exploratory investigation. *Southern Speech Communication Journal, 49,* 49-65.

Gudykunst, W. B. (1983b). Uncertainty reduction and predictability of behavior in low- and high-context cultures: An exploratory study. *Communication Quarterly, 31,* 49-55.

Gudykunst, W. B. (1985a). The influence of cultural similarity, type of relationship, and self-monitoring on uncertainty reduction processes. *Communication Monographs, 52,* 203-217.

Gudykunst, W. B. (1985b). A model of uncertainty reduction in intercultural encounters. *Journal of Language and Social Psychology, 4*(2), 79-98.

Gudykunst, W. B. (1986). Ethnicity, types of relationship, and intraethnic and interethnic uncertainty reduction. In Y. Y. Kim (Ed.), *Interethnic communication: Current research* (pp. 201-224). Newbury Park, CA: Sage.

Gudykunst, W. B., Chua, E., & Gray, A. J. (1986). Cultural dissimilarities and uncertainty reduction processes. In M. L. McLaughlin (Ed.), *Communication yearbook 10* (pp. 456-469). Newbury Park, CA: Sage.

Gudykunst, W. B., & Hammer, M. R. (1987). The influence of ethnicity, gender and dyadic composition on uncertainty reduction in initial interactions. *Journal of Black Studies, 18,* 191-214.

Gudykunst, W. B., & Nishida, T. (1984). Individual and cultural influences on uncertainty reduction. *Communication Monographs, 51,* 23-36.

Gudykunst, W. B., & Nishida, T. (1986). Attributional confidence in low- and high-context cultures. *Human Communication Research, 12,* 525-549.

Gudykunst, W. B., Nishida, T., Koike, H., & Shiino, N. (1985). The influence of language on uncertainty reduction: An exploratory study of Japanese-Japanese and Japanese-North American interactions. In M. L. McLaughlin (Eds.), *Communication yearbook 9* (pp. 555-575). Beverly Hills, CA: Sage.

Gudykunst, W. B., Nishida, T., & Schmidt, K. (1988, May). *The influence of cultural variability, self-monitoring, predicted outcome value on uncertainty reduction in ingroup vs outgroup and same vs opposite sex relationships: Japan and the United States.* Paper presented at the International Communication Association, New Orleans.

Gudykunst, W. B., Schmidt, K. L., Bond, M. H., Wang, G., Gao, G., Nishida, T., Leung, K., & Barraclough, R. A. (in press). The influence of individualism-collectivism, self-monitoring, and predicted outcome value on communication in ingroup and outgroup relationships. *Journal of Cross-Cultural Psychology.*

Gudykunst, W. B., Sodetani, L. L., & Sonoda, K. T. (1987). Uncertainty reduction in Japanese-Caucasian relationships in Hawaii. *Western Journal of Speech Communication, 51,* 256-278.

Gudykunst, W. B., & Ting-Toomey, S. (1988). *Culture and interpersonal communication.* Newbury Park, CA: Sage.

Gudykunst, W. B., Yang, S., & Nishida, T. (1985). A cross-cultural test of uncertainty reduction theory: Comparisons of acquaintances, friends, and dating relationships in Japan, Korea, and the United States. *Human Communication Research, 11,* 407-454.

Gudykunst, W. B., Yoon, Y., & Nishida, T. (1987). The influence of individualism-collectivism on perceptions of communication in ingroup and outgroup relationships. *Communication Monographs, 54,* 295-306.

Hall, E. (1959). *The silent language.* Garden City, NY: Anchor.

Hall, E. (1977). *Beyond culture.* Garden City, NY: Anchor.

Hofstede, G. (1983). National cultures in four dimensions. *Studies of Management & Organization, 13,* 46-74.

Hofstede, G. (1984). *Culture's consequences.* Beverly Hills, CA: Sage.

Imahori, T. T. (1987a, February). *An exploratory comparison of initial intracultural and intercultural interactions: Investigation of actual communication behaviors and perceptions.* Paper presented to the annual meeting of the Western Speech Communication Association, Salt Lake City, UT.

Imahori, T. T. (1987b, November). *Intracultural and interpersonal epistemology: Behavioral comparison of intimacy and interrogative strategies between initial intracultural and intercultural interactions.* Paper presented at the annual meeting of the Speech Communication Association, Boston.

Jourard, S. M. (1971). *The transparent self* (2nd ed.). Princeton, NJ: Van Nostrand.

Kellerman, K. A., & Berger, C. R. (1984). Affect and the acquisition of social information: Sit back, relax, and tell me about yourself. In R. N. Bostrom (Ed.), *Communication yearbook 8* (pp. 412-415). Newbury Park, CA: Sage.

Levine, D. N. (1985). *The flight from ambiguity.* Chicago: University of Chicago Press.

Middleton, J. (1983). One hundred and fifty years of Christianity in a Ghanaian town. *Africa, 53*(3), 47-52.

Novicki, M. A. (1987, November). Adjustment with a new face. *Africa Report,* pp. 47-52.

Triandis, H. C., Bontempo, R., Villareal, M. J., Asai, M., & Lucca, N. (1988). Individualism and collectivism: Cross-cultural perspectives on self-ingroup relationships. *Journal of Personality and Social Psychology, 54,* 323-338.

6

Stability of Romantic Relationships in China and the United States

GE GAO ● *San Jose State University*

This chapter analyzes the interactive mechanisms that contribute to stability in romantic relationships in China and the United States. Two specific research questions were asked: (1) What accounts for stability in a serious romantic relationship? (2) Do the same factors account for relationship stability in China and the United States? The findings of the study indicated that mutuality of openness, involvement, shared nonverbal meanings, and relationship assessment were the four factors that consistently explained relationship stability in both China and the United States.

Many relational studies have used social penetration theory (Altman & Taylor, 1973) to unravel some of the determinants of relationship growth and development. Social penetration theory attempts to account for relationship growth and development by examining the "breadth" and "depth" of the act of verbal disclosure over time. Recent theoretical and empirical developments (e.g., Parks, 1981) question a linear model of verbal disclosure growing from shallow and narrow to deep and wide. It can be argued that verbal exchanges between partners do not usually follow a consistently progressive pattern. Verbal exchanges take different forms in various situations.

In an attempt to move beyond the social penetration perspective, this study intends to isolate factors that explain stability in relationships by exploring some of the interactive mechanisms operating in serious romantic relationships in China and the United States. Specifically, the focus of the study aims to address two weaknesses in relationship development studies: a lack of empirical research on the factors that contribute to relationship stability and a lack of cross-cultural generalizability. First, there is little empirical research in the field on the process where both partners become interdependent and maintain some type of stability in a serious romantic relationship. Second, a cross-cultural orientation helps to increase our general understanding of

AUTHOR'S NOTE: I am indebted to my adviser, William Gudykunst, for his valuable comments and suggestions. I am also grateful to Stella Ting-Toomey for her insights and constant encouragement.

interpersonal relationships because the scope of cross-cultural studies broadens the generalizability of research findings.

PROBLEMS IN RELATIONSHIP DEVELOPMENT RESEARCH

The prototypical relationship development phases are marked by acquaintance, establishment, continuation, deterioration, and termination (Levinger, 1983). Most research on dyadic relationship development to date has been conducted in the first and the last stages as well as in the turning points in relationships (e.g., see Duck, 1982; Huston & Levinger, 1978; for a review). Studies concerning relationship initiation or disengagement and relationship turning points are often approached by the researchers from the individual's perspective. Relationship stability needs to be examined from a relational point of view because the term *relationship* is dyadic in nature. As Hinde (1979) indicates, a shift from the individual to the relational level of analysis is necessary to describe and explain relational stability and growth.

A relational unit of analysis shapes the conceptual focus of research concerning the relationship development process (Gottman, Notarius, Gonso, & Markman, 1976; Millar & Rogers, 1976; Morton, Alexander, & Altman, 1976). It also shapes the areas of research observations by the researchers. In fact, Hinde (1981) suggests that dyadic events taking place should be the emphasis of a relational level of analysis perspective. This entails what the partners do together and how partners define and differentiate types of relationships. In other words, the focus needs to be confined to events or activities in which partners mutually engage because dyadic properties have replaced individual properties in relationships. Specifically, there is a need to isolate the factors that contribute to mutual involvement and what role mutual involvement plays in the relationship. This appears consistent with previous research indicating a more frequent occurrence of behavioral exchanges in advanced relationships than in less advanced relationships (Gottman, 1979; Morton, 1978; Rausch, Barry, Hertel, & Swain, 1974). Focusing on the interactive activities that take place between both partners in a relationship is the most appropriate approach for conducting relationship development research.

Another major inadequacy of past relationship development research is failure to examine stable aspects of relationships. As Morton and Douglas (1981) indicate, difficulties in capturing relational processes have led researchers to study manageable topics such as relationship initiation, relationship disengagement, and turning points. Relationship stability suggests that a particular stage of a relationship has been achieved in which things gradually move toward a state of equilibrium. The use of a dynamic-change approach to the study of stability will inevitably result in misinterpretation. Routine, everyday interactions between both partners in the relationship stability stage should be examined as critically as those in other relationship development stages.

In addition, cross-cultural comparisons of relationship stability or relationship growth are scarce. The limited number of studies conducted in the cross-cultural domain have focused on comparisons of social penetration processes in various types of relationships (Gudykunst & Nishida, 1983, 1986; Won-Doornink, 1979, 1985). Recent developments in intercultural relationship research (Gudykunst, Gao, Sudweeks, Ting-Toomey, & Nishida, 1991; Sudweeks, Gudykunst, Ting-Toomey, & Nishida, 1990) have been limited to the examination of the importance of culture-related variables in the development of interpersonal relationships.

This study attempts to fill the void of cross-cultural relationship stability research by employing a self-report open-ended method of data collection, that is, the interview. The self-report technique is considered to be one of the most frequently used approaches to the exploration of close relationships (Harvey, Hendrick, & Tucker, 1988). Researchers who use self-report techniques often seek to understand meanings of verbal and nonverbal behaviors from the perspective of those who create them. The specific interview method employed in this study enables the researcher to interact with the participants and to clarify, elaborate, and probe interpretations going on in the process. Two specific questions were asked to guide the study: (a) What accounts for stability in a serious romantic relationship? (b) Do the same factors account for relationship stability in China and the United States?

METHODS

Respondents

The sample for the study consisted of 34 college students. Among them were nine Chinese dyads and eight North American dyads currently involved in serious romantic relationships. The average age of the Chinese respondents was 23 years, and their average length of relationship was 1.87 years. The average age of the North American dyads was 22 years, and their average length of relationship was 1.66

years. Nearly all of the North American respondents reported two or more previous relationships (93%), whereas only about half of the Chinese respondents had been involved in a previous relationship (58%).

Procedures

Both the Chinese and the North American respondents were contacted through either undergraduate classes or personal friends. The Chinese were interviewed in Chinese in China, and the North Americans were interviewed in English in the United States. All interviews were conducted separately and tape-recorded with permission. Each open-ended interview session varied from a half hour to a full hour.

Interviews were conducted for the specific purpose of gathering information about the overall relationship development process. Participants were asked to provide a historical account of their relationship and the interactive acts in which they are currently engaged, such as activities they do together, things they share, and projections they make regarding their relationship. The North American interviews were transcribed in English. Although the Chinese interviews were transcribed in Chinese, the quotes used to support the current analysis were translated to English for purposes of presentation here.

Data Analysis

Analyses of the transcripts occurred in several phases. Each dyad's set of interviews were read several times to provide a complete picture of the relationship development process and to capture the interactive properties the dyad shared. My initial treatment of the data involved a separate reading of Chinese and North American transcripts to get a sense of commonalties and differences across cultures. To focus on the current stage of the relationship and locate some of the mechanisms that were operating, I examined specific accounts of behaviors taking place in the relationships. I tried to build an understanding of meanings each partner in a dyad attributed to the interactive behaviors by comparing the shared "sphere" of the specific utterances or stories. Each interview, therefore, was interpreted from a relational perspective. Given that the study's focus was on the current stage of the relationships, I looked for common patterns of interactive acts in all dyads. As Spradley (1979) indicates, thematic (or pattern) analysis enables researchers to see a holistic picture. A number of research studies employing thematic analysis have uncovered some relationship dimensions that would have been hidden otherwise (e.g., Owen, 1984; Rawlins, 1983). In this study, each dyad's relationship was determined based on participants' own labels (e.g., casual relationship, serious relationship) and their descriptions of the relationship.

A major motif—that is, relationship stability—emerged out of all the open-ended interviews. In addition, a graph technique was used to elicit mutual assessment of a relationship within each dyad. All respondents depicted their current stage of relationship development with straight, horizontal lines in comparison with some of their curved lines in different turning-point stages.

Before presenting the results, an issue pertaining to cross-cultural studies needs to be addressed. I discovered that the North American transcripts were much more lengthy and substantive than the Chinese ones. In the interview sessions in China, my Chinese respondents would not provide elaborate answers to my questions. To get a detailed account of some aspects of the relationship, I had to "pull out sentences from their mouths" by repeatedly asking for specifics.

The Chinese responses were very brief and general even in dealing with specific happenings or stories of the relationships, even though I had been introduced to the respondents through their personal friends and I spoke the same language. In contrast, the North American respondents I interviewed were relative strangers, but they would open up and become very elaborate and explicit in telling me about their relationships, which surprised me quite a bit. In interviewing the North American respondents, most of the time I sat and listened, except when there was a need for probe or clarification. This cultural difference seems to be consistent with the commonly known assumption that, in China, you must be an intimate friend before a Chinese will open up and tell you embedded stories. To illustrate, my best friend told me everything about her romantic relationship, but she would only talk about this relationship with a limited number of people, and I doubt whether she would have given details to a stranger interviewing her about the relationship. The whole issue illustrated here evokes two culture-laden ideas relating to talk. Specifically, given a cultural context, what is involved in talk and what is valued in talk needs to be taken into consideration to understand the data being analyzed.

RESULTS AND DISCUSSION

All dyads from both cultures were in stable and highly involved romantic relationships. To provide a picture of the degree of stability present in the relationships, illustrative dyadic cases are presented. I begin with two accounts from the North American dyad:

> We do a lot of things together. We do spend a lot of time together. I was always the kind of person that I would get sick of somebody if I spent too much time with him. That's kind of weird that we spend so much time together, but we really don't get sick of each other. We go to school together and we try to study together. We love movies, always go to the dollar theater. We found out it was so easy to talk to each other. I think I know pretty much everything about him and I think that's the best thing about our relationship. That's why it has worked so far. I think we're at the point where we know each other very well just from the way I look at him and he looks at me. We can pretty much tell what the other is thinking. Hopefully, I will end up marrying him forever. He feels the same way. I think I'll probably go where he goes to continue our relationship. (NA-3, F)

> We're very compatible. We always like being together although we are not doing anything. We like driving a lot. We drove to San Diego and Sedona. That's pretty much our best time, time for us to talk and just to relax. We're very open about each other. I don't think she has things (hidden from me) and I think we're about letting 90% of our inner thoughts out. There is nonverbal communication between us all the time knowing that we don't need to start conversations. That's pretty much communication right there. There's a sense of awareness or presence. I think the relationship is getting better. I don't see her changing in such a way and me changing in such a way whereas to harm our relationship. I think as things get better beyond schooling and work there's the marriage and the family 'cause I don't see it getting worse. (NA-3, M)

Accounts given by the Chinese dyad were:

> We have fun together and we study together. Sometimes we go out and we like to cook. There are often gestures and expressions in the eyes between us. It's unnecessary to talk a lot. We certainly talk about lots of things. We talk about popular social issues, personal feelings, and everyday life. I hope the relationship will be successful and it will keep growing. I'll try my best to keep the relationship. She feels the same way. (CH-1, M)

> We play sports together. If there is a good movie, we try to go see it. We talk and exchange our opinions. We often talk about ourselves and our feelings toward each other. Sometimes we can sincerely discuss where the dissatisfaction with each other comes from, our frustrations, and uncertainties about future. There are expressions in the eyes and other nonverbal behaviors between us. I want to keep developing the relationship. It will continue and I think he does too. (CH-1, F)

Given that stability emerged as the major motif of all of the relationships in this study, I searched for factors that appeared to contribute to stability in the relationships. Both the North American and the Chinese dyadic accounts revealed the importance of openness, involvement, shared nonverbal meanings, and relationship assessment in explaining the stability present in their relationships. The fact that partners in both dyads feel free to share things demonstrates the dimension of openness in the relationship. The extensive amount of time invested in the relationship, implicit understandings of each other's nonverbal behaviors, and mutual assessment of the relationship all signify stability in the described relationships.

The four factors discussed above appeared to be salient and consistent within each individual dyad as well as across dyads in both the Chinese sample and the U.S. sample. Overt correspondence in the individuals' accounts of dyadic behaviors such as openness, involvement, and shared nonverbal meanings as well as in the assessment of relationship appear to be the dominating themes throughout the dyadic transcripts. Concurring accounts of interactions within each dyad seemed to explain why stability existed in the relationships. Given this overview, each factor will be discussed separately and their interconnections will be examined.

Openness

Mutuality of openness emerged in all dyadic accounts of the verbal interactions. The open channel of communication is actualized through both partners' willingness to reveal whatever is on their minds without the constraints of time, subject matter, or situation. For example, overt expressions of the North American respondents—such as "We find each other being able to discuss just about everything" (NA-1, M); "My father passed away a while ago so I talk about that a lot with him which I don't talk to anybody else" (NA-1, F); "We've always shared our problems with each other. I don't usually hide anything from him" (NA-9, F); and "We just know each other so well that we can feel comfortable on any topic. I couldn't think of anything we wouldn't talk about" (NA-9, M)—illustrate the open interactions that take place in stable and serious relationships.

The accounts provided by the Chinese respondents further illustrate the concept of openness: "We usually tell each other what we have in mind" (CH-2, M); "We talk about lots of things; basically we're able to disclose over 90% with each other" (CH-2, F); "When we're together, we can possibly talk about everything" (CH-3, M); "We talk about everything" (CH-3, F). An open channel of communication signifies mutual trust and feelings of comfortableness with each other. The use of "we" as a relational property suggests that some type of close behavior from one partner will inadvertently lead to a similar reaction from the other. The openness of the channel, therefore, requires bilateral efforts.

In this study, the absence of the closedness component of the dialectic was anticipated because of the stable nature of relationships. As the data above illustrated, the fact that both partners are open to each other contributes to the stability of all relationships. In other words, the interplay of openness and closedness will prevail when a relationship development process is examined over a period of time, such as from initiation to stability.

The conceptualization of openness used here is an attempt to overcome the "self-disclosure syndrome" in relationship development studies. Most research in the area of self-disclosure operates from the social exchange paradigm, which evaluates the costs and rewards as well as the reciprocal nature of disclosing (Altman, 1973; Altman & Taylor, 1973; Derlega & Grzelak, 1979). Given the current analysis, the traditional conceptualization of self-disclosure and some of its original postulations seem to be unwarranted in accounting for relationship stability. Specifically, the "depth" and "breadth" of verbal disclosing patterns proposed by Altman and Taylor (1973) were not present in the data. Respondents did not report how deeply they talked and what they talked about, but the fact that they were able to open up and express whatever was there suggested the notion of openness.

The assumption that individuals are driven by their intentionality when self-disclosing to others (e.g., there is always a reason behind an individual's eliciting a piece of personal information) also was not supported given the overt statements of respondents expressing a willingness and comfortableness with being open. In addition, the reciprocity argument (e.g., Altman, 1973) also lacked saliency. Examples in the study demonstrated that both partners in stable relationships reach a point where they are no longer conditioned by the "I disclose and you reciprocate" rule. Rather, the ability to maintain an open channel and to let information freely flow tends to be the dominating mechanisms of the relationship. The findings of the study indicate that being open to each other appeared to account for the stability in the relationships.

Involvement

Mutual involvement appeared consistently as a dyadic behavior pattern in all relationships. A willingness to invest extensive amount of time in the relationship on the part of both individuals and feelings of togetherness were the binding force of the couples. Consider the following examples: "We can do anything together. We do a lot" (NA-8, F). "[We do] basically everything. We play tennis. We bum around" (NA-8, M). "[We do] everything. We play tennis and stay together a lot during the week" (NA-2, M). "We take trips a lot. We study a lot together" (NA-2, F). "We are almost always together such as going to movies and studying together" (CH-7, F). "We're together a lot. We often sit and talk" (CH-7, M). "We see each other every day and do everything together" (CH-2, M). "We do everything together" (CH-2, F).

It appears that mutual engagement in activities and frequent interactions between partners create and maintain a sense of togetherness and stability in the relationship. This behavior pattern appears consistent with most of the work in interpersonal relationship development. Most theorists (e.g., Hinde, 1981; Kelley et al., 1983) indicate that frequency of interaction is a major component necessary for relationship development. Morton and Douglas (1981) argue that successful co-orientation such as playing sports or raising kids together is a source of attraction between partners. Several empirical studies also have found support for positive relationship between involvement and maintenance of relationships (e.g., Gudykunst et al., 1991; Rose & Serafica, 1986).

Another interesting finding regarding involvement was exemplified in statements such as "We like being together although we're not doing anything" (NA-3, M); "We can just hang out together, say, watch TV and just enjoy each other's company" (NA-1, F); and "We do whatever is there" (NA-1, M). It appears that couples who maintain some type of stability in their serious relationships tend not to do "planned activities" all the time. A number of respondents stated that they have passed the activity-oriented stage. "Being together" in a less structured or unstructured way and being aware of and enjoying the other person's presence characterize the relationship. The importance of involvement in relationship development has been largely ignored in various relational studies. As Morton and Douglas (1981) indicate, shared activities, namely, what two individuals in a relationship typically do together, need to be examined in more detail in future research.

Shared Nonverbal Meanings

Relationship stability also was characterized by shared nonverbal meanings between partners. The nonverbal meanings each partner attaches to actions, events, and settings are created in the relationship. The most innovative mechanism in a relationship emerges when mutual understanding of implicit nonverbal actions takes place. Mutuality of understanding occurs when both partners attribute the same meanings to a particular behavior, event, or situation.

For example, dyadic exchanges such as "I can tell when something is bothering him" (NA-1, F); "I can tell when something is bothering her through her grimaces or through her body tension" (NA-1, M); "We know each other so well that we know when something is wrong or something is bothering us" (NA-8, F); "We both know what each other is thinking without her telling me or me telling her" (NA-8, M); "There is an implicit understanding between two of us" (CH-8, F); "I have realized that we have an implicit understanding of each other" (CH-8, M); "We can really understand each other without using words" (CH-4, M); "I feel like we have an implicit understanding of each other" (CH-4, F). These quotes indicate that partners have acquired a deep, sensitive understanding of each other's nonverbal nuances. The extent to which two partners understand each other nonverbally can define the nature of the relationship. Mutual understanding and accurate attributions of nonverbal behaviors appear to be the essence of a stable relationship.

The emergence of the dimension of shared nonverbal meanings is consistent with previous research. Burgoon (1985) emphasizes the importance of nonverbal communication in defining relationships. She also argues that the nature of a relationship depends on the accurate interpretation of each other's nonverbal behaviors. Empirical studies also support the relationship between stability and shared nonverbal meanings. Gudykunst et al. (1991) found that the ability to understand nonverbal behaviors was the most salient factor in romantic relationships, less salient in friendships, and the least salient in acquaintance relationships. Similarly, research suggests that synchronized communication increases with relationship intimacy (Knapp, Ellis, & Williams, 1980). The emergence of shared nonverbal meanings also suggests increased attributional confidence for both partners and the appearance of idiosyncratic rule structures in intimate relationships (Gudykunst & Nishida, 1986; Miller & Steinberg, 1975).

Relationship Assessment

Stability in a relationship also was manifested in the mutuality of relationship assessment: that is, how both partners view the current status and the future development of the relationship. The importance of relationship assessment in relational research has been dealt with in a number of previous studies (e.g., Laing, Phillipson, & Lee, 1966; Littlejohn, 1983). Morton et al. (1976) propose that viable relationships require "mutuality of relationship definition," which refers to the extent to which both partners view the relationship in the same way. In this study, consistent assertions with respect to the prediction of the future of the relationship on the part of both partners in a dyad suggest the element of stability in the relationship.

The following examples illustrate this observation: "I can see this relationship having great longevity" (NA-1, M); "Hopefully it will last forever is what I'm thinking" (NA-1, F); "A good future" (NA-4, F); "I'd say the immediate future may be the next four years we'll probably stay the way it is now" (NA-4, M); "We're planning to get married" (CH-7, F); "We plan to get married" (CH-7, M); and "I'm very optimistic that our relationship will develop satisfactorily" (CH-4, M); "We plan to get married" (CH-4, F). The predictions described above imply that both partners have reached consensus about the nature of their relationships. In other words, both partners have agreed in terms of the current status of the relationship and where the relationship is heading.

Stability in a relationship is also defined by the mutual assessment of possible behavior changes on the part of each individual in a dyad. Rands and Levinger (1979) studied individuals' expectations regarding behavioral changes in different stages of relationships. They found that, the more intimate the relationship, the more probable it is that a positive association exists between the depth of a relationship and the probability of realistic expectations. The American and the Chinese dyads in the study revealed a consistent match between each other's views on the change dimension in the relationship. Some examples follow: "I don't think she'll change her mind" (NA-8, M); "I think he'll try to adapt to the situation" (NA-8, F); "I don't think she'll change" (CH-7, F); and "Right now I don't think she'll change" (CH-7, M). As the data above illustrated, this finding also seems compatible with the assertions they made regarding the future development of the relationship.

The notion of stability and relational assessment is reinforced by retrospective studies using the graph technique (e.g., Huston, Surra, Fitzgerald, & Cate, 1981; Purdy, 1978). Huston et al. (1981) reported that the upturns and downturns on the graphs often correspond to or reflect occurrences of separating events between partners in a relationship. In this study, the graph technique was used to help explain the mutual assessment of a relationship within each dyad.

Respondents were asked to draw a line that signified their romantic relationship development. The horizontal and the vertical lines, respectively, represent the length of the relationship and the perceived chance of marriage. An examination of the shape of the line reveals a number of ups and downs during the initial and turning-point stages of the relationship, but the line appears to level out in the current stage, suggesting stability in the relationship. This is consistent with Huston et al.'s (1981) findings.

To summarize, openness, involvement, shared nonverbal meanings, and relationship assessment are interdependent dimensions of relationships. For instance, the dimension of openness is contingent upon the degree of involvement, shared nonverbal meanings, and relationship assessment. An individual is reluctant to open up if he or she does not spend enough time with the partner or perceives no future for the relationship. Enhancement or decline in either of the dimensions is often determined by the nature of other dimensions. This coexisting relationship cuts across all romantic relationships in China and the United States and is clearly exemplified in the two illustrative dyadic accounts presented in the beginning of the results section.

CONCLUSION

The four factors isolated in this study consistently emerged as important dimensions in explaining relationship stability in both the United States and China (see Table 6.1). Mutuality of openness, involvement, shared nonverbal meanings, and relationship assessment occurred in both the North American and the Chinese dyadic relationships. The compatible findings across cultures indicate the generalizability of those dimensions in interpersonal relationship research. Investigations and analyses of the interactive properties of openness, involvement, shared nonverbal meanings, and relationship assessment signify the transition of cross-cultural relationship development research from the individual level to the dyadic level.

Before concluding, a number of general issues involved in the study need to be addressed. First, the compatibility of the isolated factors in the North American and the Chinese samples was anticipated. The extent to which cultural variations account for differences in relationship dimensions is expected in areas such as relationship initiation,

TABLE 6.1 Summary of Factors of Relationship Stability

Factors	Definition	Examples
Openness	An open channel of communication between both partners	We've always shared our problems with each other. I don't usually hide anything from him (NA-9, F).
		We just know each other so well that we can feel comfortable on any topic. I couldn't think of anything we wouldn't talk about (NA-9, M).
		When we're together, we can possibly talk about anything (CH-3, M).
		We talk about everything (CH-3, F).
Involvement	Strong sense of togetherness and extensive amount of time invested in the relationship	We can do anything together. We do a lot (NA-2, F).
		We do basically everything. We play tennis and stay together a lot during the week (NA-2, M).
		We're together a lot. We often sit and talk (CH-7, F).
		We see each other everyday and do everything together (CH-7, M).
Shared nonverbal meanings	Implicit understanding of each other's nonverbal messages	We know each other so well that we know when something is bothering us or something is wrong (NA-8, F).
		We both know what each other is thinking without her telling me or me telling her (NA-8, M).
		We can really understand each other without using words (CH-4, M).
		I feel like we have an implicit understanding of each other (CH-4, F).
Relationship assessment	Mutual definition of the current status and future development of the relationship	I can see this relationship having great longevity (NA-1, M).
		Hopefully it will last forever is what I'm thinking (NA-1, F).
		I'm very optimistic that our relationship will develop satisfactorily (CH-4, M).
		We plan to get married (CH-4, F).

relationship transitions, turning points, and relationship disengagement but not in relationship stability (Gudykunst & Kim, 1984). There appears to be a plausible explanation for this argument.

As indicated by the findings of this study, stability is a relational property. That is, it involves the coordinated personal efforts of both individuals in maintaining stability in order for stability to take place within the relationship. The impact of social and cultural factors, therefore, may not appear as salient as in other stages of relationships such as initiation and disengagement. This position is consistent with that of Gudykunst and Kim (1984). They argue that culture influences early stages of relationship development but, once stereotypes are broken down (e.g., the affective exchange stage), culture does not play as significant a role in explaining differences in intimate relationships. A number of empirical studies have validated the universal structure of interpersonal behavior that is consistent across cultures (e.g., Adamopoulos & Bontempo, 1986; Foa & Foa, 1974; Triandis, 1977, 1978). Intimacy, for example, has been isolated as a universal dimension embedded in interpersonal relationships across many different cultures (e.g., Triandis, 1977, 1978).

The four factors manifested in the current study appear to be compatible with findings from previous research on relationship growth and development (e.g., Hinde, 1981; Kelley, 1979; Knapp et al., 1980). For example, Hinde (1981) proposes eight useful dimensions in describing interpersonal relationships, which include the following: content of interactions, diversity of interactions, qualities of interactions, relative frequency and patterning of interactions, reciprocity versus complementarity, intimacy, interpersonal perception, and commitment. Kelley's (1979) theory of interdependence emphasizes the importance of mutuality of dependence in close relationships. The three communication-related factors suggested by Knapp et al. (1980) consist of personalized communication, synchronized communication, and communication efficiency.

Although these proposed dimensions do not strictly apply to relationship stability and have not been used in any cross-cultural relationship stability studies, it would be useful to incorporate them in future intercultural relationship research and examine them in the context of relationship stability. In addition, the relative importance of each dimension and its saliency in different stages of a relationship need to be further examined in future studies.

Finally, one methodological issue regarding cross-cultural research needs to be reinforced here. The implicit communication style exhibited by individuals from collectivistic, high-context cultures (e.g., China and Japan) creates difficulty in collecting interview data. Collectivistic, high-context individuals often are reluctant to provide strangers with elaborate and explicit responses. My personal experience in interviewing the Chinese respondents validated this point. Researchers are recommended to conduct exploratory studies in an individualistic, low-context culture first, and to develop a basic feel for the interview process. Successful research efforts in a collectivistic, high-context culture require language and cultural competency in a researcher, enabling him or her to request elaborations, as well as the use of more structured and closed-ended research technique. Alternatively, observational studies, such as those incorporating field research, need to be conducted in both individualistic, low-context cultures and collectivistic, high-context cultures. Also, both rhetorically and nonverbally sensitive styles are needed to conduct qualitatively based interpersonal-intercultural communication studies.

REFERENCES

Adamopoulos, J., & Bontempo, R. (1986). Diachronic universals in interpersonal structures: Evidence from literary sources. *Journal of Cross-Cultural Psychology, 17,* 169-189.

Altman, I. (1973). Reciprocity of interpersonal exchange. *Journal of the Theory of Social Behavior, 3,* 246-261.

Altman, I., & Taylor, D. A. (1973). *Social penetration: The development of interpersonal relationships.* New York: Holt, Rinehart & Winston.

Burgoon, J. (1985). Nonverbal signals. In M. L. Knapp & G. R. Miller (Eds.), *Handbook of interpersonal communication* (pp. 344-390). Beverly Hills, CA: Sage.

Derlega, V. J., & Grzelak, J. (1979). Appropriateness of self-disclosure. In G. J. Chelune (Ed.), *Self-disclosure* (pp. 151-176). San Francisco: Jossey-Bass.

Duck, S. W. (1982). A topography of relationship disengagement and dissolution. In S. W. Duck (Ed.), *Personal relationships: Vol. 4. Dissolving personal relationships* (pp. 1-30). London: Academic Press.

Foa, U., & Foa, E. (1974). *Societal structures of the mind.* Springfield, IL: Charles C Thomas.

Gottman, J. M. (1979). *Marital interaction: Experimental investigations.* New York: Academic Press.

Gottman, J. M., Notarius, C., Gonso, J., & Markman, H. (1976). *Couple's guide to communication.* Champaign, IL: Research Press.

Gudykunst, W. B., Gao, G., Sudweeks, S., Ting-Toomey, S., & Nishida, T. (1991). Themes in opposite-sex Japanese-North American relationships. In S. Ting-Toomey & F. Korzenny (Eds.), *Cross-cultural interpersonal communication.* Newbury Park, CA: Sage.

Gudykunst, W. G., & Kim, Y. Y. (1984). *Communicating with strangers.* Reading, MA: Addison-Wesley.

Gudykunst, W. B., & Nishida, T. (1983). Social penetration in Japanese and North American relationships. In R. Bostrom (Ed.), *Communication yearbook 7* (pp. 592-610). Beverly Hills, CA: Sage.

Gudykunst, W. B., & Nishida, T. (1986). The influence of cultural variability on perceptions of communication behavior associated with relationship terms. *Human Communication Research, 13,* 147-166.

Harvey, J. H., Hendrick, S. S., & Tucker, K. (1988). Self-report methods in studying personal relationships. In S. W. Duck, D. F. Hay, S. E. Hobfoll, W. Ickes, & B. M. Montgomery (Eds.), *Handbook of personal relationships*. Chichester: John Wiley.

Hinde, R. A. (1979). *Towards understanding relationships*. London: Academic Press.

Hinde, R. A. (1981). The bases of a science of interpersonal relationships. In S. W. Duck & R. Gilmour (Eds.), *Personal relationships: Vol. 1. Studying personal relationships*. London: Academic Press.

Huston, T. L., & Levinger, G. (1978). Interpersonal attraction and relationships. *Annual Review of Psychology, 29,* 115-156.

Huston, T. L., Surra, C. A., Fitzgerald, N. M., & Cate, R. M. (1981). From courtship to marriage: Mate selection as an interpersonal process. In S. W. Duck & R. Gilmour (Eds.), *Personal relationships: Vol. 2. Developing personal relationships*. London: Academic Press.

Kelley, H. H. (1979). *Personal relationships: Their structures and processes*. Hillsdale, NJ: Lawrence Erlbaum.

Kelley, H. H., Berscheid, E., Christensen, A., Harvey, J. H., Huston, T. L., Levinger, G., McClintock, E., Peplau, L. A., & Peterson, D. R. (1983). Analyzing close relationships. In H. H. Kelley et al. (Eds.), *Close relationships* (pp. 20-67). San Francisco: Freeman.

Knapp, M., Ellis, D., & Williams, B. (1980). Perceptions of communication behavior associated with relationship terms. *Communication Monographs, 47,* 262-278.

Laing, R. D., Phillipson, H., & Lee, A. R. (1966). *Interpersonal perception*. New York: Springer.

Levinger, G. (1979). A social exchange view of the dissolution of pair relationships. In R. L. Burgess & T. L. Huston (Eds.), *Social exchange: Advances in theory and research*. New York: Academic Press.

Levinger, G. (1983). Development and change. In H. H. Kelley et al. (Eds.), *Close relationships* (pp. 315-359). San Francisco: Freeman.

Littlejohn, S. W. (1983). *Theories in human communication*. Belmont, CA: Wadsworth.

Millar, F. E., & Rogers, L. E. (1976). A relational approach to interpersonal communication. In G. R. Miller (Ed.), *Explorations in interpersonal communication* (pp. 87-104). Beverly Hills, CA: Sage.

Miller, G., & Steinberg, M. (1975). *Between people*. Chicago: Science Research Associates.

Morton, T. L. (1978). Intimacy and reciprocity of exchanges: A comparison of spouses and strangers. *Journal of Personality and Social Psychology, 36,* 72-81.

Morton, T. L., Alexander, J. F., & Altman, I. (1976). Communication and relationship definition. In G. R. Miller (Ed.), *Exploration in interpersonal communication*. Beverly Hills, CA: Sage.

Morton, T. L., & Douglas, M. A. (1981). Growth of relationships. In S. W. Duck & R. Gilmour (Eds.), *Personal relationships: Vol. 2. Developing personal relationships*. London: Academic Press.

Owen, W. F. (1984). Interpretive themes in relational communication. *Quarterly Journal of Speech, 70,* 274-287.

Parks, M. (1981). Ideology in interpersonal communication: Off the couch and into the world. In *Communication yearbook 5* (pp. 79-108). New Brunswick, NJ: Transaction.

Purdy, T. F. (1978). *Perceptions of involvement in close relationships.* Senior honors thesis, University of Massachusetts, Amherst.

Rands, M., & Levinger, G. (1979). Implicit theories of relationship: An intergenerational study. *Journal of Personality and Social Psychology, 37,* 645-661.

Raush, H. L., Barry, W. A., Hertel, R. K., & Swain, M. A. (1974). *Communication, conflict, and marriage.* San Francisco: Jossey-Bass.

Rawlins, W. K. (1983). Negotiating close friendship: The dialectic of conjunctive freedoms. *Human Communication Research, 9,* 255-266.

Rose, S., & Serafica, F. C. (1986). Keeping and ending casual, close and best friendships *Journal of Social and Personal Relationships, 3,* 275-288.

Spradley, J. P. (1979). *The ethnographic interview.* New York: Holt, Rinehart & Winston.

Sudweeks, S., Gudykunst, W. B., Ting-Toomey, S., & Nishida, T. (1990). Developmental themes in Japanese-North American interpersonal relationships. *International Journal of Intercultural Relations, 14,* 207-233.

Triandis, H. (1977). *Interpersonal behavior.* Monterey, CA: Brooks/Cole.

Triandis, H. (1978). Some universals of social behavior. *Personality and Social Psychology Bulletin, 4,* 1-16.

Won-Doornink, M. (1979). On getting to know you: The association between stage of relationship and reciprocity of self-disclosure. *Journal of Experimental Social Psychology, 15,* 229-241.

Won-Doornink, M. (1985). Self-disclosure and reciprocity in conversation: A cross-national study. *Social Psychology Quarterly, 48,* 97-107.

7

Self-Disclosure and Reciprocity in South Korean and U.S. Male Dyads

MYONG JIN WON-DOORNINK ● *Washington State University*

This study was a replication and extension of a previous study by Won-Doornink, and it examines the association between the stage of a relationship and the depth of reciprocated self-disclosures in dyadic conversations. The subjects were 80 Korean male university students and 80 American male university students. Structured conversations were carried out at three relationship stages. The results indicated that generation and reciprocation of self-disclosures by the two national groups were virtually identical and tended to fall into the pattern predicted by Altman's self-disclosure reciprocity model (1973).

The study reported in this chapter is a replication test of two previous studies conducted by Won-Doornink (1979, 1985). The study examines the association between the stage of an interpersonal relationship and the depth of reciprocal self-disclosures in male dyads in South Korea and the United States.

Altman (1973) proposed the reciprocal self-disclosure model, which posits an inverted U-curve relationship between specific relationship stage and topical intimacy in self-disclosure. Based upon this model, I have developed two general hypotheses in a program of research to determine whether the interaction between the stage of a relationship and the incidence of topical intimacy follows this pattern. First, it was predicted that there is an overall inverse association between the stage of an interpersonal relationship and the incidence of reciprocity of *nonintimate* disclosures. Second, it was expected that there is a curvilinear association between the stage of an interpersonal relationship and the incidence of reciprocity of *intimate* disclosures. These two general hypotheses were confirmed for female dyads in South Korea, male-female dyads in South Korea, and male-female dyads in the United States in a previous series of cross-cultural interpersonal relationship studies.

The current study was conducted to determine whether South Korean male dyads use different self-disclosing and reciprocal behaviors than South Korean female or male-female dyads. In both of the previous studies, the principal subjects were women, because numerous investigators have indicated that females disclose more than males (Aries & Johnson, 1983; Arlett, Best, & Little, 1976; Chelune, 1976; Cozby, 1973; Little, 1968; McGuire & Padawer-Singer, 1976; Pelligrini, Hicks, Meyers-Winston, & Antal, 1978; Thase & Page, 1977; Walker & Wright, 1976). However, several other studies have shown no sex differences in self-disclosure (e.g., Maccoby & & Jacklin, 1974; Plog, 1966). And Cozby (1973) points out that no study has shown that males are more willing disclosures than females. Taylor and Altman (1987, p. 271) summarize differences in self-disclosure between men and women, suggesting that self-disclosure is influenced by the "target person's sex, social desirability, marital status, and topical content."

BACKGROUND OF THE STUDY

The topic of reciprocity of self-disclosures is of common interest to communication researchers and social psychologists, and this interest has lasted at least since Jourard's (1959) prediction of the dyadic (reciprocity) effect of self-disclosure. Cozby (1973) and Chaikin and Derlega (1974) reviewed the literature related to this topic and indicated that the most frequently shown determinant of disclosure is disclosure itself. Altman and Taylor (1973, p. 56), after a careful review of the same literature, concluded that reciprocity of exchange is not the sole determinant of mutual exchange: "Neither is it particularly useful to invoke a norm of reciprocity as both an explanation and description of a phenomenon residing in the individual actors, in their interpersonal relationships, in the topic of exchange, and in the situational context."

The most recently published self-disclosure study by Won-Doornink (1985) focused on cross-sex dyads in two cultural settings. It demonstrated that there are basic differences between the ways that unmarried persons interact with persons of the opposite sex in South Korea and in the United States. South Korea is a strongly segregated society and, when persons enter adolescence, the mixing of the sexes is discouraged. Because of this difference, relationships between adolescent persons in South Korea and in the United States are quite different. In the United States, it is considered part of a natural period of growth for young men and women to have a variety of dating partners (Nye & Berardo, 1973). In South Korea, this form of dating behavior is condemned. This would seem to make male-male relations much more customary in South Korea than in the United States and would suggest that relations between males in South Korea would possibly be deeper and more self-disclosive than those in the United States.

Relationships in South Korea are based upon the principles handed down by Confucius, the Chinese sage who lived during the sixth century B.C. Confucius set up an ideal ethical-moral system intended to govern all relationships within the family (Kim, 1978; Yum, 1988). it was basically a system of subordination: of the son to the father, of the younger to the elder brother, of the wife to the husband, and of the subject to the throne. The fifth relationship in the Confucian system was that of friend to friend, which was the only relationship in which there was equality. The loyalty of male friends was of great importance. The relationships expounded by Confucius were primarily based upon males relating to males, with the only relationship between males and females of importance that of husband and wife. Thus it seems probable that South Korean male relationships are of great importance, with the possibility that self-disclosing behavior among males is different in South Korea than that found in the United States. To test this hypothesis, I decided to examine relationships between young male dyads in South Korea and in the United States, to determine whether normative behavior in the two cultures affects the degree of generation and reciprocity of self-disclosures.

Henley 1973, 1977) has pointed out that norms help to maintain cultural rules by regulating expected forms of behavior, but they may also serve individual's instrumental values. Derlega and Grezelak (1979, p. 163) believe that "social norms help individuals to regulate intimacy in their relationships." Norms may affect behavior not only through a combination of positive and negative sanctions that can be imposed but also through a self-perception process (Bem & Jones, 1967). For example, if men are perceived by people to hide their feelings and not self-disclose, other men may act accordingly. Beyond the influence of societal and cultural norms on the self-disclosure process, the particular relationship stage also asserts strong influence on self-disclosure reciprocity patterns. Overall, Derlega, Winstead, Wong, and Greenspan (1987) did find that respondents in the United States disclosed significantly more intimately to friends than to strangers.

Five hypotheses were developed in this study: (a) For both the South Korean and U.S. subjects there would be an overall inverse association between the stage of an interpersonal relationship and the incidence of reciprocity of nonintimate self-disclosures. (b) For both the South Korean and U.S. subjects there would be a curvilinear association between the stage of an interpersonal relationship and the incidence of intimate reciprocal self-disclosures. (c) The South Korean subjects would generate significantly more self-disclosures at each of the stages of relationships than would the U.S. subjects. (d) The South Korean subjects would have a significantly higher rate of topical reciprocity at each of the stages of relationship than would the U.S. subjects. (e) The South Korean subjects would have a significantly higher rate of overall reciprocity of self-disclosure at each of the stages of relationship when compared with the U.S. subjects.

METHOD

The methodology used for this study was the same as that used in the previous studies (Won-Doornink, 1979, pp. 230-233; 1985, pp. 98-100). However, procedures were changed slightly to accommodate the differing conditions.

Subjects

The target number of subjects from each of South Korea and the United States was 20. The initial subjects for the experiments were South Korean male student volunteers attending a South Korean university and U.S. male student volunteers attending a U.S. university. The 40 subject groups were to be made up of one male subject and his three self-professed acquaintances or friends. To be eligible for participation in the study, each initial subject had to have an ongoing interpersonal relationship with three men, with one relationship from each of the following categories:

(1) *The early stage of relationship:* A man whom the subject had met within the previous 30 days, with whom the subject had had no more than six hours of close interpersonal interaction, and whom the subject considered as a possible candidate for a future relationship.

(2) *The middle stage of relationship:* A man whom the subject had known for at least three months but not more than one year, with whom the subject felt the relationship was still developing but not the subject's best male friend.

(3) *The advanced stage of relationship:* The person the subject said was his best male friend.

These pairings were established by describing the various stages of relationship to each subject and giving him explanatory materials specifying the characteristics that each potential candidate for each stage of relationship should possess. The subject was then asked to nominate three acquaintances or friends with whom he had separate self-disclosing interactions.

Volunteers were sought from physical education activity classes in both South Korean and U.S. universities. These classes were used because they were designed to be general education classes with students from virtually every academic area in the university. Within the U.S. setting, 145 men were invited to participate in the study and 63 volunteered (43%). Within the South Korean setting, 190 men were asked to participate and 91 volunteered (48%).

When the time arrived to nominate three acquaintances or friends for disclosing sessions, 19 of the American volunteers realized that they did not have three separate relationships of the types specified, and they withdrew; 48 Koreans withdrew for the same reason. This left 44 volunteers (30%) in the U.S. pool and 43 in the South Korean pool (23%).

Schedules were developed on each campus for the disclosing sessions. Each individual session (which included the male subject and his three acquaintances or friends) took approximately 60 minutes, so a 75-minute period was allotted for each session. All sessions were audiotaped.

Self-disclosing sessions continued until 20 had been completed for each cultural group. For a session to be completed, people representing all three stages of relationship had to be present. Twelve American disclosing groups failed to appear for their appointments, leaving 32 viable groups (22% of the initial subjects contacted). Of South Koreans, 17 disclosing groups failed to appear, leaving 26 viable groups (14% of the initial subjects contacted). The primary reason for these failures to appear was the difficulty in getting all three partners together at the same time.

Instrumentation

Korean-American intimacy scales were developed for the purpose of (a) providing topics for self-disclosing sessions and (b) determining the intimacy level of each of the statements made by the subjects in the study. The 793-item self-disclosure scale used by Ayres and Ivie (1974) had previously been translated into the Korean language by the investigator.

For this study, in the United States and South Korea, 30 male university students had scaled the 793 items according to intimacy level and sorted them into topical categories. These 60 judges were asked to imagine that they were disclosing information to a member of the same sex when they rated the intimacy of items. A seven-point scale was used to rate the intimacy of each item. The ratings were subjected to a Thurstone-type analysis (Shaw & Wright, 1967) for the purpose of obtaining a measure of interjudge agreement of each item. The topical categories were the same as those developed by Ayres and Ivie (1974) and consisted of the following: occupation, religion, social and political issues, health and appearance, sex, money, entertainment, family morals, social interaction, self (biographical, personal), feelings, opinions, school/education, and dreams and fantasy. Items not chosen by 15 or more of either cultural group of panel members as belonging to a particular category were considered to be ambiguous and were not categorized. When there was a lack of agreement such that one of the cross-national panels placed an item .5 of a point or more apart on the intimacy scale, the item was excluded. Out of the 793 items, 41 were considered to be ambiguous and 119 were placed .5 of a point or more apart with regard to intimacy by the cross-national panels. Accordingly, 160 items were excluded, leaving a pool of 633 self-disclosure intimacy items.

Procedure

For the experimental conversations, three lists of 42 self-disclosure items were randomly selected from the items previously scaled for intimacy. These lists were used as stimulus items in the interactions. Each list had six items at each of the seven levels of intimacy. Care was taken to ensure that all topics were included in each list and that no more than five items from any topic appeared on any one list. Insofar as was possible, high, low, and medium intimacy values were represented for each topic.

The order in which the subjects at various stages of relationship were involved in the conversations was determined randomly. Each subject held three conversations on the same day. The South Koreans self-disclosed in the Korean language, and the U.S. subjects self-disclosed in the English language. The structure of the disclosing sessions was such that the breadth of information was essentially controlled because each subject was allowed to discuss only four major topics per disclosing session. The duration of time spent disclosing information about a topic was controlled by placing a limit of two minutes on each discussion. Only the intimacy level of the disclosure was allowed to vary, depending upon the willingness of the subject to disclose certain types of information about himself.

The same instructions were given to each person involved in the study. The following points were made:

(1) The topic of the discussion was to be the subject himself.
(2) Each person was to speak four times.
(3) The length of each disclosing session was to be two minutes, but the subject did not have to talk for the full two minutes.
(4) Topics must be from the list given the subjects.
(5) Only one topic could be discussed by each subject, but it was possible for both persons to discuss the same topic.
(6) The disclosing sessions would be tape-recorded but would be kept strictly confidential.

To analyze the data gathered in the study, it was necessary to develop three separate measures of self-disclosure behavior for the disclosure sessions. Descriptions of these measures follow: (a) *Generation of self-disclosing statements* was classified by the intimacy of all statements, whether or not they were reciprocated, and the measure of their frequency. (b) *Topical reciprocity* was measured by the frequency with which the second speaker responded in discussing exactly the same topic as the first (and, therefore, necessarily at the same intimacy level, because intimacy is defined by topic choice). (c) *Total reciprocity* was measured by the frequency with which the second speaker responded at the same level of intimacy regardless of topic choice.

Following Bales (1950), the unit of analysis was defined as the smallest segment of verbal behavior about the self to which the judge could assign a classification. The items previously discussed were used to determine the intimacy level of each statement. The intimacy levels of statements were categorized as follows: (a) Nonintimate statements were those falling between the intimacy scale values of 1.00 to 2.99. (b) Medium-intimate statements were those falling between intimacy scale values of 3.00 and 4.99. (c) Intimate statements were those falling between the intimacy scale values of 5.00 and 7.00.

Altogether, two bilingual judges (fluent in both English and Korean languages) were used to evaluate the intimacy level of each self-disclosure statement within each cultural group. Each judge listened to the audiotaped conversation and then wrote down all disclosures made by the subjects. After the statements were written down, the judges categorized them as to intimacy level and then noted the frequency of items in each category. When categorizing statements as to intimacy, if a statement referred directly to a topic, that statement was given the same intimacy value as the topic. If the topic was changed while the person was in a disclosing session, the new topic was the factor that determined the intimacy level of statements relating to it. To determine reliability, product-moment correlation coefficients were calculated between the values independently arrived at by each judge. The minimum correlation arrived at was .87 for nonintimate items. The number of statements written down by each of the judges was summed and averaged.

A two-factor mixed analysis of variance (2 × 3) with repeated measures on the last factor was used to evaluate the main and interaction effects of nationality (South Korean and U.S.) and stage of relationship (early, middle, advanced) on the generation and reciprocity of self-disclosures. In instances when significant differences resulted from the ANOVAs, the Newman-Keuls method of multiple comparisons was used. Power for the multivariate tests was at least .86 for an effect size of .25 (Stevens, 1980). Power for the univariate tests was .92 or above with a small effect size of .10 for all of the analyses (Cohen, 1977).

RESULTS

The rules used for the disclosing sessions were such that the breadth of self-disclosing behavior was controlled to allow concentration on the intimacy level of the self-disclosing behavior. Each student had a maximum of two minutes to talk about a particular topic and a total of eight minutes to disclose information during the sessions. The amount of disclosures generated at the various stages of relationship in the two cultural settings was virtually the same. For the South Korean dyads, the mean number of self-disclosures per two-minute session was 23.93 at the early stage, 23.81 at the middle stage, and 25.32 at the advanced stage. For the U.S. dyads, the corresponding values were 23.68 at the early stage, 25.08 at the middle stage, and 23.25 at the advanced stage. Analysis of variance revealed no significant differences (F [2, 76] = .91, n.s.).

The only significant main effects were associated with stage of relationship (all F [2, 76] values > 4.47, p < .001) on self-disclosure behavior. It thus appeared that culture did not have a significant effect on the generation of self-disclosure.

Comparisons of the means within each of the cultural groups showed that, for nonintimate self-disclosures, the three stages of relationship all had significantly different rates of disclosure, with the early stage disclosing the most, followed by the middle stage, and then the advanced stage. The advanced stage of relationship had significantly more medium-intimate self-disclosures than did the early stage; the early stage had significantly more medium-intimate self-disclosures than did the middle stage; and, for intimate self-disclosures, all three stages of relationship had significantly different rates of disclosures, with the middle stage disclosing the most, followed by the advanced stage, and then the early stage.

At the early stage of relationship, the subjects preferred to talk about nonintimate and medium-intimate matters; at the middle stage, they preferred to talk about intimate matters; and, at the advanced stage, they preferred to discuss medium-intimate items.

Six ANOVAs were calculated to determine the effects of culture and stage of relationship on the reciprocity of self-disclosure at each of the three intimacy levels. Culture had no significant main effects for either topical or total reciprocity (F [1, 38] < .93, p > .10). Stage of relationship had significant main effects at each of the intimacy levels of both topical and total reciprocation (F [2, 76] > 138.27, p < .001). Table 7.1 shows the mean scores for the generation of nonintimate, medium-intimate, and intimate self-disclosure, topical reciprocation, and total reciprocation by culture and relationship stage.

Tests of Hypotheses

The test of hypotheses were of two general types. First, within each of the cultural groups, comparisons were made to determine whether or not there is an inverse association between stage of relationship and reciprocation of nonintimate self-disclosures for both topical and total reciprocity (Hypothesis 1) and whether or not there is a curvilinear association between the stage of interpersonal relationship and the incidence of topical and total reciprocity for intimate disclosures (Hypothesis 2). Second, comparisons were made between the two cultural groups to determine whether the South Korean subjects generated significantly more self-disclosures (Hypothesis 3), reciprocated significantly more topical self-disclosures (Hypothesis 4), and reciprocated significantly more total self-disclosures (Hypothesis 5) than did the U.S. subjects.

Hypothesis 1 predicted that there would be an overall inverse association between the stage of relationship and the incidence of reciprocity of nonintimate self-disclosures. Because there were two measures of reciprocity and two cultures in the study, Hypothesis 1 was tested four times and in each test was found to be tenable. As interpersonal relationships advanced, the production of reciprocated nonintimate disclosures declined. Each of the mean scores for the various stages of

TABLE 7.1 Mean Scores for Self-Disclosure by Culture and Relationship Stage

	United States			*South Korea*		
	Early	*Middle*	*Advanced*	*Early*	*Middle*	*Advanced*
Generation of self-disclosure:						
nonintimate	83.35	62.90	34.15	82.15	57.27	29.44
medium intimate	68.51	55.00	100.20	74.75	51.99	97.65
intimate	36.85	82.90	51.65	34.60	81.22	52.31
Topical reciprocation:						
nonintimate	42.11	26.34	11.36	37.25	29.21	10.06
medium intimate	31.04	23.79	31.17	31.04	20.31	32.83
intimate	16.14	39.19	24.07	16.04	37.86	23.73
Total reciprocation:						
nonintimate	47.24	34.50	17.93	47.16	31.30	15.87
medium intimate	38.88	25.77	46.41	42.84	23.81	45.87
intimate	19.31	47.46	26.40	17.87	49.00	34.84

relationship, beginning with the early stage, followed by the middle stage, and then the advanced stage, was significantly ($p < .01$) higher than that following it.

Hypothesis 2 predicted that there would be a curvilinear association between stage of an interpersonal relationship and the incidence of reciprocity of intimate self-disclosures. Stated in another way, tests were conducted to determine whether or not the reciprocation of disclosures of intimate items was significantly more evident at the middle stage of relationship than at the early or advanced stages. As was the case with Hypothesis 1, this hypothesis was tested four times (twice by culture and twice by type of reciprocity). Hypothesis 2 was confirmed for both topical and total reciprocity for both the South Korean and the U.S. subjects.

Hypothesis 3 predicted that South Korean subjects would have a significantly higher rate of generation of self-disclosures than would the U.S. subjects. This hypothesis was not confirmed, and it was found that the self-disclosing behavior of the two cultural groups was very similar.

Hypothesis 4 predicted that South Korean subjects would have a significantly higher rate of topical reciprocity of self-disclosures at each of the relationship stages than would the U.S. subjects. This hypothesis was found to be untenable. The rate of topical reciprocity between the two cultural groups was nearly the same.

Hypothesis 5 stated that, at each of the stages of relationship, South Korean subjects would have a significantly higher rate of total reciprocity of self-disclosure than would the U.S. subjects. This hypothesis was found to be untenable, and it appeared that the South Korean and U.S. male dyads were equally responsive with regard to disclosing at the same general level of intimacy.

DISCUSSION

This study was conducted to replicate and extend two previous studies (Won-Doornink, 1979, 1985). All of the studies tested two hypotheses proposed by Altman (1973). These hypotheses predicted (a) that reciprocity of nonintimate disclosures is at its highest level among those in the early stages of relationship with a steady decline thereafter and (b) that the reciprocity of intimate disclosures reaches a peak among those headed toward a close relationship and diminishes when the relationship becomes advanced.

The replication and extension were done by using male dyads from two different nations (the United States and South Korea) in experimental circumstances as much like those of the previous studies as possible. The methods and procedures were identical to those of the previous studies, with the exception that no female subjects were used in self-disclosing sessions.

Three a priori hypotheses were also tested with regard to the relative responsiveness of the two cultural groups. It was predicted that the South Korean subjects would generate significantly more (a) self-disclosures, (b) topically reciprocated self-disclosures, and (c) totally reciprocated self-disclosures.

Hypotheses 1 and 2 were confirmed. As was the case in the previous studies, it appeared that, with regard to reciprocity of self-disclosure, the most important factor was the selection of topics by the initial speaker. There were consistent and important differences in the intimacy levels of topics initiated by the first speaker that were dependent upon the stage of relationship. At the early stage of relationship, the subjects preferred to talk about nonintimate and medium-intimate matters; at the middle stage of relationship, they preferred to talk about intimate matters; and at the advanced stage of relationship, the subjects preferred to discuss medium-intimate matters.

When reciprocity was considered, the same general preferences were found as in the generation of self-disclosures (i.e., the early stage reciprocated more nonintimate self-disclosures; the middle stage reciprocated more intimate disclosures; and the advanced stage reciprocated more medium-intimate self-disclosures). It appears that, if there were any equity in preferences toward reciprocation (i.e., at what level of intimacy a person prefers to reciprocate), the general configuration of means would approximate that for the generation of self-disclosures. Results indicate that a linear inverse association exists for nonintimate self-disclosures and reciprocations, and curvilinear associations exist for medium-intimate and intimate self-disclosures and reciprocations.

When hypothesized similarities between the disclosing the reciprocal behavior were tested, it was found that there were no significant differences between the generation and reciprocation of self-disclosures by the male U.S. and male South Korean subjects. This result was somewhat of a surprise because the Korean culture encourages relationships between young males and discourages relationships between young males and young females. Given this cultural bias against male-female relationships and for the same sex relationships, it was presumed that male dyads in South Korea would be more open in their self-disclosing activities than would be male dyads in the United States. This presumption proved to be false.

The use of cross-sex dyads was, without doubt, the cause of the relative reticence of the Koreans when reciprocity of topical disclosures was considered in the 1985 study. Close personal relationships between the sexes prior to marriage is discouraged in South Korea, not only by the family but by other social institutions. Based on the Confucian code, the Koreans have an old saying *Nam yaw chil se Boo dong Suk,* which means, "at the age of seven, boys and girls are not allowed to sit side by side." The majority of middle schools and high schools in South Korea are not coeducational. The elementary schools are coeducational, but, as soon as a child reaches the age of 12 and enters middle school, he or she is segregated from the opposite sex for the next six years. By the time the student leaves high school, he or she is not accustomed to interacting with members of the opposite sex outside of the family.

The previous discussion explains why young men and women in South Korea may be lacking in the social skills necessary to communicate well with each other. Young Korean men are taught the importance of developing friendship relationships with other young men and are discouraged from developing these same relationships with young women. It was hypothesized that the differing social conditions for young males in the United States and in South Korea would result in significant differences in the way that members of male dyads in these two societies self-disclose and reciprocate self-disclosures to each other. This study indicates that, contrary to predictions, the self-disclosing behavior of young U.S. and South Korean university students is remarkably similar.

How can these findings be explained? Gudykunst and Nishida (1983, p. 591) observe that, while social penetration theory has been supported in the United States, "no systematic comparisons have been made in other cultures." In their study concerning social penetration in friendships in Japan and the United States, a number of differences were found, but there were more similarities than differences.

The similarities in communicating behavior between South Korean and U.S. university students could be, to some degree at least, attributed to the infusion of U.S. culture into South Korea. This infusion has been constant, and this gradual Americanization of South Korea has been and continues to be a consequence of available U.S. television programming.

Television is a ubiquitous medium in South Korea. It is a medium thoroughly familiar to South Koreans. According to Pinder (1984), commercial television began in South Korea in 1956. Currently, there are 26 South Korean and 6 U.S. (Armed Forces Network) television stations. South Koreans have had access to both South Korean and U.S. television programming for more than 30 years. Almost 10 million TV sets are in operation, involving almost every household. In a recent study, Won-Doornink (1988) found that Korean broadcasts are limited to 6.5 evening hours and 4 morning hours on weekdays, 11 hours on Saturdays, and 17 hours on Sundays. The limited broadcast schedule is attributed to the potentially excessive use of electricity. U.S. (Armed Forces Network) television is broadcast 20 hours a day, for a total of 140 hours a week.

Several years ago, South Korean legislators expressed fear of the influence of U.S. television programs on South Korean culture and South Korean youth. Minister of Culture and Information Won-Hong Lee said, November 8, 1985, "The programs of the American Armed Forces television in Korea have caused a 'cultural disturbance' by pouring the confounded culture of a developed nation into a developing nation" (quoted in "Gov't Hopes AFKN-TV Will Limit Service U.S. Forces Bases," *The Korea Herald,* November 10, 1985). He argued that AFKN programs have a detrimental influence on South Korean youth.

In addition, a large contingent of Korean immigrants have entered the United States, and these immigrants have been in constant contact with friends and family members in the homeland. Finally, a large number of South Korean graduate students have received advanced degrees from universities in the United States and are now back in South

Korea teaching in universities throughout the country and explaining the U.S. culture to South Korean university students.

It should be noted that the conditions under which the disclosing sessions were carried on in this study were such that real disclosures along with the selected disclosure topics were forthcoming. There was no dependence upon the memory of the subjects as to their self-disclosing behavior in the past. Neither were they asked to predict how they would disclose and reciprocate in hypothetical conditions. Both U.S. and South Korean subjects appeared to be willing self-disclosers and obviously enjoyed the sessions.

It was common for subjects to disclose for the full two minutes allowed them with regard to a topic and for their disclosing partners to bemoan the fact that the time was up and no more information on that topic would be forthcoming. This is not to say that the disclosing sessions in this study were exactly like those in real life, but, within the rules established by the procedures, they seemed to be real to the participants.

With regard to future cross-cultural interpersonal communication research in the general area of self-disclosure, more attention needs to be paid to using persons other than volunteer university students as subjects. As Babbie (1975, p. 244) has indicated, "College undergraduates are not typical of the public at large." To assume that middle-aged U.S. and South Korean persons carry on self-disclosing interactions in the same way university students do is probably faulty thinking. Variables that could be taken into account in such research planning are socioeconomic status, education, age, family system, personality factors, relational commitment, relationship attributions, and disclosure predisposition.

Overall, for U.S. and South Korean male university students, the dyadic effect of reciprocal self-disclosure seems to be universal. Whether or not this is true for all U.S. and South Korean persons must be determined by systematic testing in well-designed programs of research on cross-cultural interpersonal self-disclosure.

REFERENCES

Altman, I. (1973). Reciprocity in interpersonal exchange. *Journal of the Theory of Social Behavior, 3,* 246-261.

Altman, I., & Taylor, D. A. (1973). *Social penetration: The development of interpersonal relationships.* New York: Holt, Rinehart & Winston.

Aries, E., & Johnson, F. (1983). Close friendship in adulthood: Conversational content between same sex friends. *Sex Roles, 9,* 1183-1196.

Arlett, C., Best, J. A., & Little, B. R. (1976). Influence of interviewer self-disclosure and verbal reinforcement of personality tests. *Journal of Clinical Psychology, 32,* 770-775.

Ayres, H. J., & Ivie, R. L. (1974). [Unpublished data]. Washington State University, Department of Communications.

Babbie, E. R. (1975). *The practice of social research.* Belmont, CA: Wadsworth.

Bales, R. R. (1950). *Interaction process analysis.* Cambridge, MA: Addison-Wesley.

Bem, D. D., & Jones, J. (1967). Self-perception: An alternative interpretation of cognitive dissonance phenomena. *Psychological Bulletin, 74,* 183-200.

Chaikin, A. L., & Derlega, J. J. (1974). Liking for the norm-breaker in self-disclosures. *Journal of Personality, 42,* 117-129.

Chelune, G. J. (1976). A multidimensional look at sex and target differences in disclosure. *Psychological Reports, 39,* 259-263.

Cohen, J. (1977). *Statistical power analysis for the behavioral sciences.* New York: Academic Press.

Cozby, P. C. (1973). Self-disclosure: A literature review. *Psychological Bulletin, 79,* 73-91.

Derlega, V. J., & Grezelak, J. (1979). Appropriateness of self-disclosure. In G. J. Chelune et al., *Self-disclosers: Origins, patterns and implications of openness in interpersonal relationships.* San Francisco: Jossey-Bass.

Derlega, V., Winstead, B., Wong, P., & Greenspan, M. (1987). Self-disclosure and relationship development: An attributional analysis. In M. Roloff & G. Miller (Eds.). *Interpersonal processes: New directions in communication research.* Newbury Park, CA: Sage.

Dimond, R., & Munz, O. (1967). Race, sex, ordinal position at birth and self-disclosure in high school students. *Psychological Reports, 25,* 236-238.

Gudykunst, W., & Nishida, T. (1983). Social penetration in Japanese and North American friendships. In R. Bostrom (Ed.), *Communication yearbook 7* (pp. 592-610). Beverly Hills, CA: Sage.

Henley, N. M. (1973). The politics of touch. In P. T. Brown (Ed.), *Radical psychology* (pp. 421-433). New York: Harper & Row.

Henley, N. M. (1977). *Body politics: Power, sex and nonverbal communications.* Englewood Cliffs, NJ: Prentice-Hall.

Jourard, S. M. (1959). Self-disclosure and cathexis. *Journal of Abnormal and Social Psychology, 59,* 428-431.

Jourard, S. M., & Richman, P. (1963). Factors in the self-disclosure inputs of college students. *Merrill-Palmer Quarterly of Behavior and Development, 9,* 141-148.

Kim, S. J. (1978). *A handbook of Korea.* Seoul: Korean Information Service.

Little, K. B. (1968). Cultural variations in social schemata. *Journal of Personality and Social Psychology, 10,* 1-7.

Maccoby, E., & Jacklin, C. (1974). *The psychology of sex differences.* Stanford, CA: Stanford University Press.

McGuire, W. J., & Padawer-Singer, A. (1976). Trait salience in the spontaneous self-concept. *Journal of Personality and Social Psychology, 33,* 743-754.

Nishida, H. (1981). Value orientations and value changes in Japan and the U.S.A. In T. Nishida & W. Gudykunst (Eds.), *Readings in intercultural communication.* Tokyo: Geirinshobo.

Nye, F. I., & Berado, F. M. (1973). *The family: Its structure and interaction.* New York: Macmillan.

Pellegrini, R. J., Hicks, R. A., Meyers-Winton, S., & Antal, B. G. (1978). Physical attractiveness and self-disclosure in mixed sex dyads. *Psychological Record, 28,* 509-516.

Pinder, A. (1984). South Korea. *International Television Almanac, 18,* 116-126.

Plog, S. (1966). The disclosure of the self in the United States and Germany. *Journal of Social Psychology, 65,* 191-205.

Shaw, M. E., & Wright, J. M. (1967). *Scales for the measurement of attitudes.* New York: McGraw-Hill.

Stevens, J. (1980). Power of the multivariate analysis of variance test. *Psychological Bulletin, 88,* 728-737.

Taylor, D. A. (1968). The development of interpersonal relationships: Social penetration process. *Journal of Social Psychology, 75,* 79-90.

Taylor, D., & Altman, I. (1987). Communication in interpersonal relationships. In M. Roloff & G. Miller (Eds.), *Interpersonal processes: New directions in communication research.* Newbury Park, CA: Sage.

Thase, M., & Page, R. A. (1977). Modeling of self-disclosure in laboratory and nonlaboratory interview settings. *Journal of Counseling Psychology, 24,* 35-40.

Walker, L. S., & Wright, P. H. (1976). Self-disclosure in friendship. *Perceptual and Motor Skills, 42,* 735-742.

Won-Doornink, M. J. (1979). On getting to know you: The association between the stage of a relationship and reciprocity of self-disclosure. *Journal of Experimental Social Psychology, 15,* 229-241.

Won-Doornink, M. J. (1985). Self-disclosure and reciprocity in conversation: A cross-national study. *Social Psychology Quarterly, 48,* 97-107.

Won-Doornink, M. J. (1988). Television viewing and acculturation of Korean immigrants. *Amerasia Journal, 14,* 79-92.

Yum, J. (1988). The impact of Confucianism on interpersonal relationships in East Asia. *Communication Monographs, 55,* 374-388.

8

Conflict Competence Within African, Mexican, and Anglo American Friendships

MARY JANE COLLIER ● *Oregon State University,*
Corvallis

This study analyzes conflict in African, Mexican, and Anglo American close friendships. Similarities and differences in definitions of and competencies enacted in conflict with close friends were evident across ethnic and gender groups. Examples of norms unique to each group included a preference for directness and rational argument described by Anglo males and for situational flexibility by Anglo females. Clear argument and a problem-solution orientation were preferred by African American males, and appropriate assertiveness and respect were preferred by African American females. Finally, mutual understanding through talking over the issues was preferred by Mexican American males, and support for the relationship was preferred by Mexican American females.

Conflict is described by a variety of communication scholars as a pervasive, complex process, functional as well as dysfunctional to the relational system (Folger & Poole, 1984; Frost & Wilmot, 1978; Ting-Toomey, 1988). *Conflict* is defined here as the communication process among persons perceiving incompatible goals and interference from each other in achieving those goals (Chanin & Schneer, 1987; Folger & Poole, 1984; Frost & Wilmot, 1978). Conflict occurs when relational partners perceive incompatibility in such diverse areas as ideas, values, emotions, needs, access to resources, and constraints on actions. Relational partners, by definition, experience conflict fairly often, while the degree or intensity of conflict experienced will certainly vary across situation, topic, conflict issue, trigger event, individual goals, and relational goals.

Cultural and ethnic background are sources of socialization wherein cultural and ethnic members learn about what constitutes conflict and how it should be managed. In other words, we are taught how to define, recognize, and manage conflict by our families and peers and by representations we view in print and electronic media. Such messages occur within and across community, ethnic, and national contexts. We learn to think of conflicts as something that is good or bad, manageable or a major disruption. We learn how to avoid, confront, collaborate, negotiate, bargain, or use violence in conflict within cultural and intercultural contexts.

The influence of culture on conflict is important because increasing cultural diversity characterizes the demography of countries such as the United States. Banks (1987) as well as DeVos (1982) note that the "melting pot" theory proposed in the early part of the twentieth century, predicting that immigrants would soon assimilate into one composite culture, is more myth than reality. The *Chronicle of Higher Education* (March 1988) reported an increase of 33% of "minority" students in the United States between 1976 and 1986, with the largest gains among Asians and Hispanics. African Americans and Hispanics are categorized in most institutions of higher learning as "underrepresented" based on enrollments, rates of graduation, and professional career choice in comparison with Anglo Americans. In the last five years, media reports of racism and discrimination against Blacks in several cities in the United States have increased. Advances in the quality of media and availability of information have resulted in widespread and immediate access to national and world events, including those involving conflict within and between ethnic and national groups (Williams, 1989).

Increasing contact between cultures as well as changes in technology and economic development have resulted in changing gender roles and prescriptions throughout the world. Differences in the communication style of Anglo American males and females throughout history is well documented (Bate, 1988; Gilligan, 1982; Kramarae, 1981; Pearson, 1985; Thorne, Kramarae, & Henley, 1983), however, ethnic Asian, Hispanic, and African American male and female styles in the United States have not received detailed research attention. Although such books as *Women, Race and Class* (Davis, 1983) discuss the influence of race, socioeconomics, history, and the suffrage movement on Black women in the United States, there is a gap in the literature addressing communicative style differences among Black men and women and also a dearth of research on the African American culture from the perspective of African Americans (Hecht, Ribeau, & Alberts, 1989).

The extent to which females and males in various ethnic groups adopt patterns of behavior consistent with their traditional ethnic role models or consistent with their ideas about "mainstream" Anglo role models, is an issue faced by increasing numbers of young adults in the United States. Gender role prescriptions and role models are also changing.

Research by Cromwell and Cromwell (1978) calls into question stereotypic labeling of Black families as matriarchal and Chicano families as patriarchal in conflict and decision-making situations among husbands and wives.

National and ethnic culture and gender in interpersonal communication are receiving initial research attention by several scholars (Barnlund, 1989; Collier, 1990; Hecht et al., 1989; Ting-Toomey, 1988; Chapter 13 in this volume). Researchers are beginning to gather data about how friends and intimates develop relationships. Theories of relational development such as uncertainty reduction (Berger & Calabrese, 1975) and social penetration (Altman & Taylor, 1973) are being tested across culturally diverse samples. Gudykunst, Gao, Sudweeks, Ting-Toomey, and Nishida (in this volume) found, for example, similarities and differences in same and different sex relationships between Japanese and American respondents.

The current study is a comparative ethnic study concerning male and female perceptions of the conflict process within their close friendships. Close friendships are characterized by affective exchange as well as increasing spontaneity (Taylor & Altman, 1987). La Gaipa (1977) notes that close friends seem to be characterized by self-disclosure, helping, similarity, positive regard, strength of character, and authenticity. Adelman, Parks, and Albrecht (1990) summarize research on friendship and note that friendships in the United States are characterized by voluntariness, status equality, assistance, activity sharing, confidentiality, and emotional support.

Conflict in close friendships merits research attention from intercultural-interpersonal communication scholars. Close friends may define conflict as a threat to their relationship. Close friends may not want to risk losing a source of emotional support, assistance, and shared activities. On the other hand, close friends may view conflict as a natural and necessary phenomenon, a process that clarifies issues and relational preferences and ultimately strengthens the bond with the other.

Close friendships sometimes have a longer "life" than intimate relationships. Close friendships act as an important source for the identity development process (Ting-Toomey, 1989) and frequently provide primary support (Collier, 1990). Close friendships should be studied for an important additional reason, to test the implicit assumptions made in social penetration theories (Altman & Taylor, 1973) and uncertainty reduction theories (Berger & Calabrese, 1975). Such assumptions posit that, as relationships become more intimate, cultural predictions decrease, and self-disclosure and certainty about the relational partner as a unique individual increase.

In conflict episodes, cultural background influences may prohibit self-disclosure and prescribe avoidance or consultation with a third friend for mediation. Ethnic groups that are more collectivistic and more "feminine" (Hofstede, 1980) may view self-disclosure as rude or selfish in friendships and intimate relationships. Because the intensity and style with which ethnic identity is enacted differs across situations, and because identities are cocreated and negotiated among individuals, the extent to which persons rely on idiosyncratic predictions and rules of appropriate behavior in close friendships versus cultural predictions merits empirical research.

CONCEPTUAL AND THEORETICAL BACKGROUND

In this study, *conflict* is defined as the communication process involving persons who perceive incompatible goals and interference from each other in achieving those goals (Chanin & Schneer, 1987; Folger & Poole, 1984; Frost & Wilmot, 1978). Incompatible goals (Deutsch, 1973) can involve ideas, values, emotions, and needs (Ting-Toomey, Trubisky, & Nishida 1989).

Culture and Ethnicity

The research on conflict among and between culture groups reviewed here includes several different conceptualizations of culture. Some scholars are most interested in predicting from national affiliation to particular modes of communication (Barnlund, 1989) or styles of managing conflict (Cushman & King, 1985). Other scholars are interested in predicting from dimensions of cultural variability to conflict management style (Ting-Toomey, 1988; Ting-Toomey et al., 1989).

In this study, attention is given to two kinds of ethnic/cultural processes. *Ethnicity* is defined as the ethnic group with which a person identifies his or her heritage. Persons can be grouped on the basis of the label or group affiliation that best represents ancestral background, heritage, and roots. Certainly persons selecting the same label such as "Mexican American" are not presumed to define what the label represents in exactly the same way; however, general similarities in what the label represents are presumed. Ethnicity connotes origin from a nation-state outside of or preceding the creation of the present residence as well as involuntary membership and shared sense of tradition, people-hood, and heritage (Banks, 1987).

Three ethnic groups were given consideration in this study. Mexican Americans and African Americans were chosen because these two groups are classified as "minorities" in most educational and political institutions (Banks, 1987) and are underrepresented in several professions and disciplines (Sowell, 1981). Anglo Americans were chosen as a group of interest because they met the criteria for ethnicity even though members more typically define themselves as White Americans or mainstream Americans and trace heritage to the early settlers of the United States rather than to a country of origin outside the United States.

Anglo Americans have superordinate socioeconomic power in the United States (Folb, 1982). Most of the research on interpersonal relationships has focused on Anglo Americans (see Roloff & Miller, 1987, for a review of interpersonal research). Several research programs are being undertaken that incorporate comparisons between Asians and Asian Americans with Anglo Americans (Barnlund, 1989; Gudykunst & Nishida, 1986; Gudykunst, Nishida & Chua, 1987; Ting-Toomey, 1988) but comparisons of Mexican Americans and African Americans with Anglo Americans warrant more attention in the communication literature.

Ethnicity and Conflict Style

Just as definitions of conflict are assumed to differ across cultural contexts, cross-cultural research has suggested that conflict style is a culture-relative construct and differs across ethnic groups (Ting-Toomey, 1986; Ting-Toomey et al., 1989). In this study, conflict style (pattern of communication conduct in conflict episodes) is conceptualized as a culture-general theoretical construct while the manifestations and particular stylistic modes of conduct adopted by members of different ethnic groups are defined as culture specific.

Anglo Americans are described as typically using one of two styles in conflict: dominating, which is confrontation based, and integrating, which is solution oriented (Ting-Toomey et al., 1989). Ting-Toomey (1986) compared Anglo American with Black American respondents and noted that Black Americans tend to use more controlling strategies and Anglo Americans tend to use more solution-oriented strategies.

Cushman and King (1985) found that members of the Japanese culture emphasized the importance of face and used a collaborative style, while North Americans used a competitive style. Accommodation and relatively passive messages characterize Japanese interaction in criticism and conflict contexts while North Americans employ active, confrontational strategies (Kumagi & Straus, 1983). Kagan, Knight, and Martinez-Romero (1982) described Mexicans' conduct in conflict as including more passive, avoidance messages than active confrontation.

Ethnic Identity and Conflict

The second kind of cultural affiliation and process discussed here is the ethnic identity evident in conflict episodes among persons with similar ethnic backgrounds. Ethnic identity is defined consistently with what can be thought of as emergent culture, a system of symbols, meanings, and norms that is historically passed down and contextually influenced (Collier, 1989; Geertz, 1973; Schneider, 1976). Ethnicity can be thought of as the heritage with which individuals identify and trace their history, and ethnic identity can be thought of as a pattern of communicative conduct that is recognizable and contextually emergent. The messages, meanings, and rules about what it takes to be an "African American" or "Chicano" evolve and are handed down and taught to newcomers.

Ethnic identity here has two major components: (a) a constitutive component—institutions, symbols, and beliefs that describe what the cultural/ethnic identity "is"—and (b) a normative component—values, rules, and competencies regarding how to behave and what "should and should not be said and done" (Collier & Thomas, 1988). Ethnic identity patterns may be studied in particular contexts or speech communities such as organizations, neighborhoods, family systems, or friendships.

As Hymes (1972) has noted, cultural membership, and hence ethnic identity, is a product of the context, type of episode, and goals of participants. The ethnic identity being addressed here is limited to the communication process in conflict episodes among friends. The question essentially becomes: "To what extent do individuals who share similar ethnicity also enact a similar ethnic identity in conflict with friends?"

Ethnic identity was operationalized in this study by attention to the two overlapping dimensions of cultural identity discussed above—constitutive and normative dimensions. The constitutive dimension includes definitions of friendship, conflict, and issues within the conflict. The question that emerges here is this: "What constitutes conflict for ethnically similar friends?"

The normative dimension includes impressions of communicative competence—conduct that is appropriate and effective in a particular context (Collier, 1989; Spitzberg & Cupach, 1984). Appropriate and inappropriate conduct as well as outcome of the conflict and effect of the conflict on the friendship are all a part of the normative dimension of ethnic identity given attention here. Essentially the question becomes: "What does it take to competently enact a particular ethnic identity in conflict with friends?"

Gender and Conflict

Gender of the friends may affect conflict processes and enactment of ethnic identity. Putnam and Jones (1982) argue that biological sex signifies a set of expected behaviors derived from male-female socialization. Belenky, Clinchy, Goldberger, and Tarule (1986) demonstrate that females from a variety of ethnic backgrounds in the United States view reality and draw conclusions about truth, knowledge, and authority in different ways than their male counterparts. Gilligan (1982) and Lyons (1983) have shown that males and females differ in their definitions of what constitutes concepts of morality, responsibility, and rights. Maltz and Borker (1987) and Tannen (1987) attribute differences in male and female communication features not only to social power but also to their conceptualization of genders as culture groups.

Fitzpatrick and Winke (1979) show that Anglo American males in the U.S. culture are viewed as more competitive, forceful, and deceptive than Anglo American females. The generalizability of such findings, however, to males from other ethnic or cultural backgrounds is open to question. Cross-ethnic comparisons of gender differences in conceptualizations of and styles in conflict thus merit study.

Interpretive Perspective

An interpretive cultural perspective is being used in this study. The respondents' descriptions and interpretations of conduct were obtained. Such a focus is intended to provide information about how ethnic males and females make sense of their conflict with close friends. Such a focus increases representational validity and helps set appropriate limits on generalizability. Conceptual equivalence of constructs (Gudykunst & Ting-Toomey, 1988; Lonner & Berry, 1986; Olebe & Koester, 1989) is addressed here through attention to respondents' descriptions and interpretations of such terms as *friendship* and *conflict*.

The identification of how close friends perceive conflict, and in turn, how it affects their relationship, is an important ontological problem. Conflict can be defined as a relatively common occurrence that is "managed" to various degrees, or it can be defined as rare and something to be "resolved" as soon as possible. Style of management or resolution is affected by definitions of and beliefs about the conflict process.

For the purposes of this study, respondents from various ethnic backgrounds were asked to describe their definitions of *friendship* and *conflict* and to describe their impressions of their friend's and their own appropriate/inappropriate and effective/ineffective behavior in recalled conflict episodes. Such a perspective focuses on recurrent themes and norms inherent in respondents' descriptions of their experience. Such an approach is intersubjective (Collier & Thomas, 1988) in that patterns and systematic symbols, norms, and meanings shared by ethnic friends are identified. In addition, the manner in which ethnic friends construct and interpret their experience (Baxter, 1987; Carbaugh, 1988) is the focus. Finally, descriptions of self and other's conduct were used because of the emphasis upon ethnic friends' accounts and experiences. Such an approach has been used in several current research programs (Baxter, 1987; Hecht, Ribeau, & Alberts, 1989; Shotter, 1989; Ting-Toomey, 1986; van Dijk, 1987).

Research Questions

A major component of ethnic identity is assumed to be found in definitions of friendship. Identity is based upon ideas of self in relationship to others (Cooley, 1968; Stewart, 1990). Definitions of friendship are thus a part of social and ethnic identity. Because the respondents' perspectives and interpretations were important, the first research question addresses respondents' definitions and descriptions of what close friendship meant to them:

> *R1*: Do Anglo, African, and Mexican Americans differ in their descriptions of close friendships?

The second research question concerned the constitutive dimension of ethnic identity in conflict episodes with friends. Constitutive beliefs include how conflict is defined and issues that become the focal point in conflict.

It has been argued that persons who share similar ethnic backgrounds may enact similar identities in conflict episodes. However, the extent to which African American, Mexican American, and Anglo American friends conduct themselves in similar ways, that is, enact similar or different ethnic identities, is a question as yet unanswered by communication scholars. Conflict episodes may be defined by close friends as intensely negative experiences (Frost & Wilmot, 1978) that call the relationship into question—that is, close friends may expect that they should not experience conflict—so it is important to get a sense of how respondents define their own relationships as well as define conflict.

Males and females have been shown to differ in their perspectives on decision making, morality, rights, and responsibility (Belenky et al., 1986; Gilligan, 1982). Maltz and Borker (1987, p. 212) note, "What we are suggesting is that women and men have different cultural rules for friendly conversation and that these rules come into conflict when women and men attempt to talk to each other as friends and equals in conversation." The second research question in this study asks:

> R2: Do male and female Anglo, African, and Mexican American close friends differ in their constitutive ideas about conflict?

A third area of investigation involved the normative component of ethnic identity, operationalized as impressions of communication competence. Attention was devoted to self and other appropriate/inappropriate and effective/ineffective conduct as well as outcomes of the conflict. Because members of ethnic groups and males and females may differ in their ideas about what it takes to be a competent communicator in conflict with close friends, the following research question is posed:

> R3: Do male and female Anglo, African, and Mexican American close friends differ in their impressions of competent conduct in conflict episodes?

METHODS

Respondents

Total respondents included 70 student volunteers (29 males and 41 females) recruited from a large, urban university in the western United States. Respondents were retained for analysis when they identified themselves as Anglo American, African American, or Mexican American. Mexican Americans were second and third generation, African Americans were third and fourth generation, and Anglo Americans were third and fourth generation. Ethnicity was determined through open-ended questions in which respondents provided their own label for their background. In all, 24 Anglo Americans, 21 African Americans, and 25 Mexican Americans were retained for analysis.

The majority of respondents in the Mexican American group defined themselves with that label; others used terms such as *Chicano, Chicana,* or *American of Mexican descent.* African Americans used labels including *Black American, Pan African,* and *African American.* Anglo

Americans described themselves as *White American, European American,* and *Anglo.* There were 10 Anglo males and 14 Anglo females, 9 African American males and 12 African American females, and 10 Mexican American males and 15 Mexican American females. A slight majority of males recalled conflicts with other males, but, overall, males and females in each group recalled an equal number of conflicts with same gender and different gender close friendships. The respondents varied in age from 20 to 54 years of age.

Procedures

An open-ended questionnaire was created and pretested on a small sample of students who were from diverse ethnic backgrounds. Three research assistants representing each ethnic group were selected to administer the questionnaire and conduct individual interviews with members of their own ethnic background. Three of the research assistants identified themselves as Anglo Americans, two as Mexican American, one as American of Mexican descent, two as African American, and one as Black American. Each group of research assistants included both males and females.

The research assistants met individually with respondents from their own ethnic groups. Respondents were solicited from various communication classes and a peer mentoring program for African American and Mexican American students. The research assistants first explained the research project and asked the respondent to fill out the open-ended questionnaire in his or her own words. The research assistant clarified questions and probed for more information where appropriate after the respondent completed the questionnaire. The research assistants also read over the questionnaire in the presence of the respondent to ensure that responses were understood.

The questionnaire included the following kinds of questions. First, respondents were asked to describe their definition of *close friendship* and when they considered someone to be a close friend. Then they were asked to define *conflict.* The next series of questions asked them to recall a conflict they experienced recently with someone who was a close friend (but not a spouse or person with whom they were living) who was from the same ethnic group. They were asked to describe the place or places where the conflict took place, what "triggered" the conflict or was said and done to start the conflict, the basic issues in the conflict, their goals, and their perceptions of the other's goals in the conflict.

The next series of questions addressed self and other's inappropriate and ineffective conduct, and things that were said and done or could have been said and done that were (could have been) appropriate and effective in managing the conflict. They were also asked to explain why these behaviors were (would be) appropriate and effective and then describe the outcome and effect of the conflict on the friendship.

Demographic questions were also asked about respondent and close friend in the recalled conflict including age, gender, ethnic background, and generation. Finally, respondents were asked to explain whether they thought that males and females think about or manage conflict differently.

Analysis of Data

The research assistants also acted as coders in the study for several reasons. Because the focus was upon close friends from the same ethnic group and the research assistants were familiar with the interview data, research assistants from each ethnic group coded data from that particular ethnic group. Also, cultural validity is strengthened when coders have some experience with the ethnic group being given attention.

The first step in the coding process was to have the coders read all of the questionnaires from their ethnic group to provide a sense of the ethnic group as a whole. Next, each coder took the questionnaires and made a transcription of each definitional theme, appropriate and inappropriate speech act, outcome, and so on onto separate slips of paper. The result of this step was a stack of responses for each questionnaire item.

Each coder did an individual sort of all the slips of paper corresponding to each questionnaire item for respondents from their own ethnic group. Coders identified similar responses and placed them into similar piles. Coders were instructed to identify three to five themes as an estimated number of piles. The category range was suggested to coders to establish a set of boundary conditions to increase validity (Holsti, 1969) and was also based upon previous research utilizing similar coding procedures (Collier, 1988; Hecht et al., 1989).

The intent in the coding process was to identify the meaning of the particular theme or norm of the respondent in the context of the conflict and close friendship (Geertz, 1973). When repetition of key words or phrases or what was interpreted as similar meaning was evident, then a category or "pile" of responses emerged (Owen, 1984).

After each individual coder completed his or her individual sort and recorded the sort on a summary sheet, then all three coders for each ethnic group met to discuss their individual sorts. The coders were then asked to reach consensus on their sorts. In other words, they derived a final sort on the basis of consensus that each particular definitional theme, speech act, outcome, and so on belong in a particular category of similar responses (see Collier, 1988; or Hecht et al., 1989, for examples of similar coding processes).

Analysis of the responses for gender differences occurred as a last step. Coders separated males and females in their ethnic group and discussed responses and came up with a consensus sort. The themes identified to address the research questions are neither mutually exclusive categories (Agar & Hobbs, 1982) nor exhaustive. The themes reported here are a result of the joint discussion of the three coders. The researcher interpreted the themes as provided by the research assistants. Examples are provided to illustrate the themes.

RESULTS AND INTERPRETATIONS

In all, 85% of the respondents recalled a conflict episode that had occurred within the previous six months. This high percentage lessens the danger of recall bias. Results and interpretations are presented in the following section.

Definitions of Close Friendship

With regard to the first research question and definitions of *close friendship,* some similar and different themes emerged for respondents. All respondents described close friendships as including a high degree of trust. Examples typifying what all the coders identified as trust included, "will keep my secrets" and "knows things about me no one else ever will." Respondents in all groups also mentioned acceptance, "of all of me including my least attractive parts," "total and unconditional acceptance," "knows me and accepts me."

In addition to emphasizing trust and "being able to confide in the other person about anything and everything," Anglo Americans also described close friends as persons "who are there for you, you can rely on them." Also, many Anglos referred to what the coders labeled as freedom of expression: "I can freely express my thoughts, ideas, and feelings" and "I share my thoughts and other forms of self expression without a fear of being turned against." "I can behave however I need to." "A close friend will let me be me."

African Americans described close friendships as acceptance, "knows me and accepts me for all of who I am," as well as problem solving, "when I can talk to him/her and know that possible solutions can come out of it," and "a person who will help with all of life's problems." "Close friends are people who support you and help you and you help them through life."

Mexican Americans, in addition to mentioning trust and acceptance, also described what the coders called supportiveness: "will defend me if it ever became necessary," "is my best ally," and "will listen and support and encourage me on a wide range of issues." Another unique category and theme associated with Mexican Americans was that of sharing feelings. Examples included "mutual affection, joy in each other's company," "can share emotionally intense highs and lows," and "a person that I can share my intimate feelings with" and "share happiness, sorrow, anxieties etc. etc.!!"

Constitutive Ideas About Conflict with Close Friends

The second research question addressed similarities and differences in constitutive ideas about conflict with friends. The issues and events triggering the conflict (Frost & Wilmot, 1978) were similar across all respondents. Respondents described particular behaviors of the other or self as trigger events. A wide variety of issues were described by all respondents including expectations for the relationship between the close friends; expectations for other friends and family members; spiritual beliefs and practices; use of time, money, and other resources; life-style; and work ethic.

Males and females appeared to differ slightly only in the Anglo American group regarding constitutive definitions of conflict. Anglo American males defined conflict with what the coders noted as a problem or issue emphasis. Examples included "difference of opinion," "attack on one's beliefs and opinions," "unresolved situation," and "inability to compromise."

Anglo American females also talked about issues and lack of goal accomplishment, "disparity in goals or means for achieving a goal," and "two or more individuals who desire clearly a different outcome" but also included descriptions of the relationship between persons. For example, females described "two or more people who have control/input to a situation are at odds in how to manage each other" as well as "prolonged disagreement resulting in exceptional discomfort for both parties," "an impasse comes between two people causing a connection to be lost," and "an opposition of wills and desire to win at expense of relationship."

African American males and females were extremely consistent in their definitions of conflict. Examples included "disagreement," "different views," "contrary or differing views," and "misunderstanding, difference in ideas." African American respondents reflected the most agreement and the shortest descriptions of what conflict meant to them. "Lack of understanding" was a commonly mentioned theme.

Mexican American males and females reflected more of a relational definition of what conflict was all about. The coders noted that Mexican Americans described conflict as a disagreement, similar to the other groups, but also frequently described conflict in terms of its implications for the relationship. "Being out of balance with the other person," "a clash about an idea or thought," "when people lose respect for the other person's viewpoint and become closed," "not understanding or considering each other's needs," and "opposition of desires, enough to cause distress and unhappiness." The coders also noted a theme of loss of harmony in that respondents mentioned things like "not in harmony," "out of balance," "negative, uncomfortable, frustrating for our friendship," "clash," and "both person's values don't mix in harmony."

Conflict Competence

The normative patterns reflecting conflict competence were given attention through discussion of several items on the questionnaire. Coders identified themes in self and other's incompetence as well as competent conflict management conduct. The results of the various questionnaire items were discussed together. What follows here is a general summary of themes regarding competent conflict management.

Males and females in the Anglo American group both emphasized the importance of taking responsibility for behavior. Males mentioned "accept[ing] responsibility for being wrong"; also "I apologized," and "When you're wrong you should say so, and he did." Males also mentioned that "following through on commitments is essential" and "he kept his agreement." Females' descriptions: "She admitted it was her fault," and, "She felt sorry for herself and that was not OK," and, "She has to be willing to accept the consequences of her action."

Anglo American males frequently mentioned the importance of being direct as an appropriate conflict management behavior. Examples were "getting things in the open," "say no right up front," "state[ing] clearly what I saw and then he did the same," and "we should have gotten right to the issue" or "directly asked questions." Equality and shared control was identified by the coders as a theme for males: "Don't condescend to me." "He didn't give me any credit for a brain." "His sarcasm wasn't necessary." "His tone indicated disrespect and judgment." "Acting like my superior and giving my advice didn't set well."

Rational decision making as opposed to emotional decision making was also described as appropriate by Anglo males: "be clear," "keep your temper and discuss things calmly," and "explain . . . reasons for his actions." "She listened to the evidence I gave her to get her to change her mind."

Anglo American females overall indicated a concern for the other, the relationship, and situational flexibility as appropriate. Concern for the other was revealed in such comments as "sometimes it's better to agree to disagree and change the subject" and "she showed respect for my position and I showed respect for hers." "Being combatant isn't worth it. I don't want to lose the friendship." Inappropriate behaviors here included "when I told her I couldn't believe my ears."

Several females mentioned the appropriateness of reaffirming the relationship. "I told her how much I valued our friendship." "She reminded me how long we had been friends." "She told me that my opinion had always been important to her."

Expressing feelings, requesting information about other's feelings, and responding positively to those feelings were all mentioned by females. "Expressing exactly how I feel," "*I feel* statements would have been more appropriate than the *you are* accusing statements I used." "Not responding to her feelings was wrong of me." "She didn't have empathy for how I was feeling." "Asking the other person their thoughts and feelings."

The responses to the question about whether males and females in general think about and manage conflict differently were revealing. Males noted, "Women are more rational and more intuitive." "Women are better listeners." "Women try to solve problems without controlling the other person." Women made the following comments: "The most important thing to males in conflict is their egos." "Men don't worry about feelings." "Females are more concerned with others' feelings." "Men are more direct."

African American males and females were similar in their description of problem solution as appropriate behavior in conflict management. "I told him to stay in school and that I would help him study." "We decided to study together for the class." "We decided together how to solve the problem and deal with our friend." "She admitted she needed my help." "He helped me put together a pros and cons list."

African American males emphasized that appropriate arguments should be given, information should be offered, and opinions should be credible: "His case was full of holes." "He overgeneralized and tried to tell me Black Americans and Africans are the same." "When I didn't get a satisfactory explanation . . . I rejected him." "You shouldn't try to make a case when you are uninformed."

African American females pointed out that criticism is not appropriate: "She told me I was selfish." "I offended her because I said she was naive." Also, assertiveness was viewed as appropriate but only when the other's rights and views were considered. "She pushed her own way and opinion and totally disregarded mine." "He made no effort to understand my situation." "I went too far by telling my friend she should stop smoking if she cared at all about her health." "She kept telling me what she thought over and over."

The comments from male and female African Americans regarding gender differences were similar. These comments typified the responses: "Females don't always have to play win/win like males do." "Females make more of an attempt to resolve the conflict." "Females are more compassionate and honest." "Men manage by facts only." "Women are more emotional than men."

Male Mexican Americans described the importance of talking to reach a mutual understanding: "make a better effort to explain" or "stuck to problem until we solved it together." "He asked my perspective and then gave his." Males also described taking responsibility for actions in comments such as "apologize when you're wrong." "She shouldn't blame others for her mistake." "He should have kept his word."

Mexican American females described several kinds of reinforcement of the relationship that were appropriate: "She said, 'I really care' " and "thanked me for hanging in there with her," and "could have started out by telling me that our friendship was important." Also, females gave several examples of criticism or "put downs" that were clearly inappropriate. "She laughed and didn't care," "sarcastic remarks toward me," "told me I was oversensitive," "got this judgmental look and glared down at me."

Finally, Mexican American females, like Anglo American females, noted the importance of situational flexibility in combination with concern for the relationship and the other person. "Stay away but be available" was appropriate, along with "stayed away and let time heal." "We avoid the topic now." Also, however, confrontation was felt to be appropriate in some situations. "I could have been more serious, more confrontive." "I should have made a direct request."

Both male and female Mexican Americans gave detailed examples of how gender affects thoughts about and management of conflict. "Women can argue verbally while men try to get their point across physically." "Men are more selfish and don't consider the consequences of the conflict for the relationship." "Men are more 'up front' in handling conflict." "Females communicate feelings and emotions more directly." "Men seem to [be] more ego involved—right versus wrong—female emotions play a big part in their conflict."

Anglo American males and females did not differ in their descriptions of the outcome of the conflict and the effect of the conflict upon the friendship. Of the 25 Anglo respondents, 21 noted that the conflict was finished or the issue resolved. Four indicated that the conflict was still going on or that "the situation no longer exists but the conflict was never really resolved."

It is interesting to note that only three respondents described negative effects of the conflict on their friendship: "no friendship remaining," "made it stagnate," and "we kept our distance for a long, long while." The vast majority of the comments described little or no effect or a positive effect: "*None*," "no effects, bad or good and no guilt," "deepened our sensitivity, understanding and love for one another," and "solidified our friendship," "brought us closer."

African American males and females had mixed responses with regard to the outcomes from the conflict. Descriptions included "[it] will never be resolved in my lifetime," "[we] will need several more meetings," and "it is still going on"; also "finished and forgotten" and "resolved with a good outcome."

The effects of the conflict on the friendship for Mexican Americans were primarily negative: "Our friendship ended," "unsure of whether or not to continue friendship," "made us both stop and think about what friendship is," "friendship became strained," and "we don't spend as much time together." Three respondents described positive effects such as "we are not closer friends."

DISCUSSION

Respondents had similar and different definitions of *close friendship*. The characteristics of trust and acceptance mentioned by members of all ethnic groups are similar to confidentiality and emotional support (Adelman et al., 1990) and positive regard (La Gaipa, 1977) and may be reflective of culture-general beliefs about close friendship. The difference included Anglos also emphasizing freedom in expression of ideas, African Americans emphasizing problem solving, and Mexican Americans emphasizing support and expression of feelings.

These themes are consistent with Collier's (1989) findings, in which Anglo Americans agreed upon honesty and confidentiality as important characteristics of friendships, African Americans described sincerity and respect for the individual, and Latinos described respect and support for the relationship. The freedom of expression described by Anglos is consistent with a preference for honesty and trust. The problem-solving theme discussed by African Americans included an emphasis on sincere help and advice based upon respect for the individual rather than advice or criticism. The support described by Mexican Americans included implicit reinforcement for the relationship and mutual interdependence.

The constitutive ideas about conflict identified here show consistency with other research programs on ethnic friendships. The task orientation of Anglo Americans is consistent with individualism and emphasis on masculinity (Hofstede, 1980). In addition, Stewart (1972) has described North Americans as a "doing" rather than "being" culture, which places emphasis on achievement and linear definitions of time.

Hecht and Ribeau (1984) described African American communication style as including deep topical involvement; Hecht et al. (1989) noted authenticity and understanding as important themes for African Americans in conversations with Whites. The short descriptions of conflict as "differences in views" by African Americans in this study may reflect a high-context dimension of their ethnic communication style.

Collier (1990) proposed a theme of bondedness as describing communication among Mexican American families, which is illustrated here by the category of support for the relationship and a probable emphasis of this ethnic group on collectivism. In particular, the descriptions of conflict from this group included metaphors and emotionally laden terms such as "clash" and "loss of harmony."

Male and female ethnic friends differed in their ideas about conflict competence. While Anglo American males and females seemed to focus upon taking responsibility for behavior, males talked more about being direct and using rational argument, and females talked more about situational flexibility and conflict management based on concern for task and relationship. African American friends described joint and responsible problem solution, while males referred most often to the use of appropriate argument and females to appropriate assertiveness without criticism. Mexican American males and females differed in that males emphasized talking directly and responsibly and females emphasized reinforcing the relationship. Males and females in all groups described females as more compassionate and concerned for feelings and males as more concerned with winning the conflict and being "right."

The ethnic differences identified here may call into question some of the previous research on conflict style used by males and females. Kagan et al. (1982) found that Mexican Americans used passive or avoidance styles in conflict. In the current study, females spoke about situational flexibility and appropriate confrontation, and males described the need to collaborate and reach understanding through discussion. African American males emphasized the need for clear argument; however, African American females described criticism and attempts to control as inappropriate. Further research is needed to explain apparent contradictions of past findings that African Americans prefer active confrontation and the use of controlling styles (Kagan et al., 1982; Ting-Toomey, 1986) with the results identified here.

The Anglo American responses clearly reflect individualistic, low-context dimensions through the emphasis on self-face concern and the use of directness and a controlling style (Ting-Toomey, 1988). Males, in particular, commented on the need for equality in decision making and directness, which is consistent with the results of Ting-Toomey et al. (1989).

The outcomes experienced from conflict reflected differences across ethnic lines but not gender lines. Anglo Americans described positive or neutral effects of the conflict on the friendship, while both African Americans and Mexican Americans described negative effects that were long and short term. Conflict may be experienced as more natural and expected by Anglos and, with the emphasis on individualism, a necessary part of individual self-expression in friendships.

Overall, more information on gender differences within and across ethnic groups is warranted. Females and males define *conflict* differently and enact different norms. Collier and Thomas (1988) propose that different identities are salient in different situations; it may be that conduct is a product of dialectics between gender and ethnic identities (Baxter, 1987).

Taken together with the results of other exploratory studies, the findings of the current study do lend support to the notion that there are differences in emergent ethnic and gender identities in conflict between close friends. Cross-cultural research on such ethnic differences provides insights about conflict and friendships from the respondents' perspectives and experiences. The preferred styles with which close friends manage conflict show that not only does ethnic background emerge as a salient conflict issue for some close friends but males and females may be considered to be distinct "cultural" groups in that males and females view themselves as separate groups and apparently share some of the same definitions of and norms for conflict management. To understand conflict processes more fully, it is essential to consider, among other variables, both ethnic background and gender identities.

Several limitations are apparent in this study; for example, sample size prohibits extensive generalization. Also, future research should give adequate attention to salience of ethnic background and extent to which close friends consider their ethnicity a factor in their relational conduct and conflict management. Additional subjects and comparisons of same and different gender friendships is warranted. Additional information from interviews and ethnographic observation would increase confidence in interpretations and assumptions about intersubjective meanings of such labels as "responsibility for behavior."

The findings of this study, when considered along with previous research on ethnic communication, nonetheless, are provocative. Constitutive beliefs about conflict as well as management behaviors and consequences experienced differ across ethnic and gender boundaries. Past research on interpersonal conflict, grounded for the most part in data about Anglo American marriages and interpersonal relationships, can benefit from attention to ethnicity and gender. Insights gained through cross-cultural comparisons and interpretive studies can become the basis for research that is more representative of the changing cultural demography throughout the world and can become a foundation upon which intercultural conflict can be studied and management and mediation models designed.

REFERENCES

Adelman, M. B., Parks, M. R., & Albrecht, T. (1990). The nature of friendship and its development. In J. Stewart (Eds.), *Bridges not walls* (5th ed.), (pp. 283-292). New York: McGraw-Hill.

Agar, M., & Hobbs, J. R. (1982). Interpreting discourse: Coherence and the analysis of ethnographic interviews. *Discourse Processes, 5*, 1-32.

Altman, I., & Taylor, D. A. (1973). *Social penetration: The development of interpersonal relationships*. New York: Holt, Rinehart & Winston.

Banks, J. A. (1987). *Teaching strategies for ethnic studies* (4th ed.). Boston: Allyn & Bacon.

Barnlund, D. C. (1989). *Communicative styles of Japanese and Americans*. Belmont, CA: Wadsworth.

Bate, B. (1988). *Communication and the sexes*. New York: Harper & Row.

Baxter, L. A. (1987). Symbols of relationship identity in relationship cultures. *Journal of Social and Personal Relationships, 4*, 261-280.

Belenky, M. F., Clinchy, B. M., Goldberger, N. R., & Tarule, J. M. (1986). *Women's ways of knowing*. New York: Basic Books.

Berger, C. R., & Calabrese, R. J (1975). Some explorations in initial interaction and beyond: Toward a developmental theory of interpersonal communication. *Human Communication Research, 1*, 99-112.

Carbaugh, D. (1988). Cultural terms and tensions in the speech at a television station. *Western Journal of Speech Communication, 52*, 216-237.

Chanin, M., & Schneer, J. (1987). Manifest needs as personality predispositions to conflict-handling behavior. *Human Relations, 40*, 575-590.

Collier, M. J. (1988). A comparison of conversations among and between domestic culture groups: How intra- and intercultural competencies vary. *Communication Quarterly, 36*, 122-124.

Collier, M. J. (1989). Cultural and intercultural communication competence: Current approaches and directions for future research. *International Journal of Intercultural Relations, 13*, 287-302.

Collier, M. J. (1990, June). *Ethnic friendships: Enacted identities and competencies.* Paper presented at the annual International Communication Association Conference, Dublin, Ireland.

Collier, M. J., Ribeau, S., & Hecht, M. L. (1986). Intracultural communication rules and outcomes within three domestic cultures. *International Journal of Intercultural Relations, 10*, 439-458.

Collier, M. J., & Thomas, M. (1988). Identity in intercultural communication: An interpretive perspective. In Y. Kim & W. Gudykunst (Eds.), *Theories of intercultural communication* (pp. 99-120). Newbury Park, CA: Sage.

Cooley, C. H. (1968). The social self: On the meanings of "I." In C. Gordon & K. Gergen (Eds.), *The self in social interactions* (pp. 87-91). New York: John Wiley.

Cromwell, V. L., & Cromwell, R. E. (1978). Perceived dominance in decision-making and conflict resolution among Anglo, Black and Chicano couples. *Journal of Marriage and the Family, 40*, 749-759.

Cushman, D., & King, S. (1985). National and organizational cultures in conflict resolution: Japan, the United States and Yugoslavia. In W. Gudykunst, L. Stewart, & S. Ting-Toomey (Eds.), *Communication, culture and organizational processes* (pp. 114-133). Newbury Park, CA: Sage.

Davis, A. (1983). *Women, race and class.* New York: Random House.

Deutsch, M. (1973). Conflicts: Productive and destructive. In F. Jandt (Ed.), *Conflict resolution through communication* (pp. 155-197). New York: Harper & Row.

DeVos, G. (1982). Ethnic pluralism: Conflict and accommodation. In G. DeVos & L. Romanucci-Ross (Eds.), *Ethnic identity* (pp. 5-41). Chicago: University of Chicago Press.

Fitzpatrick, M. A., & Winke, J. (1979). You always hurt the one you love: Strategies and tactics in interpersonal conflict. *Communication Quarterly, 27*, 3-11.

Folb, E. (1982). Who's got the room at the top? Issues of dominance and nondominance in intracultural communication. In L. Samovar & R. Porter (Eds.), *Intercultural communication: A reader* (3rd ed., pp. 132-141). Belmont, CA: Wadsworth.

Folger, J., & Poole, M. S. (1984). *Working through conflict: A communication perspective.* Glenview, IL: Scott, Foresman.

Frost, J., & Wilmot, W. (1978). *Interpersonal conflict.* Dubuque, IA: William C Brown.

Geertz, C. (1973). *The interpretation of cultures.* New York: Basic Books.

Gilligan, C. (1982). *In a different voice: Psychological theory and women's development.* Cambridge, MA: Harvard University Press.

Gudykunst, W. B., & Nishida, T. (1986). The influence of cultural variability on perceptions of communication behavior associated with relationship terms. *Human Communication Research, 13,* 147-166.

Gudykunst, W. B., Nishida, T., & Chua, E. (1987). Perceptions of social penetration in Japanese-North American dyads. *International Journal of Intercultural Relations, 11,* 171-189.

Gudykunst, W. B., & Ting-Toomey, S. (1988). *Culture and interpersonal communication.* Newbury Park, CA: Sage.

Hall, E. T. (1976). *Beyond culture.* Garden City, NY: Doubleday.

Hecht, M. L., & Ribeau, S. (1984). Ethnic communication: A comparative analysis of satisfying communication. *International Journal of Intercultural Relations, 8,* 135-151.

Hecht, M. L., Ribeau, S., & Alberts, J. K. (1989). An Afro-American perspective on interethnic communication. *Communication Monographs, 56,* 385-410.

Hocker, J., & Wilmot, W. (1985). *Interpersonal conflict.* Dubuque, IA: William C Brown.

Hofstede, G. (1980). *Culture's consequences: International differences in work-related values.* Newbury Park, CA: Sage.

Holsti, O. (1969). *Content analysis for the social sciences and humanities.* Reading, MA: Addison-Wesley.

Hymes, D. (1972). Models of the interaction of language and social life. In J. Gumperz & D. Hymes (Eds.), *Directions in sociolinguistics: The ethnography of communication* (pp. 1-72). New York: Holt, Rinehart & Winston.

Kagan, S., Knight, G., & Martinez-Romero, S. (1982). Culture and the development of conflict resolution style. *Journal of Cross-Cultural Psychology, 13,* 43-59.

Kramarae, C. (1981). *Women and men speaking.* Rowley, MA: Newbury House.

Kumagi, F., & Straus, M. (1983). Conflict resolution tactics in Japan, India, and the U.S.A. *Journal of Comparative Family Studies, 14,* 337-387.

La Gaipa, J. J. (1977). Testing a multidimensional approach to friendship. In S. Duck (Ed.), *Theory and practice in interpersonal attraction* (pp. 250-270). London: Academic Press.

Lonner, W. J., & Berry, J. W. (1986). Preface. In W. J. Lonner & J. W. Berry (Eds.), *Field methods in cross-cultural research* (pp. 11-16). Newbury Park, CA: Sage.

Lyons, N. (1983). Two perspectives on self, relationships and morality. *Harvard Educational Review, 53,* 125-145.

Maltz, D. N., & Borker, R. A. (1987). A cultural approach to male-female miscommunication. In J. J. Gumperz (Ed.), *Language and social identity* (pp. 195-216). Cambridge: Cambridge University Press.

Olebe, M., & Koester, J. (1989). Exploring the cross-cultural equivalence of the behavioral assessment scale for intercultural communication. *International Journal of Intercultural Relations, 13,* 333-348.

Owen, W. F. (1984). Interpretive themes in relational communication. *Quarterly Journal of Speech, 70,* 274-287.

Pearson, J. (1985). *Gender and communication.* Dubuque, IA: William C Brown.

Putnam, L., & Jones, T. (1982). Reciprocity in negotiations: An analysis of bargaining interaction. *Communication Monographs, 49,* 171-191.

Roloff, M. E., & Miller, G. R. (Eds.). (1987). *Interpersonal processes: New directions in communication research.* Newbury Park, CA: Sage.

Schneider, D. (1976). Notes toward a theory of culture. In K. Basso & H. Selby (Eds.), *Meaning in anthropology* (pp. 197-220). Albuquerque: University of New Mexico Press.

Shotter, J. (1989). Social accountability and the social construction of "you." In J. Shotter & K. Gergen (Eds.), *Texts of identity* (pp. 133-151). Newbury Park, CA: Sage.

Sowell, T. (1981). *Ethnic America.* New York: Basic Books.

Spitzberg, B., & Cupach, W. (1984). *Interpersonal communication competence.* Beverly Hills, CA: Sage.

Stewart, E. (1972). *American cultural patterns: A cross-cultural perspective.* Pittsburgh: University of Pittsburgh.

Stewart, J. (1990). Interpersonal communication: Contact between persons. In J. Stewart (Ed.), *Bridges not walls* (5th ed., pp. 13-31). New York: McGraw-Hill.

Tannen, D. (1987). Ethnic style in male-female conversation. In J. J. Gumperz (Ed.), *Language and social identity* (pp. 217-231). Cambridge: Cambridge University Press.

Taylor, D., & Altman, I. (1987). Communication in interpersonal relationships: Social penetration processes. In M. Roloff & G. Miller (Eds.), *Interpersonal processes: New directions in communication research* (pp. 257-277). Newbury Park, CA: Sage.

Thorne, B., Kramarae, C., & Henley, N. (Eds.). (1983). *Language, gender and society.* Rowley, MA: Newbury House.

Ting-Toomey, S. (1986). Conflict styles in Black and White subjective cultures. In Y. Kim (Ed.), *Current research in interethnic communication* (pp. 75-89). Newbury Park, CA: Sage.

Ting-Toomey, S. (1988). Intercultural conflict styles: A face negotiation theory. In Y. Kim & W. Gudykunst (Eds.), *Theories in intercultural communication* (pp. 213-238). Newbury Park, CA: Sage.

Ting-Toomey, S. (1989). Identity and interpersonal bonding. In M. Asante & W. Gudykunst (Eds.), *Handbook of international and intercultural communication* (pp. 351-373). Newbury Park, CA: Sage.

Ting-Toomey, S., Trubisky, P., & Nishida, T. (1989, November). *An analysis of conflict styles in Japan and the United States.* Paper presented at the meeting of the Speech Communication Association, San Francisco.

van Dijk, T. A. (1987). *Communicating racism: Ethnic prejudice in thought and talk.* Newbury Park, CA: Sage.

Williams, F. (1989). *The new communications.* Belmont, CA: Wadsworth.

9

The Emergence of
Interpersonal Behavior
Diachronic and Cross-Cultural Processes
in the Evolution of Intimacy

JOHN ADAMOPOULOS ● *Indiana University*
at South Bend

Many current theories of the structure of interpersonal behavior assume the existence of universal dimensions along which meaning is communicated. There is psychological and historical evidence, however—gleaned from the literature of different cultures—that some of these "universal" structures may have changed considerably over the past few thousand years. This chapter presents a framework for the systematic investigation of such changes, with special emphasis on the understanding of intimacy and some of its correlates. Changes over time, as well as cross-cultural differences in the experience of intimacy, are considered in the context of this framework.

In recent years, psychological science has begun to confront a fundamental problem in the analysis of interpersonal behavior: the attribution of "universal" status to certain aspects of human conduct, previously assumed—but not shown—to be pancultural phenomena. That it took psychology so long to take notice of the words of Herodotus (ca. 490-425 B.C./1954, p. 115) about differences and similarities in "the ordinary practices of mankind [humankind]" may reflect a certain ethnocentric arrogance in modern science or other, perhaps more admirable, qualities. Whatever the reason, it is at the same time exciting and surprising that an almost infinite variety of interpersonal behavior can be described by a rather small number of dimensions of social interchange.

Recent approaches to this problem in psychology have grown out of rather diverse perspectives and have produced different theoretical and methodological conceptualizations. Despite such differences, however, an impressive degree of convergence in research findings suggests that interpersonal behavior may display consistencies, which, in turn, may

AUTHOR'S NOTE: The writing of this chapter was facilitated by a Hewlett Foundation Summer Faculty Fellowship Grant, Indiana University.

imply the possibility of behavioral "universals." Ultimately, then, different conceptualizations may be reducible to a more or less common manner in which human beings communicate and understand meaning when they interact with their social environment. A related problem that stems naturally from such speculation, and that, unfortunately, has received very little attention from social scientists, concerns the *origins* of commonalities in the structure of interpersonal exchange and their significance for understanding the evolution of human social behavior.

The following analysis will attempt to summarize findings on the structure of interpersonal behavior from different perspectives and to work toward an integrative framework for the explanation of behavioral commonalties and their emergence over long periods of time. A second part of the analysis will focus on some general implications of the framework for the study of intimacy and its diverse meanings across cultures and time.

PERSPECTIVES ON THE STRUCTURE OF INTERPERSONAL BEHAVIOR

Most structural analyses of interpersonal behavior have been motivated by the assumption that all human action can be described by a limited number of semantic features or "common denominators" (Lonner, 1980). Such features—usually presented in the form of dimensions—presumably reflect the meaning that humans want to communicate to the world around them. This simple assumption, which is completely compatible with current theories of cognitive functioning, has led to a very large number of monocultural and cross-cultural investigations of an exploratory nature. Generally, theory has followed research in this approach, which I will call the empirical/inductive perspective.

Other approaches are theory driven but have not always led to greater insights about the meaning of interpersonal behavior because of methodological weaknesses, inadequate data bases, or other problems. There are a variety of such perspectives, and it is beyond the modest goals of this chapter to review them. Instead, I will discuss briefly issues related to two theoretical approaches that have made important contributions to our understanding of the structure of social action and have inspired to some extent the model that will be presented in a later section: the ethogenic and the resource-exchange perspectives.

The Empirical/Inductive Perspective

Following the classic work of Osgood and his colleagues on affective meaning (e.g., Osgood, Suci, & Tannenbaum, 1957), a number of social psychologists applied a similar methodology to the analysis of social behavior. Most notably, Triandis (1972, 1978) has produced persuasive evidence from a number of different cultures that interpersonal behavior is understood along the dimensions of association-dissociation (affiliation), superordination-subordination (dominance), and intimacy-formality.

These dimensions, of course, do not account for all variability in social behavior, but they do appear to reflect commonalties in the human meaning system. Other dimensions have also emerged in many studies around the world, but it is always difficult to distinguish methodological artifact, stemming from the multivariate procedures employed, from culture-specific meaning systems. The three dimensions mentioned above, however, appear with surprising frequency in cultures as diverse as Japan, India, and the United States and may, therefore, be included in the data base of a universal theory of interpersonal structure (Adamopoulos, 1988).

Triandis (1972) has labeled the particular way in which members of a specific group perceive their social environment as "subjective culture"—a cultural ideograph, so to speak. Cross-cultural commonalities in subjective culture are often implicitly thought to reflect something fundamental among all human beings, but, in general, this approach has not offered a systematic account of the origins of such culture-common structures. It is possible that Osgood's (1969) speculation on the evolutionary significance of the dimensions of affective meaning may be of some help here. For example, telling friend from foe (association-dissociation) and controlling and manipulating the social environment (superordination-subordination) surely must have been prerequisites for survival among our distant ancestors (and are probably even more so in our times). However, such an account of the emergence of interpersonal structure does not easily lead to verifiable theoretical predictions and is clearly based on the arguable assumption that evolutionary models from biology can also explain psychocultural evolution (Adamopoulos, 1988).

In more recent work, Triandis (1980) has attempted to link the three pancultural dimensions of interpersonal behavior to resource-exchange theory (e.g., resource availability may be associated with the formation of affiliation), but no theoretical framework for the systematic linkage of resources to dimensions has been developed. Nevertheless, the empirical/inductive approach has contributed to the creation of a rich data base for the analysis of social relations across cultures. In recent years, other, somewhat less ambitious research programs have confirmed many of Triandis's findings using different methodologies and definitions of social-interaction units (e.g., Wish, Deutsch, & Kaplan, 1976).

The Ethogenic Perspective

Offered as an alternative to psychological determinism, the ethogenic method relies on the descriptive analysis of social situations to identify particular routines or rules that individuals use in constructing their interaction with the environment (e.g., Harré, 1977,1980). Thus this perspective, by definition, focuses on the structure of action, which it hopes to articulate through the use of ethnomethodology and account analysis. Unfortunately, however, the emphasis that the ethogenic perspective places on individual construction of action results in a rather skeptical attitude toward the possibility of establishing universal structures of interpersonal behavior (e.g., Schlenker, 1977). This skepticism, which is also shared by Gergen (1982), is based on the assumption that structures of meaning develop in different ways across cultures and time in accordance with the variety of human experience.

Pessimism notwithstanding, this is an important criticism that should be heeded by all theories aspiring to explain universal psychological phenomena. Diachronic processes that account for historical and cultural changes in interpersonal behavior must be incorporated in the analysis of the structure of action systems because they provide the macro context for interpersonal behavior.

Ethogenics and ethnomethodology have influenced the work of a number of investigators of interpersonal interaction. In recent years, Forgas (1982) has employed quantitative methodology to obtain the cognitive representation of "social episodes," or daily interaction routines, for individual members of subcultures and other social groups. His findings confirm those of the empirical/inductive perspective: intimacy, formality, pleasantness (affiliation), and self-confidence (superordination) are among the most frequently obtained perceptual dimensions of interpersonal relations across sociocultural groups (Forgas, 1985).

The Resource-Exchange Perspective

One of the most important theoretical contributions to the analysis of the structure of social interaction is the circumplex developed by Foa and Foa (1974, 1980). In this model, social interaction is conceptualized as the exchange of six classes of resources: love, status, information, money, goods, and services. These resources vary along the dimensions of particularism-universalism and concreteness-abstractness.

Particularism refers to the extent to which a specific resource exchange may be affected by the relationship between actor and target of action. Thus love is the most particularistic resource (e.g., *who* your sexual partner is matters a great deal these days), whereas money is the most universalistic one (e.g., the *specific* individual who was the teller in your last bank transaction made no difference, I hope, to whether or not you received your worth). The dimension of *concreteness-abstractness* describes the material (goods, services) or symbolic (information, status) nature of resources.

The resource-exchange model provides systematic predictions about the nature, course, and experience of interpersonal interaction. Several investigations within and among cultures have found support for some of these predictions (e.g., Brinberg & Castell, 1982; Foa et al., 1987). Most empirical studies, however, have failed to relate model predictions to the more general conclusions on interpersonal structure established by the other perspectives. Attempts to link the resource circumplex to the three pancultural dimensions of social behavior have been, for the most part, unsystematic and rather awkward (Adamopoulos, 1984). Still, this model is very useful in explaining both the organization and the emergence of social behavior across cultures and over time (Adamopoulos, 1988; Foa & Foa, 1980). In addition, it has been used successfully in explaining the specific structure of the interpersonal domain of personality (Wiggins, 1979), which has also been found to share many common features across cultures (e.g., Goldberg, 1981).

Toward an Integration

Each of the three perspectives presented so far provides significant information on interpersonal structure and raises important challenges for any theory that attempts to explain the pancultural dimensions of human behavior. Specifically, the empirical/inductive perspective provides the interpersonal dimensions that must be organized and explained. The ethogenic perspective underscores the importance of recognizing formally in any such theory the role of history and culture (time and social context). Finally, the resource-exchange perspective provides an alternative meaning system for social behavior and an infrastructure for the analysis of interpersonal relations.

I have proposed elsewhere (Adamopoulos, 1984, 1988; Adamopoulos & Bontempo, 1986) a framework for the organization of interpersonal behavior that attempts to address many of the findings and concerns raised by the three perspectives. This framework can also be used to account for the emergence of particular behavior features over time by assuming that the successive differentiation of fundamental constraints on human behavior results in relatively stable, local behavior structures.

A Model for the Differentiation of Interpersonal Behavior

The following integration of the perspectives outlined earlier has two major aims: (a) the definition of the functional relationships among pancultural dimensions of social behavior and (b) the description of processes that result in the emergence of particular interpersonal structures over time.

Theoretical assumptions. The model is based on the following set of assumptions, many of which have been discussed previously. Additional justification for many of these assumptions has been derived from the general literature in social science, history, and literary criticism and has been presented in earlier reports (Adamopoulos, 1988; Adamopoulos & Bontempo, 1986).

First, interpersonal behavior is viewed as a means of communicating the intentions that motivate resource exchange between two or more individuals. Thus the emphasis is on the meaning that is communicated through action rather than on the overt act itself. The six resource classes identified by Foa and Foa (1974) are assumed to be universal and exclusively defined by the attributes of universalism-particularism and concreteness-abstractness.

Second, behavior is naturally constrained by a number of variables that are fundamental to any social interchange. Three of these have been identified so far: *exchange mode, interpersonal orientation,* and *resource type.* During interpersonal interaction, a concrete or symbolic resource (type) is given or denied to another individual (exchange mode). This behavior may be oriented toward a very specific person or toward any individual who happens to fill the appropriate social role (interpersonal orientation).

Third, over time, the three constraints may undergo a process of differentiation into increasingly fine discriminations. This process occurs in successive stages, as shown in Figure 9.1, moving from the first discrimination between giving and denying a resource to the relationship between actor and target (orientation) and, finally, to the type of resource being exchanged.

The specific order in which constraints are differentiated is not arbitrary. It reflects the assumption that the distinction between concrete and symbolic forms of exchange is a rather late development in human social evolution, dating perhaps to the formation of culture (e.g., Etkin, 1954). In contrast, the distinction between particular individuals (e.g., members of a reference group) and generalized others as targets of interpersonal behavior may have occurred much earlier, in a critical

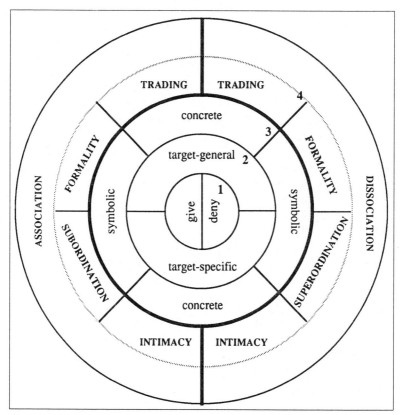

Figure 9.1: The emergence of interpersonal behavior from constraint differentiation.

NOTE: 1 = exchange mode, 2 = interpersonal orientation, 3 = resource type, and 4 = interpersonal behavior features.

point of our evolutionary history (Hogan, 1975). Furthermore, the particular order of constraint differentiation yields specific and testable functional relationships among emerging behavior dimensions.

The emergence of interpersonal structures. The behavioral patterns that result from the differentiation process are presented in the two outer circles in Figure 9.1. The most general structure, the association-dissociation dimension, emerges as *giving* is differentiated from *denying*. Affiliation, then, is assumed to be a very early form of behavior that is correlated with, but distinct from, several other interpersonal dimensions.

The model provides theoretical definitions of all three pancultural dimensions of social behavior. For example, *subordination* is defined as the giving of symbolic resources to a specific target, whereas *super-ordination* is characterized by the denial of such resources. The model also indicates that a basic behavioral dimension defined by the exchange of concrete and target-general resources (trading) has been largely ignored in cross-cultural studies of interpersonal structure.

In general, behavioral structures are assumed to remain relatively stable within particular historical periods, thus constituting *synchronic* universals. However, the diachronic processes involved in the differentiation of constraints may result in the emergence of new behavior patterns over time.

Major sociocultural changes often stimulate differentiation. For example, the invention of the printing press had dramatic effects in fifteenth-century Europe (Eisenstein, 1979). A complex resource, at once both concrete (in the print culture it enables) and symbolic (in the information it perpetuates), printing is clearly target general. The model predicts that formality and trading are the most likely behavioral structures to be affected by this process. Eisenstein (1979), viewing the phenomenon as a continuous process of incremental change following a revolution in communication, has presented an elaborate account of such effects. First, a completely new set of trading networks was set up as printing workshops sought to increase profits by entering new markets. Then, over the course of several decades and perhaps centuries, there emerged new formal social relationships that guided the professional and cross-cultural interaction of the specialist workers required for the application of the new technology. What we see, in other words, is the "saturation" of society with a new resource, which leads to further differentiation of those interpersonal behaviors that are defined through the constraints associated with that resource.

Along the same lines, the revolution in information technology in the late twentieth century will focus a great deal of interpersonal interaction on the exchange of symbolic resources. This may result in the emergence of a highly differentiated power structure and of social relationships that are based on interpersonal distance and formal interaction.

Empirical evidence. There have been few experimental tests of the model so far. One cross-cultural investigation with Greek and U.S. participants found support for the predicted relationships between resource classes and the pancultural interpersonal dimensions (Adamopoulos, 1984). The experimental method, however, cannot be used to test the model's description of diachronic processes.

I have developed a different methodology to explore such long-term processes. Interpersonal behavior, and its social context, are carefully and exhaustively recorded in various literary pieces from different cultures and historical periods. Structural analyses can then be performed on behavior frequencies across social situations. A number of such analyses have been applied to interpersonal behavior depicted in the Homeric epics (the *Iliad* and the *Odyssey*), in medieval epic poetry (*Beowulf* and *The Song of Roland*), and in a number of other literary masterpieces (e.g., Adamopoulos, 1982; Adamopoulos & Bontempo, 1986). The results have generally been supportive of model predictions. The dimension of association-dissociation, which is the earliest pattern to form according to the differentiation model, always emerged as the clearest structure, followed occasionally by dominance. In most cases, intimacy and formality were not clearly differentiated but were reflected in a psychological complex that represented ritualistic tendencies for interpersonal closeness and distance.

Despite assurances that literary works are good sources of information about sociocultural practices (e.g., Jeay, 1979; Langland, 1984), a number of criticisms can be voiced against the approach advocated here. Perhaps the most significant of these concerns the validity of the obtained structures as well as the imposition of the coders' own conceptual frameworks on the data.

The possibility that coders introduce their own, contemporary view of the structure of human behavior in the data implies that a high degree of congruence will be obtained among the dimensions of different data sets. At the same time, however, we would not expect any *systematic* differences between data sets from different historical periods and those of the same period. We *would* expect such differences if, in fact, this coding procedure resulted in at least a partially accurate depiction of social behavior in different eras.

To explore this possibility further, I selected seven behavioral items that were common in the investigations of the four epic works mentioned earlier. Dimensions obtained in the original factor analyses were matched on the basis of labels initially assigned to them, and coefficients of congruence (Harman, 1967) of the factor structures were compared for all pairs of literary sources. The average coefficient was .60, suggesting that the psychological structures uncovered may, indeed, be universal modes of behavior. In addition, as expected, the average congruence coefficient for works that were written in the same (more or less) historical period (i.e., congruence between the *Iliad* and the *Odyssey* and between *Beowulf* and *The Song of Roland*) was .80, whereas the average coefficient for the other combinations (i.e., pairs of works written in different time periods) was .51.

In a further analysis, coefficients of congruence for each pair of literary sources were correlated with the approximate time difference (in centuries) between the works of the pair. It was expected that there would be a significant negative correlation, such that the greater the historical distance between the works, the less similar the obtained behavioral structures would be. This correlation was $-.75$ ($p < .05$, one-tailed).

These results, however tentative, imply that there is merit to this approach for obtaining valuable information about the universal components of human interaction. In addition, they provide support for the assumption that pancultural behavioral patterns may be stable or "universal" only for limited, if long, periods of time (hence the use of the term *synchronic universals* in an earlier discussion). Clearly, interpersonal behavior has undergone at least some changes in our recorded history. The remainder of this chapter will explore the potential of the model in explaining interpersonal structure by focusing on the dimension of intimacy.

THE STRUCTURE OF INTIMACY

Most modern theories of close personal relationships in social psychology and related disciplines define *intimacy* as an interpersonally rewarding process characterized primarily by mutual self-disclosure (e.g., Derlega & Chaikin, 1975; Reis, Senchak, & Solomon, 1985). The role of many hostile behaviors that have strong connotations of intimate interaction is usually considered only in the investigation of dissolution processes.

The differentiation model outlined in the previous section defines *intimacy* in rather different terms: It is conceptualized as the giving or denying of target-specific and primarily concrete resources. This definition raises two significant theoretical issues that should be discussed in some detail.

First, the model definition emphasizes both positive and negative characteristics of this behavior dimension. Cross-cultural research has shown repeatedly that intimacy can be correlated with both poles of the association-dissociation continuum (e.g., Triandis, 1972; Triandis, Shanmugam, & Tanaka, 1966).

Second, the model also emphasizes concreteness as the type of resource most likely to be exchanged in intimate transactions. It is assumed that intimacy involves primarily the exchange of love and, to a lesser extent, the exchanges of status and services. Finer discriminations in resource type—the last stage of differentiation—may lead to other kinds of intimate relations of a more symbolic nature.

The Emergence of Intimacy

The model implies the possibility that the distinction between intimacy and formality occurred at a fairly late stage in cultural evolution. In contrast to association and dissociation, or superordination and subordination, which differ only in terms of the exchange mode employed, intimacy and formality differ in both interpersonal orientation and resource type. It is reasonable to assume that more complex interpersonal structures require much longer periods of time to evolve.

The analyses of literary works from different ages summarized earlier in fact never derived a clear dimension of intimacy-formality, though they almost always yielded the other two pancultural structures. Furthermore, correlations between matched dimensions in different literary pieces showed that association-dissociation enjoyed the greatest congruence across time, with superordination and subordination a distant second. Thus what little empirical evidence is available on this issue seems to support the model's prediction of the evolutionary order of interpersonal structures: affiliation, dominance, and intimacy.

Relationship Between Intimacy and Dominance

As can easily be seen in Figure 9.1, the psychological meaning of intimacy is closely related to that of superordination and subordination. This relationship has frequently been identified in the psychological literature on interpersonal relations (e.g., Gudykunst & Ting-Toomey, 1988). Rohner (1986) has established a direct connection between parental control and behavioral intimacy in children in his hologeistic study of parental acceptance-rejection theory. Brown (1965) has also noted the close link between the two forms of behavior in his discussion of the dual function of various forms of address across cultures. Typically, familiarity communicates the denial of status, whereas formal forms of address communicate respect. Similarly, Henley and LaFrance (1984) have reported that smiling, and other nonverbal behaviors that convey warmth and intimacy, may at the same time signal subordination.

Historical analyses of the structure of close relationships have also established a connection between intimacy and status in medieval Europe (e.g., Secord, 1984) and in Homeric Greece (Adamopoulos & Bontempo, 1986). Perhaps more important, Aristotle explicitly discussed close relationships of "unequal status" in the *Nicomachean Ethics* along with recommendations for their proper handling (his favorite was equity).

An Old-Fashioned Analysis: Aristotelian
Attributes of Close Relationships

The preceding analysis points to the possibility that intimacy may be defined by the exchange of resources that vary somewhat along the concreteness-abstractness continuum. Therefore, we may be able to distinguish between two types of intimacy—each associated with the exchange of more or less concrete resources. In fact, early comprehensive discussions of close relationships focused on both types. Among the best known is, no doubt, Aristotle's analysis of *philia,* which refers to friendship, affection, and love (Wheelwright, 1951).

Aristotle (ca. 384-322 B.C./1962) described three major attributes of personal relationships: usefulness, pleasure, and goodness (altruism). It should no longer come as a surprise that a modern analysis of the structure of heterosexual relationships has identified similar characteristics. Forgas and Dobosz (1980) found that individual perceptions of common relationships (e.g., "a long-lasting, close platonic relationship"; "a one night sexual encounter") varied along the dimensions of sexuality (pleasure), evaluation and balance (usefulness), and love (goodness).

Consideration of these attributes in the context of the two types of intimacy identified previously results in a classification scheme that can accommodate most close interpersonal relationships. Some examples of such relationships appear in Table 9.1.

Aristotle's analysis of *philia,* developed at a time when intimacy, ritual, and formality may still have been indistinguishable to some extent, encompasses all six categories of personal relationships. It is clear that, in past centuries, many close relationships were based on concrete exchanges. For example, wives were often seen as property in ancient Greece, and arranged marriages for material gain were the norm (e.g., Ehrenberg, 1962). In Aristophanes' *Lysistrata,* women used a "sex strike" to accomplish their goal of bringing men back from war (Seldes, 1930). In the *Odyssey,* Penelope was clearly considered an object— much like a scepter—whose possession would bring the kingdom of Ithaka within reach. And let us not forget the *Iliad,* in which a confrontation over the rights of warriors to the spoils of war—including concubines—started the great feud between Agamemnon and Achilles.

It should be remembered that Aristotle also considered close relationships of more symbolic nature, as indicated by his discussion of the link between intimacy and social status. Over time, many patterns of intimate behavior acquired an increasingly symbolic form. An interesting case is the connection between physical attractiveness and romantic

TABLE 9.1 Aristotelian Attributes of Two Types of Intimacy: Some Examples

	Resource Type	
Aristotelian Attributes of Close Relationships	*Type I More Concrete*	*Type II Less Concrete (symbolic)*
Usefulness	arranged marriages	social penetration; reciprocal self-disclosure; communication of status
Pleasure	mutually desired sexual relationships	physical attractiveness-attraction paradigm; romantic love
Altruism	unusual philanthropy; self-sacrificing behavior	companionate love; commitment and trust

love (not particularly worthy of attention for Aristotle). Physical attractiveness is not a concrete, material resource, but, rather, it conveys a variety of information about personality dispositions and life experiences. Consider Hawthorne's (1852/1983, p. 27) description of Miles Coverdale's first encounter with Priscilla, with whom he proclaimed to be in love in the final line of *The Blithedale Romance*:

> Her brown hair fell down from beneath a hood, not in curls, but with only a slight wave; her face was of a wan, almost sickly hue, betokening habitual seclusion from the sun and free atmosphere, like a flower-shrub that had done its best to blossom in too scanty light. . . . In short, there has seldom been seen so depressed and sad a figure as this young girl's. . . . The fantasy occurred to me, that she was some desolate kind of creature, doomed to wander about in snowstorms.

Modern theories of intimacy concentrate on the second type, possibly as a result of the importance of symbolic exchanges in Western society. Altman and Taylor's (1973) theory of social penetration, typifying contemporary approaches, emphasizes the role of self-disclosure, which, eventually, may lead to the development of mutual trust and commitment.

Clearly, then, we notice a movement away from concern with the concrete aspects of exchange in intimate interaction within Western psychology. This tendency may very well reflect a societal trend toward an increasing reliance on symbolic exchange. On the other hand, it may reflect a Western academic tradition of accentuating the significance of symbolic interaction. In either case, the study of the evolution of intimacy across time and across cultures is a matter worth pursuing further.

REFERENCES

Adamopoulos, J. (1982). Analysis of interpersonal structures in literary works of three historical periods. *Journal of Cross-Cultural Psychology, 13,* 157-168.

Adamopoulos, J. (1984). The differentiation of social behavior: Toward an explanation of universal interpersonal structures. *Journal of Cross-Cultural Psychology, 15,* 487-508.

Adamopoulos, J. (1988). Interpersonal behavior: Cross-cultural and historical perspectives. In M. H. Bond (Ed.), *The cross-cultural challenge to social psychology* (pp. 196-207). Newbury Park, CA: Sage.

Adamopoulos, J., & Bontempo, R. N. (1986). Diachronic universals in interpersonal structures: Evidence from literary sources. *Journal of Cross-Cultural Psychology, 17,* 169-189.

Altman, I., & Taylor, D. (1973). *Social penetration: The development of interpersonal relationships.* New York: Holt, Rinehart & Winston.

Aristotle (1962). *Nicomachean ethnics* (M. Ostwald, Trans.). Indianapolis: Bobbs-Merrill. (Original work appeared ca. 384-322 B.C.)

Brinberg, D., & Castell, P. (1982). A resource exchange theory approach to interpersonal interactions: A test of Foa's theory. *Journal of Personality and Social Psychology, 43,* 260-269.

Brown, R. (1965). *Social psychology.* New York: Free Press.

Derlega, V. J., & Chaikin, A. L. (1975). *Sharing intimacy.* Englewood Cliffs, NJ: Prentice-Hall.

Ehrenberg, V. (1962). *The people of Aristophanes.* New York: Schoken.

Eisenstein, E. L. (1979). *The printing press as an agent of change: Communications and cultural transformations in early-modern Europe* (Vol. 1). Cambridge: Cambridge University Press.

Etkin, W. (1954). Social behavior and the evolution of man's mental faculties. *American Naturalist, 88,* 129-142.

Foa, E. B., & Foa, U. G. (1980). Resource theory: Interpersonal behavior as exchange. In K. J. Gergen, M. S. Greenberg, & R. H. Willis (Eds.), *Social exchange: Advances in theory and research* (pp. 77-94). New York: Plenum.

Foa, U. G., & Foa, E. B. (1974). *Societal structures of the mind.* Springfield, IL: Charles C Thomas.

Foa, U. G., Salcedo, L. N., Tornblom, K. Y., Garner, M., Glaubman, H., & Teichman, M. (1987). Interrelations of social resources: Evidence of pancultural invariance. *Journal of Cross-Cultural Psychology, 18,* 221-233.

Forgas, J. P. (1982). Episode cognition: Internal representations of interaction routines. In L. Berkowitz (Ed.), *Advances in experimental social psychology* (Vol. 15, pp. 59-101). New York: Academic Press.

Forgas, J. P. (1985). *Interpersonal behavior: The psychology of social interaction.* Sydney: Pergamon.

Forgas, J. P., & Dobosz, B. (1980). Dimensions of romantic involvement: Towards a taxonomy of heterosexual relationships. *Social Psychology Quarterly, 43,* 290-300.

Gergen, K. J. (1982). *Toward transformation in social knowledge.* New York: Springer-Verlag.

Goldberg, L. R. (1981). Language and individual differences: The search for universals in personality lexicons. In L. Wheeler (Ed.), *Review of personality and social psychology* (Vol. 2, pp. 141-165). Beverly Hills, CA: Sage.

Gudykunst, W. B., & Ting-Toomey, S. (1988). *Culture and interpersonal communication.* Newbury Park, CA: Sage.

Harman, H. H. (1967). *Modern factor analysis.* Chicago: University of Chicago Press.

Harré, R. (1977). The ethogenic approach: Theory and practice. In L. Berkowitz (Ed.), *Advances in experimental social psychology* (Vol. 10, pp. 284-314). New York: Academic Press.

Harré, R. (1980). *Social being: A theory for social psychology.* Totowa, NJ: Littlefield, Adams.

Hawthorne, N. (1983). *The Blithedale romance.* Harmondsworth, England: Penguin. (Original work published 1852)

Henley, N. M., & LaFrance, M. (1984). Gender as culture: Difference and dominance in nonverbal behavior. In A. Wolfgang (Ed.), *Nonverbal behavior: Perspectives, applications, intercultural insights* (pp. 351-371). Lewiston, NY: C. J. Hogrefe.

Herodotus (1954). *The histories* (A. de Selincourt, Trans.). Baltimore: Penguin. (Original work appeared ca. 490-425 B.C.)

Hogan, R. (1975). Theoretical egocentrism and the problem of compliance. *American Psychologist, 30,* 533-540.

Jeay, M. (1979). Sexuality and family in fifteenth-century France: Are literary sources a mask or a mirror? *Journal of Family History, 4,* 328-345.

Langland, E. (1984). *Society in the novel.* Chapel Hill: University of North Carolina Press.

Lonner, W. J. (1980). The search for psychological universals. In H. C. Triandis & W. W. Lambert (Eds.), *Handbook of cross-cultural psychology: Vol. 1, Perspectives* (pp. 143-204). Boston: Allyn & Bacon.

Osgood, C. E. (1969). On the whys and wherefores of E, P, and A. *Journal of Personality and Social Psychology, 12,* 194-199.

Osgood, C. E., Suci, G. J., & Tannenbaum, P. H. (1957). *The measurement of meaning.* Urbana: University of Illinois Press.

Reis, H. T., Senchak, M., & Solomon, B. (1985). Sex differences in the intimacy of social interaction: Further examination of potential explanations. *Journal of Personality and Social Psychology, 48,* 1204-1217.

Rohner, R. P. (1986). *The warmth dimension: Foundations of parental acceptance-rejection theory.* Beverly Hills, CA: Sage.

Schlenker, B. R. (1977). On the ethogenic approach: Etiquette and revolution. In L. Berkowitz (Ed.), *Advances in experimental social psychology* (Vol. 10, pp. 315-330). New York: Academic Press.

Secord, P. F. (1984). Love, misogyny, and feminism in selected historical periods: A social-psychological explanation. In K. J. Gergen & M. M. Gergen (Eds.), *Historical social psychology* (pp. 259-280). Hillsdale, NJ: Lawrence Erlbaum.

Seldes, G. (1930). *Aristophanes' Lysistrata: A new version.* New York: Farrar & Rinehart.

Triandis, H. C. (1972). *The analysis of subjective culture.* New York: John Wiley.

Triandis, H. C. (1978). Some universals of social behavior. *Personality and Social Psychology Bulletin, 4,* 1-16.

Triandis, H. C. (1980). Values, attitudes, and interpersonal behavior. In H. E. Howe, Jr., & M. M. Page (Eds.), *Nebraska Symposium on Motivation 1979* (pp. 195-259). Lincoln: University of Nebraska Press.

Triandis, H. C., Shanmugam, A. V., & Tanaka, Y. (1966). Interpersonal attitudes among American, Indian, and Japanese students. *International Journal of Psychology, 1,* 177-206.

Wheelwright, P. (1951). *Aristotle.* Indianapolis: Bobbs-Merrill.

Wiggins, J. S. (1979). A psychological taxonomy of trait-descriptive terms: The interpersonal domain. *Journal of Personality and Social Psychology, 37,* 395-412.

Wish, M., Deutsch, M., & Kaplan, S. J. (1976). Perceived dimensions of interpersonal relations. *Journal of Personality and Social Psychology, 33,* 409-420.

10

Unexplored Barriers
The Role of Translation in Interpersonal Communication

ANNA BANKS ●
STEPHEN P. BANKS ● *University of Idaho*

This chapter addresses the frequent use of translation in interpersonal-intercultural encounters. A scheme is developed that identifies three primary approaches to translation—translation as mediation, translation as creation, and translation as domination. The central problem, relevant contexts, and researcher demands for each approach are explored. Translation is viewed as an intervening variable in intercultural research. As such, the process of translation is considered to be a threat to the reliability and validity of data gleaned from material that has been translated.

At first it seems difficult to identify instances when translation is immediately relevant to interpersonal-intercultural communication. Journal articles, edited volumes, and monographs that address intercultural communication are conspicuously devoid of translation as an interactional phenomenon. It is understandable that accounts of translation are rare in such reports because, logically, interpersonal communication requires a degree of mutual familiarity to be "interpersonal" (Miller, 1978), and the obvious barrier of different languages and cultures that would call for the services of a translator[1] could be assumed to forestall the development of familiarity.

On the other hand, a bit of probing reveals that translation often is active behind the scenes of very significant interpersonal exchanges in intercultural settings. At least three types of situations link up interpersonal communication, intercultural settings, and translation. The existence of these types of situations serves as the warrant for our exploration of translation as an intervening variable in the communicative experience per se and in research on interpersonal communication in intercultural contexts.

The first type of situation involves third party translation of discourse produced (typically) by one person for another person when neither knows the other's language. Although, for most researchers, this is likely to be the epitomizing case of interpersonal-intercultural communication that entails translation, it is not particularly commonplace. Interlingual service encounters, of course, are becoming widespread in the United States and elsewhere; however, only a few types of service encounters approach "interpersonalness," such as those in health care and legal settings, which tend to foster repeated contacts between practitioner and client. A nonservice encounter that qualifies as the first type of translation situation is found in the experience of one of the authors while a graduate student in California. A friend introduced him to a student who is speech and hearing disabled. Because the author does not know American Sign Language, and the friend is an ASL translator, the friend translated for the author and the new acquaintance. Over the course of a year, the three met for dinner regularly before evening seminars and enjoyed many interpersonal, interlingual conversations.

The second and third types of situations are perhaps more common to intercultural communication researchers. The second type comprises translations of interpersonal communication by speakers who share a common language but whose conversation is translated for an audience who does not know their language. The paradigm case of this situation is the translation of drama, film, interviews, documentary video, or other interaction for a radio or television audience in a different language setting.

The third type of situation involves translation that is crucial to scholars of intercultural communication—the translation of data from the source language to the language of analysis or reporting. Intercultural communication research by its very nature entails crossing boundaries—cultural and linguistic—and, as Klein (1982, p. 134) aptly stated, "when data cross borders, translation is needed." Consequently, most of the work currently being conducted in the field of intercultural communication involves, at some level, the use of translated data.

Despite the occurrence of translation in these communication situations, translation itself remains a field "in search of theory" (Toury, 1980). The thesis of this chapter is that, in translated conversations and in the analysis of data that have been subjected to translation, the translation process is not an innocent party but potentially acts as an intervening variable and deserves study as such. Below we set forth three approaches to translation and demonstrate that aspects of all three are relevant to the analysis of interpersonal communication in intercultural contexts. We position each approach, however, as being particularly relevant to specific types of context and as deserving focused attention when understanding translated interaction in each type of context. Most centrally, we hope to sensitize intercultural researchers to the need to include translation as a key threat to validity in their scholarship.

The age of translation studies is "very much in its infancy" (Schulte, 1985, p. 1), and one of the key questions facing intercultural scholars— but one all too often left unaddressed—is this: What is translation? We take *translation,* in its simplest sense, to be the rendering of information in one linguistic code into another code (see Carbaugh, 1985). However, we recognize and make central to our argument that translation is interpretive, constitutive, and ideological. Translation in this perspective is "so much more than a word-for-word code-switching process" (Gonzalez, 1989, p. 487). Thus we concur with Nida (1964, p. 97) that "the model for [translation] . . . must be a communication model, and the principles must be primarily sociolinguistic in the broad sense of the term."

THE NATURE OF TRANSLATION

There is widespread disagreement among scholars as to how translation should be conceptualized. The broadest, most encompassing definitions come from a hermeneutic perspective. For example, Gadamer states, "The process of translation comprises in its essence the whole secret of human understanding of the world and of social communication" (in Schulte, 1985, p. 1).

Other researchers, such as Gerver (1976), prefer to avoid the term *translation* altogether, substituting *interpretation*—in the general sense of the word. Thus, by implication, from this perspective, the translation of one language to another is opened up for ideological, cultural, and personal biases.

Some scholars, like Roman Jakobson, take a more overtly political approach to translation. Jakobson (1966) asks, "Translation of what messages? betrayer of what values?" (in Kelly, 1979, p. 219). In the same vein, Glassgold (1987, p. 20) proposes that "there is a direct connection between politics and translation" and warns that, while the practice of translation facilitates the actualization of the "global village," it can just as easily be an instrument of "obfuscation and propaganda" (p. 21).

Other approaches to translation are more explicitly communicational in their orientation. For example, Pergnier (1977, p. 203) emphasizes that "translation is an interplay between a message and two linguistic systems," and the translator is a mediator between the languages and between the individuals and their communities as well.

Pergnier's approach is echoed by Ross (1981), who believes that, while translation acts to bridge the gap between one individual or group and another, we must acknowledge the translator as an active third party in that interaction. Thus he says, "Translation does not mediate transparently between author and audience, but is itself articulative and judicative" (Ross, 1981, p. 17).

While the foregoing perspectives on translation vary in some of their basic assumptions, they are not entirely inconsistent with each other. Several similarities among them can be deduced. First, each view recognizes that translation is an active, ongoing process. Second, the process involves a series of decisions and judgments that must be made by the translator. Third, by implication, all translations encompass an element of interpretation. Fourth, the process of translating from one linguistic system to another is also the process that facilitates interaction between one culture and another. In that process, the translator functions as the controller and source of an intervening variable who has the potential to influence the nature of the ensuing communication.

Despite the similarities drawn above, the debate over the nature and role of translation has not been concluded. Philosophers, linguists, and others interested in translation theory continue to question its relation to meaning and social action (e.g., Kirk, 1986; Malone, 1988; Newmark, 1988; Rose, 1981; Warren, 1989). As a way to impose some structure on this debate, we organize these views into three major approaches to translation. The term *approaches* here refers globally to one's philosophy about, account of, and interests in the activity of translating; consequently, the approaches are not necessarily mutually exclusive. The approaches can be identified by their treatment of translation's function in discourse, its relation to meaning, and its central problematic. We label the three approaches *translation as mediation, translation as creation,* and *translation as domination.*

Translation as Mediation

Quine (1959) argues that the correlation of semantics between different languages is indeterminate and also that whether meanings expressed in one language can be transformed into the same meanings expressed in another language is undecidable. Quine (1959, p. 169), therefore, advocates linguistic transfer as a pragmatic matter, a semantic correlation in the form of a "working dictionary" between languages.

Quine's approach to translation is in the tradition of Wittgenstein, who viewed translation as "a mathematical task" and the translation of one language to another as "quite analogous to a mathematic *problem* [italics in original]" (quoted in Steiner, 1975, p. 275).

The line of thought exemplified by Wittgenstein supports the belief that translation is a mechanical transfer of meanings from one language to another. Meanings are assumed to inhere in texts, and the act of translating mediates between systems, ferrying meaning back and forth. From this perspective, meaning is treated as ostensive reference (Bagwell, 1986) in messages, and its central problematic is accuracy.

One of the most basic problems faced by researchers using data in a language other than that in which the analysis will be conducted is whether the translation they are working with is accurate. All language is characterized by ambiguity, and any researcher using language data must deal with problems of denotation and connotation, or what Gonzalez (1989, p. 495) calls "invariance of content" and "stylistic equivalence." The problems of ambiguity are amplified when the data require not only interpretation but also translation. Steiner (1975, p. 45) somewhat negates this issue when he states that "any model of communication is at the same time a model of translation, of a vertical or horizontal transfer of significance." We think it is more complex than this and an issue worthy of further consideration.

Accuracy of translation is paramount in interpersonal communication situations. Most translations in this context are cases of simultaneous translation, such as that conducted at summit conferences of world leaders and in certain service encounters. In a review of empirical studies on the process and results of simultaneous translation, Gerver (1976, p. 183) found that, when translators devote at least 75% of their time to simultaneous listening and speaking, "over 85 percent of the source-language text was correctly interpreted."

Gerver categorized the 15% inaccuracies into six types: (a) omission, or not processing the information when there is overload; (b) escape, or cutting off the input; (c) error, or incorrect processing and failure to correct; (d) queuing, or delaying responses during heavy load periods and catching up during any lulls that occur; (e) filtering, or systematic omission of certain types of information; and (f) approximation, or less precise response when there is not time for details.

Although Gerver considers 85% correct as a good average, we find it problematic. A 15% error in conversational understanding could mean the difference between a friend being sent to the *gallery* or being sent to the *galley* or the *gallows*. Moreover, if a 15% error rate is not acceptable in other forms of data reduction in research, it should not be acceptable for translated data used in social science studies.

The 15% rate of inaccuracies becomes crucial in situations where issues of national and international concern are being discussed and where the life of the interactants is concerned. Simultaneous translation facilitates communication between national leaders who do not speak each other's language. It is also the method by which leaders of other nations and cultures are able to communicate their message beyond their own cultural and linguistic boundaries. For example, after the recent elections in Nicaragua, former president Daniel Ortega gave a series of interviews to U.S. reporters. What the national television audiences heard on the nightly news or in the lengthy interview Ortega granted the *MacNeil/Lehrer NewsHour* was not just Ortega's voice but also the voice of a translator. Moreover, what the audience made sense of was the text created by the translator, not the Sandinista leader. As Newmark (1980) stated: "In the search for equivalence of an appropriate linguistic match the translator himself [herself] acts as both reader of the source text and the author of the target text." In other words, Newmark emphasizes that the text that results from the translation from one language to another is "created" by the translator, and any inaccuracies are, in this approach, assignable to the translator.

As the population of the United States becomes increasingly multilingual, the need for translation between individuals in service encounters is growing exponentially (Sanders, 1989). One area of particular concern is in the health care industry. Diaz-Duque (1989) studied the problems faced by monolingual Spanish-speaking patients seeking medical attention at the University of Iowa Hospitals and Clinics. Although the hospital offers some Spanish/English translation services and a "language bank" to help those needing translation services in other languages, the author found that the services are inadequate in terms of numbers and competence of translators:

> A widespread misconception exists that bilingualism automatically qualifies a person to interpret in any setting. Few health professionals and their patients are aware of the complexities involved in interpreting or translating from one language to another. (Diaz-Duque, 1989, p. 95)

Based on her own experiences as a translator in a medical setting, Diaz-Duque identified a number of problems associated with accuracy in translation for interpersonal encounters between patient and physician. She demonstrated that inaccurate translation in the medical context can result in misdiagnoses, reduced patient-physician rapport, inferior treatments, and poor patient compliance with treatments.

Similar problems are found in the legal/judicial context. According to a recent *Time* magazine estimate, 43,000 requests for translation in 60 languages are made annually in federal courts alone. Municipal courts in major cities each issue between 40,000 and 50,000 translation requests per year.

The problem is not only the sheer volume of requests for translation but the quality of the translators provided. Often a defendant will bring a family member who speaks some English, or an employee at the courtroom who has knowledge of the source language will be hired as a translator for the duration of the trial. There is no standard certification of translators required by the U.S. justice service at this time, and only a few states test their translators for language skills. Consequently, as Sanders (1989, p. 65) notes, "Horror stories regularly fill court dockets." Sanders cites one case in which the prosecutor asked whether the testimony of a Polish-speaking witness was lengthier than the English translation. "Yes," responded the Polish interpreter, "but everything else was unimportant." Such inaccuracies in interpretation have consequences that go beyond simple cases of misunderstanding, because it is on the basis of written and oral testimonies—in their translated form—that guilt or innocence is determined.

The task, then, for intercultural researchers and practitioners alike is twofold. It is not only to strive for semantic fidelity in translation through the use of experts in the languages involved and in translation as a professional practice but it also is to bear in mind that meaning equivalency entails accounting for cultural and situational differences when translation occurs.

Translation as Creation

Translation has been strongly influenced by recent work in hermeneutics, poststructuralism, and postmodernism. Scholars who adhere to these perspectives argue that all discourse is a form of translating previous texts into new texts (Steiner, 1975), and no text is ever repeated identically (de Man, 1985). Translating thus becomes transmuting; the translator becomes an author/speaker; and sociocultural features of discourse become central to meaning.

The first approach, translation as mediation, focuses on discourse in which participants are aware of the need for and occurrence of translation in their communication. Translation as creation, on the other hand, is an approach that is especially apt for understanding contexts in which participants are unaware of the translation of their communication. We reemphasize that all three approaches are relevant to every instance of translation; our claim is that each approach is particularly suited to the analysis of translation in specific kinds of circumstances.

Translation as creation takes meaning to be socioculturally conditioned and independent of the intentions of sources. Its central problematic is the preservation of the life of the original: Scholars and practitioners alike struggle with the incommutability of social and cultural knowledge that creates and is expressed in different languages. When historical, cultural, or political documents are translated for a new linguistic community, or when intercultural data acquired in one language setting are translated for analysis and reporting in another, problems of cultural equivalency become paramount.

The distinction between linguistic equivalency and cultural equivalency is compounded by the emic-etic distinction discussed by Brislin (1983, 1986). Borrowing from the original sense of the term in linguistics and modifying it somewhat, Brislin frames the *etic* as those aspects of a phenomenon that have a common meaning across cultures—that is, the "core meaning." The *emic* refers to those aspects of a phenomenon that are different across cultures.

Brislin uses the etic-emic distinction in a discussion of how standard measures for use in structured interviews or questionnaires (common tools in interpersonal-intercultural research) are translated for use in different cultures and language groups. Brislin (1986, pp. 143-149) provides 12 guidelines for preparing items or modifying existing items for use in a variety of different cultures. Briefly, these guidelines are as follows: (a) Use short, simple sentences of fewer than 16 words; (b) employ the active rather than the passive voice; (c) repeat nouns instead of using pronouns; (d) avoid metaphors and colloquialisms; (e) avoid the subjunctive; (f) add sentences to provide context for key ideas; (g) avoid adverbs telling *where* and *when*; (h) avoid possessive forms where possible; (i) use specific rather than general terms; (j) avoid words indicating vagueness regarding some event or thing, for example, *perhaps* or *maybe*; (k) use wording familiar to the translators; and (l) avoid sentences with two different verbs if the verbs suggest two different actions.

We list these guidelines because, while they indicate a strong concern for the accuracy of translated data, they are unrealistic if researchers wish to study issues of interpersonal communication across cultures. Our criticism is not so much aimed at the use of these guidelines for translating items used to *collect* data (although some of Brislin's assumptions might be problematic even for data collection), our concern is more with their application to data already collected.

A careful review of Brislin's suggestions reveals that his guidelines do not reflect all practices by members of a culture in their everyday speech. For example, in the last few years, a host of studies have demonstrated that metaphors are part of everyday talk and that the speaker's choice of metaphor is significant to the ongoing meanings in communication (e.g., Lakoff & Johnson, 1980; Sacks, 1978; Smith & Eisenberg, 1987). The problem is that, because everyday language is littered with colloquialisms and metaphors, cross-cultural interpersonal researchers inevitably will be forced to translate them in interview and questionnaire responses. We agree with Brislin that these items are very difficult to translate; the fact remains, however, that most researchers must make sure that they are translated in some form, and the goal, therefore, becomes one of preserving the meaning of the original.

In addition, some of Brislin's guidelines are not applicable in all language communities. For speakers of Mandarin Chinese, for example, to avoid using passive constructions where English speakers would use the active voice would be considered grammatically incorrect or socially impolite. Most troublesome is the assumption that there are conceptual equivalencies across cultures in all situations. Obviously, this is not the case. The Navaho do not include the idea of "relocate" in their semantic repertoire; when translators searched for a term to convey the idea that the Navaho should be relocated to settle a long-standing conflict over sacred lands with the Hopi, the best Navaho term selected connoted "disappear and never be seen again" (Lujan, personal communication, 1989; also see Steinfatt, 1989, for a review of relevant literature).

The usual method used by scholars of intercultural communication to counteract problems such as these is back-translation (Brislin, 1986, p. 160). Back-translation, however, only tests the reliability of coders to provide lexical equivalencies in the first language (L1) from those derived in the second language (L2) by a translator when moving from L1 to L2 originally. As such, back-translation optimally confirms semantic correspondences but cannot confirm whether cultural equivalencies have been accomplished. Back-translating the Navaho term reliably yielded the concept "relocate" in the translation context; however, it consistently failed to yield the sense of loss and longing in the Navaho sociocultural experience with the term. We advocate sensitivity to key cultural terms and concepts and recommend discussion among translators and researchers to derive both equivalence and incompatibilities of cultural meanings. These derivations and discussions should be reported in research studies as explications of translated data.

Translation as Domination

Translation as domination considers more fully than the approaches mentioned above the nature of the translator and the influence of the actual instance of sourcing and receiving translated discourse. Evolving from the line of inquiry called "the politics of interpretation" in literary criticism (e.g., Mitchell, 1983), this politically oriented approach to translation recognizes that meanings are emergent in hearers'/readers' experience of the text but that, simultaneously, speakers/authors constrain meanings by their communicative actions. Moreover, this approach explicitly recognizes that power relations are both encoded in and partially constituted by discourse.

The main problematic for translation in this approach is "to find the ideological devices that permit elements from one discursive formation (or register) to become part of another" (Klor de Alva, 1989, p. 144). Klor de Alva (1989, p. 144) illustrates the point by the example of preserving "colonial discourse" through translation, in which the ways of expression permit ideologies "to pass from one discourse (say religion or philology) to another (like politics or economics) in order to authorize and make possible the ends of colonial control."

Shaw (1987) addressed ideology in translation by calling for greater attention to "anthropological issues" by translators. That is, a greater emphasis needs to be placed on accounting for the interactive nature of culture and its effect on the communication process and on subjects' meanings.

Addressing these concerns in social science research, Shaw criticizes the typical approach that has the researcher (and not the members of the culture) as the final authority on a given practice. In Shaw's (1987, p. 26) model, *ideology* is defined as "a system of beliefs and observances relating to origins, present conditions, and the future." He proposes that researchers consider more fully surface- and deep-structure issues. Surface-structure issues are products and activities of a culture that can easily be viewed by an outside observer. Deep-structure concerns are the implicit meanings and assumptions held by members of a culture. Intercultural communication scholars have examined both surface- and deep-structure issues, but often the two levels—one explicit and easily available, the other implicit and hard to access—are not accounted for when translation takes place.

Because the translator acts as a mediator, his or her function affects both the surface-structure and the deep-structure levels, but it is at the level of deep structure that the role of the translator becomes most problematic. Deep-structure issues often remain unarticulated, and the translator may be unconscious of his or her own ideology and influences on the translated text at this level.

Issues of ideology permeate both surface-structure and deep-structure aspects. At the surface level, Glassgold (1987) notes, many myths about a given culture have developed from a mistranslation of the cultural icons of one people by another. At the deep-structure level, ideological issues are closely allied with the issues of interpretation and preservation and the issues of accuracy discussed above. That is, the translator must make a decision about how a word or phrase will be translated, and that decision invokes not only the linguistic and cultural knowledge of the translator but also the translator's own cultural, political, and value orientation to the world.

An example from a recent news story illustrates these issues of ideology at both the surface-structure and the deep-structure levels. The example centers on the translation of letters exchanged between two Chinese students, both graduate students at a university in the western United States.

In October 1989, following the previous summer's turmoil in the People's Republic of China, one Chinese student received a threatening letter in Chinese from one of his countrymen at the same university. He reported the incident to the police and presented the unsigned letter as evidence. The police decided to investigate the matter and quickly identified the author. After consulting with two Chinese-speaking professors at the students' university, the authorities decided to drop the incident, stating "the professors indicated the anonymous nature of the letter, coupled with recent events in China, could have implied a veiled threat. . . . Both agreed the content and apparent meaning of the letter had been correctly interpreted by authorities during the initial investigation" (Olsen, 1989, p. 12).

Several details add to the complexity of this debate over the "correct" translation of the initial letter. The recipient of the letter, WKW, had become an unofficial spokesperson for Chinese students at his university. He had recently attended a national meeting of Chinese students and was gaining high visibility on campus. The author, JL, a former Chinese student organization leader at the same university, had recently resigned from his post because of differences with other students. The letter cautioned WKW to "stop showing off." Other Chinese students at the university were upset with the authorities' decision to drop the matter. They said the letter's intent and force were not accurately conveyed in a literal translation. Moreover, they argued, the letter echoed language used in the *People's Daily,* a Chinese Communist party newspaper that had warned overseas Chinese students not to criticize the government. A local newspaper editor's sage understatement observed the "police officers are at a disadvantage in this situation due to their lack of fluency in Chinese" (Bird, 1989). Yet another Chinese student from the same university retorted, "A normal American wouldn't understand how much pressure the Chinese students here are under . . . I don't think anyone in his right mind would take this as a caution" (Olsen, 1989, p. 12).

This incident illustrates one aspect of the ideological elements in all translation: Translators can miss the ideological implications of texts they are translating. If we accept the claim that all discourse contains ideological elements, the job of the translator becomes all the more complex and all the more influential. To effectively deal with issues pertaining to ideology, intercultural researchers using translated data must acknowledge and account for the pervasiveness of ideology and focus not just on the surface-level words and the text but on the historical, political, and cultural circumstances under which that text was created.

CONCLUSION

The central argument of this chapter is that the process of translation acts as an intervening variable in intercultural interaction and research. As such, the process should be considered a threat to the reliability and validity of data gleaned from material that has been translated. Our scheme can be summarized as in Table 10.1.

Each of the three approaches contributes much to the understanding of the role translation plays in everyday social life and social research. Any instance of translation benefits from analysts asking pertinent questions that are grounded in all three approaches. Certain contexts of interaction, however, demand that special attention be given to particular facets of the translation problem. This scheme aligns representative contexts with the conceptual approach that focuses most directly on the problems inherent in the context type. For each context/approach pair, we have included a specific caveat for researchers in terms of the peculiar demands that pair places on responsible analysis and reporting of research encompassing translation.

TABLE 10.1 Approaches to Analyzing Translation

·Approach	Problematic	Relevant Contexts	Researcher Demands
Translation as mediation	accuracy	simultaneous translation	translator linguistic and professional competence
Translation as creation	preservation	translated research data	cultural differences in sources
Translation as domination	ideology	news reports political, social and cultural analyses	translators' and sources' deep structural meanings

In translation-as-mediation contexts, where simultaneous translation occurs and the parties are aware of the intervening role of the translator, the accuracy problematic demands that researchers assess translators' competence in both the languages involved and the professional techniques of translation. In translation-as-creation contexts, the signal issue is the integrity of translated texts as research data. As such, researchers need to focus attention on assessing how well cultural differences in the sources of data are reflected in the process of translation. Mere back-translating will not always assure full transfer of cultural meaning, and reporting of discussions and the bases of translation decisions is required. Finally, in translation-as-domination contexts, such as the production of news items or analyses of political, social, and cultural institutions, analysts should strive to account for translators' and data sources' deep structural meanings as they might affect the creation of texts in translation.

All of the translation contexts we have encountered have been assignable to one of these three context/approach pairs. We are hopeful that our assemblage of theoretical positions on translation and related implications in this scheme will contribute to improved research on intercultural-interpersonal communication. Research on translation per se no doubt will focus on specific aspects of theory and practice; intercultural research will benefit by remaining cognizant of the potential impacts of all three approaches to translation.

NOTE

1. We acknowledge the commonplace use of the term *interpretation* to mean the rendering of oral communication from L1 to L2. However, we use the term *translation* to include the rendering of both oral and written texts from L1 to L2 not because interpretive work is any less present or influential in the rendering of oral discourse (we would argue that, after all, every instance of communication entails interpretation) but to retain the common label of *translation* as the practice of mediating between code systems and to avoid confounding *interpretation* in the sense of meaning-construction with its sense of providing a rendition of a text.

REFERENCES

Bagwell, J. (1986). *American formalism and the problem of interpretation.* Houston: Rice University Press.

Bird, K. (1989, October 29). Letter a warning to Chinese student. *The Idahonian,* p. A4.

Brislin, R. W. (1983). Cross-cultural psychology. *Annual Review of Psychology, 34,* 363-400.

Brislin, R. W. (1986). The wording and translation of research instruments. In W. J. Lonner & J. W. Berry (Eds.), *Field methods in cross-cultural research* (pp. 137-164). Newbury Park, CA: Sage.

Carbaugh, D. (1985). Cultural communication and organizing. In W. B. Gudykunst, L. P. Stewart, & S. Ting-Toomey (Eds.), *Communication, culture, and organizational processes* (pp. 30-47). Beverly Hills, CA: Sage.

de Man, P. (1985). *The lesson of Paul de Man: Yale French studies.* New Haven, CT: Yale University Press.

Diaz-Duque, O. F. (1989). Communication barriers in medical settings: Hispanics in the United States. *International Journal of the Sociology of Language, 79,* 93-102.

Gerver, D. (1976). Empirical studies of simultaneous interpretation: A review and model. In R. W. Brislin (Eds.), *Translation: Applications and research* (pp. 165-207). New York: Gardner.

Giesbers, H. (1985). Sociolinguistics and ideology. *Sociolinguistics, 15,* 2-11.

Glassgold, P. (1987). Translation: Culture's driving wedge. *Translation Review, 23,* 18-21.

Gonzalez, C. F. (1989). Translation. In M. Asante & W. B. Gudykunst (Eds.), *Handbook of international and intercultural communication* (Vol. 14, 2nd ed., pp. 484-501). Newbury Park, CA: Sage.

Kaye, L. (1990, February). Automating translators. *World Press Review,* p. 75.

Kelly, L. G. (1979). *The true interpreter: A history of translation theory in the West.* New York: St. Martin's.

Kirk, R. (1986). *Translation determined.* Oxford: Clarendon.

Klein, F. (1982). Trends in translation. *Babel, 28*(3), 134-139.

Klor de Alva, J. (1989). Language, politics, and translation: Colonial discourse and Classical Nahuatl in New Spain. In R. Warren (Ed.), *The art of translation: Voices from the field* (pp. 143-162). Boston: Northeastern University Press.

Lakoff, G., & Johnson, M. (1980). *Metaphors we live by.* Chicago: University of Chicago Press.

Malone, J. (1988). *The science of linguistics in the art of translation.* Albany: State University of New York Press.

Miller, G. R. (1978). The current status of theory and research in interpersonal communication. *Human Communication Research, 4,* 164-178.

Mitchell, W. (Ed.). (1983). *The politics of interpretation.* Chicago: University of Chicago Press.

Newmark, P. (1980). The translation of metaphor. *Babel, 26*(2), 93-100.

Newmark, P. (1988). *A textbook of translation.* New York: Prentice-Hall.

Nida, E. (1964). *Toward a science of translation.* Leiden: E. J. Brill.

Olsen, K. (1989, October 9). Warning letter's author identified. *The Idahonian,* p. A1.

Pergnier, M. (1977). Language-meaning and message-meaning: Toward a sociolinguistic approach to translation. In D. Gerver & H. W. Sinaiko (Eds.), *Language interpretation and communication.* New York: Plenum.

Quine, W. (1959). Meaning and translation. In R. Brower (Ed.), *On translation* (pp. 148-172). Cambridge, MA: Harvard University Press.

Rose, M. (Ed.). (1981). *Translation spectrum: Essays in theory and practice.* Albany: State University of New York Press.

Ross, S. D. (1981). Translation and similarity. In M. G. Rose (Ed.), *Translation spectrum: Essays in theory and practice* (pp. 8-22). Albany: State University of New York Press.

Sacks, S. (1978). (Ed.). *On metaphor.* Chicago: University of Chicago Press.

Sanders, A. (1989, May 29). *Libertad* and *justicia* for all. *Time,* p. 65.

Schulte, R. (1985). Editorial: Translation and reading. *Translation Review, 18,* 1-2.

Shaw, R. D. (1987). The translation context: Cultural factors in translation. *Translation Review, 23,* 25-29.

Smith, R. C., & Eisenberg, E. M. (1987). Understanding conflict at Disneyland: Analyzing employee interpretations of root metaphors. *Communication Monographs, 54,* 367-380.

Steiner, G. (1975). *After Babel: Aspects of language and translation.* New York: Oxford University Press.

Steinfatt, T. (1989). Linguistic relativity: Toward a broader view. In S. Ting-Toomey & F. Korzeny (Eds.), *Language, communication, and culture: Current directions* (pp. 35-75). Newbury Park, CA: Sage.

Toury, G. (1980). *In search of a theory of translation.* Tel Aviv: Porter Institute.

Warren, R. (1989). Introduction. In R. Warren (Ed.), *The art of translation: Voices from the field* (pp. 3-9). Boston: Northeastern University Press.

II

INTERCULTURAL-INTERPERSONAL COMMUNICATION

11

Social Information for Uncertainty Reduction During Initial Interactions

HYUN O. LEE • *Wake Forest University*

FRANKLIN J. BOSTER • *Michigan State University*

Past research on uncertainty reduction theory produced conflicting results regarding the effect of cultural similarity on subsequent uncertainty reduction behavior, primarily due to its methodological shortcomings. Employing face-to-face interaction, the current study attempts to recast uncertainty reduction theory from a cognitive perspective. The data indicate that people perceive intercultural partners to be less similar to themselves and that they report less attributional confidence and interpersonal attraction as compared with intracultural partners. As for information-seeking behavior, the study shows that the social penetration process is more difficult in intercultural initial interaction as participants who interacted with intercultural partners rarely requested intimate information. Unexpectedly, however, the effect of anticipation of future interaction upon information-seeking behavior is found to be minimal in this study.

A considerable amount of research attention has been given to communication processes during the early stages of acquaintanceship (Berger & Calabrese, 1975; Duck, 1976; Kellerman, 1986; Osterkamp, 1980; Sunnafrank & Miller, 1981). In particular, scholars endeavor to understand the epistemology of relationship development during an initial interaction. Several researchers suggest that the principle of similarity-attraction explains how an actor decides whether to pursue or to avoid new relationships. It is well documented that, the higher the perceived similarity level between two individuals, the greater their attention to each other (Byrne, 1971; Byrne & Clore, 1966). Scholars provide three explanations of this finding. First, Heider (1958) emphasizes the homeostatic characteristics of the elements within the dyad. According to him, we are cognitively consistent if we like those who hold attitudes similar to our own. Second, Byrne (1971) proposes a reinforcement explanation. He contends that attraction is a function of the extent to

AUTHORS' NOTE: An earlier version of the chapter was presented at the annual meeting of the International Communication Association, Dublin, Ireland, 1990.

which reciprocal rewards occur during interaction, with attitudinal similarity being a major source of reward in dyadic encounters (Clore & Bryne, 1974). Third, Berger and Calabrese (1975) advocate uncertainty reduction theory to explain the similarity-attraction hypothesis.

Uncertainty reduction theory by Berger and Calabrese (1975) approaches the process of an initial interaction from a communication perspective. Originally, the theory postulated 7 axioms and 21 theorems specifying relationships among the amount of communication, nonverbal affiliative expressiveness, information seeking, intimacy level of communicative content, reciprocity, similarity, liking, and uncertainty reduction. Subsequent research and conceptualizations elaborated the theory, including specific antecedents and strategies of uncertainty reduction (Berger, 1979), events that increase uncertainty in personal relationships (Planalp & Honeycutt, 1985), the role of language (Berger & Bradac, 1982; Sherblom & Rheenen, 1984), and shared communication networks (Parks & Adelman, 1983). Moreover, the theory has been extended to well-established relationships, such as friendships (Parks & Adelman, 1983; Planalp & Honeycutt, 1985).

Berger and Calabrese (1975) argue that, when strangers meet, their primary concern is to reduce uncertainty and hence increase predictability about the behavior of both themselves and others. Uncertainty reduction theory asserts that reducing uncertainty is central to at least two processes: prediction and explanation. At the beginning of an encounter, one important task for interactants is to predict the other's actions; a second task is to develop causal explanations for observed behaviors. In this model, the perceived similarity reduces uncertainty, which enhances interpersonal attraction. Because uncertainty itself is left as a nominal construct in the theory, Clatterbuck (1979) developed an operationalization of uncertainty in an initial interaction through measures of attributional confidence. Even though there are several variations of Clatterbuck's original scale (e.g., Parks and Adelman's measure), researchers generally equate uncertainty reduction with attributional confidence.

UNCERTAINTY REDUCTION THEORY IN INTERCULTURAL INITIAL INTERACTION

This study applies uncertainty reduction theory to intercultural initial interaction to test the theory's generalizability. There are at least two significant implications of examining the initial stage of intercultural relationships. First, recent developments in theories of intergroup behavior suggest that intercultural initial interaction occurs in the matrix of the perceived dissimilarity between interactants (Allen & Wilder, 1979; Billig & Tajfel, 1973; Brown & Turner, 1981). Allen and Wilder (1979), for example, demonstrated that persons assumed a fellow in-group member possessed more beliefs similar to their own than did a member of the out-group even when they were categorized into groups on the basis of an arbitrary task. Billig and Tajfel (1973) reported similar findings. Accordingly, if the mere categorization of persons into groups without a realistic pretext for the classification is sufficient to lead to the perception of intergroup differences in beliefs and attitudes, then, it is necessary for intercultural scholars to address the functions of perceived dissimilarity for subsequent intercultural behaviors, as intercultural relationships render many differences between interactants—such as skin color, language, and communication styles—tangible.

Second, several intercultural studies indicate that, once intercultural communicators overcome the barriers of the initial interaction, culture is not a major factor in subsequent interaction. When close intracultural and intercultural relationships were compared, no difference was observed in either perceived similarity or perceptions of social penetration (Gudykunst, 1985b; Gudykunst, Chua, & Gray, 1987). Summarizing social penetration studies in the intercultural context, Gudykunst, Nishida, and Chua (1987, p. 176) stated that

> when relationships reach the point of close friendship, and the individuals are basing their predictions about their partner on psychological data, the degree of social penetration in which people engage should not differ in intracultural and intercultural relationships as a function of culture.

Therefore, investigating the initial stage of intercultural relationships may uncover an optimum way of overcoming the intercultural initial interaction barrier.

Of particular interest in this study is the function of cultural similarity to subsequent uncertainty reduction behavior during initial interactions. Because Berger and Calabrese (1975) did not specify the types of similarity to which their axioms apply, various operationalizations of similarity are observed. Although attitudinal similarity has received most attention in intracultural studies, intercultural scholars have paid special attention to the function of cultural similarity in determining subsequent attributional confidence and interpersonal attraction during an initial interaction. According to the axioms of uncertainty reduction theory, it is expected that persons in intracultural interaction (the culturally similar condition) will report a higher degree of attributional confidence and interpersonal attraction toward their partners when compared with those in intercultural interaction (the culturally dissimilar condition).

Nevertheless, results testing uncertainty reduction theory are mixed (Gudykunst, 1985a; Gudykunst & Nishida, 1984; Gudykunst, Yang, & Nishida, 1985). In a study of Japanese and North Americans, Gudykunst and Nishida (1984) discovered that cultural similarity did not have a significant effect on attributional confidence. Similarly, with Japanese subjects, Gudykunst, Nishida, Koike, and Shiino (1986) found an insignificant effect of cultural similarity on the uncertainty reduction variables. On the other hand, two studies yielded opposite results. In a study comparing intraethnic and interethnic relationships, Gudykunst (1986) reports that there is significantly more attributional confidence in intraethnic relationships than in interethnic ones. This finding is consistent with the prediction based on an axiom of uncertainty reduction theory. Yet, another study of Gudykunst (1985a) revealed a significant effect of cultural similarity on attributional confidence, with the mean score higher for culturally dissimilar acquaintances than for similar ones.

In addition, studies reveal that cultural similarity has no impact on interpersonal attraction. Gudykunst and Nishida (1984), for example, report that persons become attracted to their intercultural partners as much as they do to their intracultural partners. Similarly, surveying Japanese subjects, Gudykunst et al. (1986) report that intercultural partners are perceived to be no less attractive than intracultural partners by the Japanese subjects. Moreover, Gudykunst (1985a) reports that the culturally dissimilar condition elicited higher attraction than the culturally similar condition in an acquaintance relationship, a result that is also in conflict with previous findings that ethnic similarity is positively related to interpersonal attraction and relational intimacy during an initial interaction (Allen, 1976; Jones & Diener, 1976; Ting-Toomey, 1981).

This study postulates that these seemingly conflicting and negligible effects of cultural similarity on attributional confidence and interpersonal attraction can be attributed to the nature of the methods used in previous studies. The majority of these studies employed the bogus-stranger technique to manipulate cultural similarity. For instance, Gudykunst and Nishida (1984) asked subjects how they would behave when introduced to a stranger from their own (the culturally similar condition) or another culture (the culturally dissimilar condition) in a social gathering. However, this method suffers from a low degree of experimental realism. As a result, contrary to many findings in intergroup behavior research (Allen & Wilder, 1979; Billig & Tajfel, 1973), persons did not perceive the intercultural partners to be dissimilar to themselves (e.g., Gudykunst, 1985a). This failure to manipulate cultural similarity adequately, therefore, might have contributed to the negligible effect of cultural similarity on attributional confidence and interpersonal attraction.

Another frequently used method in previous studies was a retrospective technique in which subjects were instructed to select specific persons with whom they had relationships and to keep these individuals in mind while answering the questions. But relying on the subject's retrospective report is also a questionable strategy as one's ability to remember information in describing past events is not necessarily accurate (Fiske & Taylor, 1984) or unbiased (Snyder & Uranowitz, 1978). Given the absence of studies designed to systematically compare intracultural and intercultural face-to-face interactions, the effect of cultural similarity on subsequent attributional confidence and interpersonal attraction is difficult to assess.

Moreover, previous studies do not consider the role of many other important variables (e.g., language) for uncertainty reduction in intercultural initial interaction. Berger and Bradac (1982) argue that language plays a multifaceted role in reducing uncertainty. Similarly, Giles and Johnson (1981) suggest that the language, or dialect, spoken is a major factor employed by the member of one group to categorize others into an in-group/out-group dichotomy. Consequences of this categorization for subsequent intercultural interaction need to be addressed. Nevertheless, the role of language in intercultural initial interaction has been overlooked because previous methods do not allow the issue to be investigated.

A study by Imahori (1987) reinforces this contention. After comparing initial intracultural and intercultural interactions, he reported that one of the major factors that differentiated intercultural communication from intracultural communication is the language barrier observed in the former. The data revealed that subjects in intercultural interactions were involved far more frequently in clarification acts than those in intracultural settings. Imahori (1987) concluded that the major difference between intracultural and intercultural interactions was the language barrier effect. Similarly, Schneider and Jordan (1981) reported that English proficiency of the nonnative sojourner is one of the major predictors of interpersonal attraction in intercultural relationships. Taken together, it is possible that the weak effect of cultural similarity on the uncertainty reduction variables is due to subjects in previous studies responding to their culturally dissimilar partners based on cognitive scripts of initial interaction (Street & Giles, 1982) rather than on the presence of communication obstacles, such as language.

Finally, if the primary goal of the actors involved in the acquaintance process is to process information as a means of assessing the similarity between them so that uncertainty may be reduced, then the question of the extent to which intercultural and intracultural interactions are similar in information processing behavior is raised. In spite of recurrent claims that social information influences persons' attributions (Berger & Calabrese, 1975) and judgments (Hewes & Planalp, 1982; Sillars, 1982), the process by which intercultural interactants use social information to reduce uncertainty and make important social judgments has been ignored. Thus this study attempts to recast uncertainty reduction theory by examining the process of intracultural and intercultural face-to-face interactions with respect to the type and amount of social information processed to reduce uncertainty.

AN INFORMATION-BASED APPROACH TO UNCERTAINTY REDUCTION THEORY

It was mentioned earlier that the motivation of social actors to process information about their partners needs to be addressed to better understand the process of uncertainty reduction. This study contends that there are several reasons to expect the level of motivation to reduce uncertainty to be relatively low in intercultural initial interaction. First, if social actors are motivated to generate more knowledge about a target person when rewards are present (Berger, 1979), communication difficulties (Gudykunst, 1983a; Simard, 1981) and the language barrier (Imahori, 1987) may contribute to the lack of motivation to reduce uncertainty in intercultural interaction, as the cost to reduce uncertainty is too high. Second, Pettigrew (1986) suggests that affective reactions, such as anxiety, are one of the major by-products of inter-group communication. Similarly, Gudykunst (1987) contends that the intergroup relationship is characterized by the high level of anxiety experienced by the participants. Accordingly, it is speculated that the initial affective responses (e.g., anxiety) to out-group members in intercultural interaction may impede further uncertainty reduction attempts (Berger, 1986b). Finally, summarizing studies related to the contact hypothesis, Amir (1969) lists some of the favorable conditions that tend to render positive outcomes in intercultural interactions. However, because most intercultural initial interactions do not contain these favorable conditions (Hewstone & Brown, 1986; Rose, 1981), the motivational level to reduce uncertainty is expected to be low.

Consistent with the previous arguments, Chaikin, Derlega, Harris, Gregorio, and Boone (1973; cited in Chaikin & Derlega, 1976) obtained evidence of restricted communication in interethnic dyads, reporting that there is less self-disclosure within interethnic settings. Word, Zanna, and Cooper (1974) also indicated that subjects were found to be less verbally immediate, to make more speech errors, and to give shorter interviews to the interethnic partner compared with the intraethnic partner in a simulated job interview situation. Based on the previous discussion, therefore, the following hypothesis is posed:

> *Hypothesis 1:* Persons will seek less information in intercultural initial inter-action than they will in intracultural initial interaction.

In addition to quantitative differences in the amount of information required for uncertainty reduction, the current study also posits that the quality of interaction differs in initial intracultural and intercultural interactions. First, Sherif (1966) contends that out-group members are responded to in terms of their group identification. One of the major consequences of category-based intergroup communication is the deindividuation of out-group members (Miller & Brewer, 1984; Wilder, 1981). For example, Wilder (1981) shows that subjects recalled fewer individual characteristics of out-group members than of in-group members. Moreover, Rubin (1977, 1979) demonstrates that people process different kinds of information depending on the context in which their interaction occurs. She found that the use of demographic and background questions predominated in ambiguous situations. Recognizing that intercultural communication is characterized by its ambiguity (Ruben & Kealey, 1979), it is expected that demographic information will be used more extensively by social actors. Gudykunst's (1983a) finding that persons ask more questions about their partners' background in intercultural initial interaction is consistent with Rubin's findings. Taken together, the following hypothesis is advanced, given the contention that information concerning a target's demographic background is regarded as nonintimate (Altman & Taylor, 1973; Miller & Steinberg, 1975):

> *Hypothesis 2:* Persons will seek less intimate information in intercultural initial interaction than they will in intracultural initial interaction.

Consequently, because of low motivation to reduce uncertainty, there will be little information available to intercultural interactants to effectively predict the other's future behavior. Furthermore, if social actors primarily process demographic and nonintimate information about their intercultural partners, uncertainty will remain high, and the intercultural relationship will be unlikely to develop to the interpersonal level. This reasoning is consistent with Miller and Steinberg's (1975) developmental theory of interpersonal relationships. According to them, communicators need psychological-level data (intimate information) to move from a noninterpersonal relationship to an interpersonal relationship. Therefore, given the previous argument that information processing behavior in intercultural interaction is characterized by low motivation to reduce uncertainty as well as by relatively nonintimate information transfer, the following hypothesis is advanced:

Hypothesis 3: Persons in intercultural interaction will report less attributional confidence and interpersonal attraction toward their partners than those in intracultural interaction.

ANTICIPATION OF FUTURE INTERACTION AND UNCERTAINTY REDUCTION

This chapter explores the possibility that intercultural initial interactions differ from intracultural ones in the amount and type of information required to reduce uncertainty. Moreover, both attributional confidence and interpersonal attraction are expected to be mediated by the type and amount of information processed during the interaction. Given the argument that intercultural interaction is apt to suffer from a lack of motivation to reduce uncertainty, it is important to investigate the conditions under which persons actively seek information to reduce uncertainty in intercultural interaction. Researchers suggest that one of such situations is when future interaction is anticipated. Berger (1979) contends that persons will increase uncertainty reduction efforts as the perceived probability of future interaction with conversational partners increases. Consistent with Berger's (1979) contention, several researchers report that anticipation of future interaction influences subsequent recall (Douglas, 1985; Harvey, Yarkin, Lightner, & Town, 1980), attention (Berscheid, Graziano, Monson, & Dermer, 1976), and communication behavior (Douglas, 1987). Harvey et al. (1980) found that persons who expected future interaction with a stranger reported higher recall scores than persons who did not anticipate further interaction. Similarly, Douglas (1985) indicates that subjects recalled more information concerning a target's background and opinions/preferences when they anticipated future interaction. Berscheid et al. (1976) also reported that persons paid more attention to and recalled more detailed information about the anticipated date than the nondate. Furthermore, they liked their anticipated date significantly more than they liked their nondate.

Hypothesizing that uncertainty reduction appears most important when the probability of future interaction is not situationally fixed (e.g., instructed by researchers either to anticipate or not to anticipate future interaction), Douglas (1987) found that persons required to negotiate a second interaction asked significantly more questions than those in the other conditions. Moreover, the intergroup contact research suggests that superordinate goals (e.g., the future interaction) override cultural differences and thus reinforce the positive outcomes of intergroup contact (Amir, 1969; Miller & Brewer, 1984). Hence it is hypothesized that anticipation of future interaction with an intercultural partner enhances the social actor's motivation to process information:

> *Hypothesis 4:* Persons will seek more information in intercultural interaction if they anticipate future interaction with their intercultural partner than if they do not.

In addition, several studies have documented that the variable of dyadic composition (i.e., same sex versus opposite sex dyad) influences the social actor's communicative behavior in an initial interaction. For instance, a study by Shuter (1982) revealed that people ask more questions, especially regarding demographic types of information, in the opposite sex dyad than they do in the same sex dyad. On the other hand, Cline (1983) reports that females tend to make more self-disclosures in same sex dyads. Conversely, employing a retrospective technique, Gudykunst, Sodetani, and Sonoda (1987) found no significant effect of dyadic composition on the uncertainty reduction variables in intercultural interaction. With a more realistic research design, this study advances the following research question to discern the relative effects of dyadic composition on subsequent uncertainty reduction behavior in initial intracultural and intercultural interactions:

> *Research Question 1:* What are the effects of dyadic composition on attributional confidence, interpersonal attraction, and information-seeking behavior during initial intracultural and intercultural interactions?

Finally, this study includes the measure of one's extraversion as it is believed to influence an individual's information-seeking behavior. According to Eysenck (1973), the extravert is a person who is sociable, needs people with whom to talk, and craves excitement. On the other hand, the introvert is a person who is reserved, is distant toward other persons, and does not like excitement. Thus the extravert is apt to ask more questions than the introvert, and the amount of information obtained will subsequently influence attributional confidence and interpersonal attraction. However, due to the paucity of empirical studies on which to draw a specific hypothesis, the following research question is posed:

> *Research Question 2:* What are the effects of one's extraversion on attributional confidence, interpersonal attraction, and information-seeking behavior during initial intracultural and intercultural interactions?

METHODS

Subjects

Eighty undergraduate students (U.S. citizens) at a midwestern university participated in the experiment. They received extra credits for their participation.

Procedure

Upon arriving at the laboratory, each subject was matched randomly with one of four confederates. Prior to interaction, all subjects were informed that they would participate in a two-part experiment, the first part concerning impression making. They were asked to conduct two interviews to form an impression of their partners. Subjects were also told that their conversation would be audiotaped, and they could end the interview whenever they wished. The experimenter then described the experiment in one of two ways. For the future-interaction condition, subjects were told that they would be working with their interviewees on a small group problem-solving task after completing the interview. For the no-future-interaction condition, subjects were led to believe that the second phase of the study was a separate social perception experiment in which they would be working independently on different tasks. After the instructions, subjects were taken to a room where their interviews were audiotaped. To control for a possible order effect, one-half of the subjects interviewed the intracultural partner first, while the other half interviewed the intercultural partner first. Upon completion of each interview, subjects were asked to fill out a questionnaire measuring their perceptions of similarity, attributional confidence, interpersonal attraction, information on the introvert-extravert scale, and demographic information.

Design

This study employed a 2 × 2 × 2 mixed factorial design with a covariate (the introvert-extravert scale) in which anticipation of future interaction and dyadic composition are between-subjects factors and cultural similarity is a within-subjects factor. In manipulating cultural similarity, four students (two U.S. and two Korean students) previously unknown to the subjects were used as confederates. Each subject was matched with both a U.S. confederate (intracultural interaction) and a Korean confederate (intercultural interaction). Confederates were trained to standardize their verbal and nonverbal behaviors during the interviews. Specifically, they were trained to answer in three sentences or less per question and were also asked not to provide any unnecessary information or nonverbal behaviors. A check of the confederates' interviewing behavior was made by a rater, and it was found that 98% of the statements made by the confederates conformed to the instructions. Anticipation of future interaction was manipulated by differing instructions given to the participants before they interacted with the confederate. Finally, one-half of the subjects were matched with same sex partners, while the other half were paired with opposite sex partners. A total of 160 dyads were formed and analyzed for the study.

Instrumentation

The perception of similarity was assessed by five, seven-point Likert items developed by Parks and Adelman (1983). The mean of this distribution was 20.28 with a standard deviation of 5.18. The scores were distributed normally. The reliability of this index was estimated by coefficient alpha and found to be .83.

Attributional confidence was measured by six, seven-point Likert items developed by Parks (1978). The mean of this distribution was 18.59 with a standard deviation of 6.64. This distribution showed slight positive skewness. Coefficient alpha was .82.

Interpersonal attraction was assessed by two, seven-point Likert items from Byrne and Clore's (1966) Interpersonal Judgment Scale. The mean of this distribution was 10.81 with a standard deviation of 1.84. The scores were negatively skewed. The reliability of this index was found to be .76.

Finally, a subject's degree of extraversion was measured by Eysenck's (1973) short version of the introvert-extravert scale. The mean of the distribution was 8.65 with a standard deviation of 2.49.

The scores were negatively skewed. The reliability coefficient alpha was .52.

Identification of Questions

Recordings of the interviews were transcribed and analyzed by a specially designed coding scheme.[1] Two independent judges listened to each of the conversations and identified all questions requesting information from the interviewee. Only the participants' verbal behavior was included in the data analysis. The judges identified 2,199 questions for intracultural interaction and 2,167 questions for intercultural interaction, respectively.

RESULTS

Manipulation Check

The manipulation of cultural similarity was checked by asking participants to indicate on a seven-point Likert scale the extent to which they perceived the culture of their interview partner to be similar to or different from their own. The data were broken down by the culture of confederates and the participant's gender. Subsequently, an analysis of variance was performed. The results of the test revealed a substantial main effect of cultural similarity, such that participants perceived intracultural partners as being much more similar to themselves than intercultural partners ($F = 220.67$; df = 1, 78; $p < .000$). All other effects were trivial in magnitude. Because this study used multiple confederates to manipulate cultural similarity, it is necessary to break down these data by confederates to check for confederate effects. The results of Tukey's test indicate no main effect for confederates at either level of cultural similarity. Thus the manipulation of cultural similarity in this study was successful.

The participants were also asked to indicate whether or not they would be interacting with their current partner in the second phase of the study as a means of checking the manipulation of anticipation of future interaction. None of the participants failed to conform to the instruction of the anticipation of future-interaction manipulation.

In addition, because this study involves a repeated measure, the effect of the order of interaction on information-seeking behavior was assessed to delineate the possible testing effect. There was no main effect of the order of interaction ($F < 1$; df = 1, 78; $p = $ ns). Moreover, it did not interact with cultural similarity ($F = 1.82$; df = 1, 78; $p = $ ns) as well.

Thus the order of interaction did not influence the participants' information-seeking behavior.

Finally, as judgments of physical attractiveness are believed to influence the process of first impressions (Maruyama & Miller, 1981), this study employed the perception of the partner's physical attractiveness as a covariate to assess its effect on information-seeking behavior. No significant covariate effect was observed, indicating that the perception of physical attractiveness did not influence the social actors' information-seeking behavior in this study.

Perceptions of the Uncertainty Reduction Variables

A $2 \times 2 \times 2$ (the culture of the interviewee $\times$ dyadic composition $\times$ anticipation of future interaction) analysis of covariance (introversion-extraversion) was the basic analysis performed to discern the effects of the treatments on the dependent variables. First, the study shows that participants perceived intracultural partners as much more similar to themselves ($M = 23.19$) than intercultural partners ($M = 17.38$) when they engaged in a face-to-face interaction ($F = 76.64$; df = 1, 76; $p < .000$). This finding bolsters the contention that the manipulation of cultural similarity needs to be interaction based. Moreover, the data indicate a significant main effect of cultural similarity on attributional confidence ($F = 67.86$; df = 1, 76; $p < .000$) as participants reported a higher degree of attributional confidence for intracultural partners ($M = 21.38$) than for intercultural partners ($M = 15.81$). It was also found that persons reported a higher degree of attributional confidence when they were interacting with the same sex partner ($M = 19.83$) than with the opposite sex partner ($M = 17.39$), a difference statistically significant at the .05 level ($F = 5.27$; df = 1, 75; $p = .024$). Finally, the data reveal that participants perceived intracultural partners as more attractive ($M = 11.64$) than intercultural partners ($M = 9.99$)—a finding consistent with the hypothesis proffered ($F = 56.44$; df = 1, 76; $p < .000$).

Number and Types of Questions Asked

It was also hypothesized that the effects of cultural similarity on the uncertainty reduction variables would be mediated by social actors' information-seeking behavior. However, this study reveals no difference in the total number of questions asked between the intracultural interaction ($M = 27.45$) and intercultural interaction ($M = 26.04$) conditions. Thus the data do not support the hypothesis that persons will process less information in intercultural interaction due to the lack of

TABLE 11.1 The Number of Total Questions by Independent Variables: Means and Standard Deviations

	Intercultural Interaction		Intracultural Interaction	
	Same Sex	Opposite Sex	Same Sex	Opposite Sex
No future interaction	25.00 (8.45)	23.90 (13.89)	24.20 (9.92)	30.03 (16.24)
Future interaction	23.90 (10.09)	31.30 (8.30)	24.60 (14.44)	30.95 (10.89)

motivation to reduce uncertainty. The only factor approaching significance is the dyadic composition effect ($F = 3.40$; df = 1, 75; $p = .069$), with more questions being asked in opposite sex dyads ($M = 29.05$) than in same sex dyads ($M = 24.44$).

To investigate whether participants were motivated to process more information when they anticipated future interaction, the data were broken down by the culture of the interviewee, and an analysis of covariance was performed for intercultural dyads. No significant effect of anticipation of future interaction was observed ($F = 1.50$; df = 1, 75; p = ns), although people in the anticipation-of-future-interaction condition asked slightly more questions ($M = 27.63$) than those in the no-anticipation condition ($M = 24.45$).

As for the intracultural data, a similar pattern was observed; that is, participants did not change their information-seeking behavior as a function of anticipation of future interaction ($M = 27.13$ for the no-anticipation condition; $M = 27.78$ for the anticipation condition). The data did indicate a significant effect of dyadic composition, however ($F = 3.97$; df = 1, 75; $p = .05$). When interacting with opposite sex partners, persons asked significantly more questions ($M = 30.50$) than they did with same sex partners ($M = 24.40$). The means and standard deviations for all variables are displayed in Table 11.1.

Given the insignificant effect of cultural similarity on the total number of questions, the data were broken down by three levels of intimacy to see whether persons ask different types of questions depending upon the culture of their interview partners. Analyses of covariance were performed for each type of question to elicit the qualitative effects of cultural similarity on information-seeking behavior. First, a significant main effect of cultural similarity on nonintimate information was observed ($F = 12.44$; df = 1, 76; $p < .000$). Overall, persons asked nonintimate questions (e.g., general request and regarding

TABLE 11.2 Number of Questions by Three Intimacy Levels: Means and Standard Deviations

	Low Intimacy		Moderate Intimacy		High Intimacy	
Cells	M	SD	M	SD	M	SD
IE, SS, NI	10.85	3.91	11.30	6.35	2.85	1.87
IE, SS, FI	11.25	4.45	9.75	6.16	2.90	2.28
IE, OS, NI	11.90	6.44	9.30	5.90	2.70	2.87
IE, OS, FI	12.44	5.17	11.05	4.16	4.50	3.29
IR, SS, NI	8.95	3.68	10.40	5.54	4.55	3.35
IR, SS, FI	9.20	5.25	10.00	4.48	5.20	6.25
IR, OS, NI	10.35	4.31	12.95	9.06	6.55	6.91
IR, OS, FI	11.80	4.54	12.55	5.29	6.35	5.07

NOTE: IE = intercultural interaction; IR = intracultural interaction; SS = same sex dyad; OS = opposite sex dyad; NI = no future interaction, and FI = Future Interaction.

demographic type of information) more frequently in intercultural interaction ($M = 12.44$) than in intracultural interaction ($M = 10.08$). Second, the data show no difference between intercultural and intracultural interactions in the amount of moderately intimate information (e.g., activity, experience, preference type of questions). Third, it was also observed that highly intimate information (e.g., attitude, opinion, personality type of questions) was more extensively sought in intracultural interaction ($M = 5.66$) than in intercultural interaction ($M = 3.25$), consistent with the proposed hypothesis ($F = 17.34$; df = 1, 76; $p < .000$). Finally, this study also demonstrated that, in intercultural interaction, participants experienced more difficulties understanding their partners ($F = 32.10$; df = 1, 75; $p < .000$), as more clarification questions were observed in the intercultural condition ($M = 1.14$) than in the intracultural condition ($M = .24$). Table 11.2 summarizes the means and standard deviations for all variables broken down by three levels of intimacy.

DISCUSSION

This study approached the uncertainty reduction process during initial interactions from a cognitive perspective. In particular, efforts were made to learn the function of information-seeking behavior on the perception of similarity, attributional confidence, and interpersonal attraction in initial intercultural and intracultural interactions. It was shown that participants found intercultural partners to be less similar to themselves and, consequently, reported less attributional confidence and interpersonal attraction. These findings indicate strongly that the effect of cultural similarity on the uncertainty reduction variables, such as perceptions of similarity, attributional confidence, and interpersonal attraction, is robust when social actors are engaged in a face-to-face interaction. These findings help clarify the conflicting results of previous studies concerning the effect of cultural similarity on the uncertainty reduction variables, because the current findings not only are consistent with many of the interaction-based intergroup studies (Allen & Wilder, 1979; Billig & Tajfel, 1973) but are based on a more realistic research design.

However, the effect of cultural similarity on subsequent information-seeking behavior was found to be very limited, as participants asked almost an equal number of questions to same and different culture interviewees. This finding is surprising, given the argument that intercultural communication will be characterized by little motivation to seek information due to communication difficulties (Imahori, 1987; Simard, 1981) and high uncertainty at the onset of interaction (Gudykunst, 1983a). It is possible that at least two factors are responsible for this finding.

First, the task of impression-making may override the effect of cultural similarity. Many intergroup contact studies advocate the role of context for intergroup behavior (Amir, 1969; Hewstone & Brown, 1986). These studies generally indicate that intergroup discrimination is most evident when subjects are led to compete with out-group members. For instance, Word et al. (1974) report that subjects gave shorter interviews to culturally dissimilar partners in a job interview situation. Given the fact that participants in this study were faced with a noncompetitive task, an impression-making interview, the weak effect of cultural similarity on the amount of information-seeking behavior is understandable. In other words, in spite of communication difficulties, participants seem to continue to ask questions to fulfill the task of impression-making.

Second, on the average, the impression-making interview lasted less than five minutes. Thus the interaction may have been too short to discern the effect of cultural similarity on information-seeking behavior. If participants were induced to interact longer, there might have been a significant effect of cultural similarity on the amount of information-seeking behavior.

On the other hand, the effect of cultural similarity became evident when the data were broken down by three levels of intimacy. The data show that the social penetration process in intercultural interaction is more difficult than in intracultural interaction. It was found that partic-ipants asked significantly fewer questions concerning the partners' attitudes, opinions, and personalities in intercultural interaction. The process of social penetration reached only up to the point when partic-ipants requested somewhat moderately intimate information such as questions concerning the partner's activities, preferences, and behav-ioral intentions. These findings are consistent with many social pene-tration studies of the intercultural relationship (Gudykunst, 1985b; Gudykunst, Chua, & Gray, 1987). Moreover, as Imahori (1987) ob-served, intercultural interaction can be characterized by communica-tion difficulties as participants in the intercultural interaction condition were involved in far more frequent clarifications than those in the intracultural condition.

To summarize, the effects of cultural similarity on qualitative fea-tures of subsequent information-seeking behavior are most striking. Even though participants require an equal amount of information for uncertainty reduction, they use different types of information to reduce uncertainty depending upon the culture of their partners. Thus these findings reinforce the necessity of approaching the process of uncer-tainty reduction from an information processing perspective to better understand the consequence of group memberships upon information-seeking behavior during an initial interaction.

Next, contrary to Berger's (1979) contention that anticipation of future interaction will elevate the social actor's motivation to seek information from the partner, this study reports that the effect of antic-ipation of future interaction on several uncertainty reduction variables is minimal in both intercultural and intracultural interactions. A few comments are necessary to interpret this null result.

First, as Tedeschi (1981) suggests, individuals expecting future in-teraction with a stranger are likely to be concerned with impression management. Therefore, anticipation of future interaction with con-versational partners is apt to bind social actors to social norms and constrain nonnormative behavior (Kellermann, 1986). According to Berger, Gardner, Parks, Schulman, and Miller (1976), there are limits on the extent to which persons can use interrogation as a means to gaining knowledge about another during an initial interaction. Asking too many questions of a stranger violates a social norm of initial interaction. Although this study allowed the participants to ask as many questions as they wished, it is possible that, when social actors have reached an upper limit of interrogation in the no-anticipation-of-future-interaction condition, there is not much room for anticipation of future interaction to have an impact on interrogation in this study. Moreover,

Shaffer and Ogden (1986) report that social actors rated themselves as being less comfortable and less relaxed during an initial interaction if they anticipated future interaction with their partners. Taken together, the weak effect of anticipation of future interaction in this study can be attributed to the fact that participants in the anticipation-of-future-interaction condition might have been more cautious in conducting their behavior so as not to violate appropriate social norms of initial interactions.

Second, even though none of the participants misunderstood the anticipation-of-future-interaction induction, they somehow did not believe strongly that they would actually be interacting with their partners in the second part of the study. In fact, during the debriefing session, several participants reported that they guessed that there would be no second part of the study despite the instruction. This observation raises a serious question concerning the validity of the manipulation of anticipation of future interaction in an artificial experimental setting. Kellermann (1986, p. 69) comments that "problems with the operationalization of the construct of anticipation of future interaction suggest its limited value in understanding interaction behavior." Therefore, further research is required to develop an operationalization of anticipation of future interaction with a more realistic research design.

This study also explores the possibility that persons manifest different patterns of uncertainty reduction behavior depending upon the gender of their partners. The data show that participants felt less confident in understanding their partner's behavior in the opposite sex dyad condition. Accordingly, they asked more questions to cope with the high degree of uncertainty. Contrasting this finding with the Cline's (1983) report that persons tend to self-disclose more in same sex dyads, it is possible that persons use more subtle ways of acquiring such information in the same sex dyad, while they are direct in their information-seeking behavior in the opposite sex dyad. More future research needs to be done to scrutinize this possibility.

Finally, this study did not support the hypothesis that extraverts would be more active than introverts in their information-seeking behavior. Introverts were not different from the extraverts in their information processing behavior either quantitatively or qualitatively. This finding can be attributed to the fact that this study used a structured context—a formal interview—for information-seeking behavior. It is possible that introverts felt more comfortable in a well-structured situation, because there were specified rules for appropriate behavior. Moreover, it is also possible that a relatively low reliability of the scale observed in this study might have contributed to the null effect.

Discussion of the several limitations of this study and the corollary recommendations for future studies is in order. First, this study investigates social actors' information-seeking behavior by interrogation only. According to Berger (1979), persons can use other interactive strategies, such as self-disclosure, to acquire information from their partners during an initial interaction. In particular, given the small effect of anticipation of future interaction in this study, it may be fruitful for future studies to investigate whether the prospect of future interaction would produce any impact on subsequent frequencies and intimacy of self-disclosure in initial intercultural and intracultural interactions. Research reports by Shaffer and Ogden (1986) support this argument, as they found that male participants became more intimate and emotionally invested in their disclosures when they expected to interact with their partners in the future.

Second, the context used also needs to be scrutinized carefully. As illustrated earlier, the intergroup contact literature consistently advocates the importance of context in intergroup behavior. Thus it should be emphasized that an impression-making interview is a noncompetition situation, and it may be important to find out how social actors vary their information-seeking behavior in more competitive situations. In addition, the role of the prospect of future interaction in such a context deserves attention in the future studies.

Third, based on Hall's (1976) distinction, this study investigated information-seeking behavior for uncertainty reduction in low-context cultures only. Several researchers speculate that uncertainty reduction strategies might vary depending upon one's cultural background. For instance, Gudykunst and Ting-Toomey (1988) suggest that persons in high-context cultures tend to reduce uncertainty about the target person through in-group relationships rather than through frequency of communication. Moreover, nonverbal aspects of communication are more valued than verbal communication in high-context cultures (Condon, 1984; Kang & Pearce, 1983; Yum, 1987). Thus it is important to find out the roles and patterns of information-seeking behavior for the uncertainty reduction processes in high-context cultures such as Korea, Japan, and China.

To conclude, the significance of this study is in its efforts to compare and contrast the patterns of uncertainty reduction behavior between intercultural and intracultural interactions from an information processing perspective. Therefore, the current data are believed to have higher external validity because they were obtained from a face-to-face interaction. In particular, given the fact that an understanding of the uncertainty reduction process in initial intercultural and intracultural interactions is not yet clear, mainly due to the low degree of both experimental and mundane realism of the research methods employed in previous studies, more future studies are needed to investigate uncertainty reduction behavior from an information processing perspective in numerous contexts. By so doing, we not only enhance our knowledge of how social actors use information for the purpose of uncertainty reduction but also provide useful guidelines for conducting one's behavior during the initial stages of relationship development.

NOTE

1. The coding scheme used in this study is based on the works of social penetration studies (e.g., Altman & Taylor, 1973). First, questions dealing with requests for information known to most people and unrelated to the interviewee (e.g., What is the population of New York city?) and questions dealing with the partner's demographic background, family background, and roles (e.g., Where are you from?) are classified as *nonintimate*. Next, questions about the partner's past and current activities and experiences (e.g., Have you been to France?), questions about the partner's preference (e.g., Do you like sports?), and questions requesting explanations for the partner's past behavior or future plans (e.g., What made you decide to go to Michigan State University?) are classified as *moderately intimate*. Finally, questions dealing with the partner's attitudes, opinions (e.g., What do you think about American politics?), and personality (e.g., Do you like to interact with others?) are coded as *highly intimate*. In addition, questions dealing with the identification of meaning or clarification of the previous responses are classified as *request for clarity* (e.g., Could you repeat what you said before?). Two judges independently coded all the questions into one of the four categories. Using Scott's (1955) formula, the intercoder reliabilities were .95 for the intracultural data and .94 for the intercultural data.

REFERENCES

Allen, B. (1976). Race and physical attractiveness as criteria for White subjects' dating choices. *Social Behavior and Personality, 4,* 289-296.

Allen, V., & Wilder, D. (1979). Group categorization and attribution of belief similarity. *Small Group Behavior, 10,* 73-80.

Altman, I., & Taylor, D. A. (1973). *Social penetration: The development of interpersonal relationships.* New York: Holt, Rinehart & Winston.

Amir, Y. (1969). Contact hypothesis in ethnic relations. *Psychological Bulletin, 71,* 319-342.

Berger, C. R. (1979). Beyond initial interaction: Uncertainty, understanding, and the development of interpersonal relationships. In H. Giles & R. St. Clair (Eds.), *Language and social psychology.* Oxford: Basil Blackwell.

Berger, C. R. (1986a). Social cognition and intergroup communication. In W. Gudykunst (Ed.), *Intergroup communication.* London: Edward Arnold.

Berger, C. R. (1986b). Uncertain outcome values in predicted relationships: Uncertainty reduction theory then and now. *Human Communication Theory, 13,* 34-38.

Berger, C. R., & Bradac, J. J. (1982). *Language and social knowledge: Uncertainty in interpersonal relations.* London: Edward Arnold.

Berger, C. R., & Calabrese, R. J. (1975). Some explorations in initial interaction and beyond: Toward a developmental theory of interpersonal communication. *Human Communication Research, 1,* 99-112.

Berger, C. R., Gardner, R. R., Parks, M. R., Schulman, L., & Miller, G. R. (1976). Interpersonal epistemology and interpersonal communication. In G. R. Miller (Ed.), *Explorations in interpersonal communication.* Beverly Hills, CA: Sage.

Berscheid, E., Graziano, W., Monson, T., & Dermer, M. (1976). Outcome dependency: Attention, attribution, and attraction. *Journal of Personality and Social Psychology, 34,* 978-989.

Billig, M., & Tajfel, H. (1973). Social categorization and similarity in intergroup behavior. *European Journal of Social Psychology, 3,* 27-52.

Brown, R., & Turner, J. (1981). Interpersonal and intergroup behavior. In J. Turner & H. Giles (Eds.), *Intergroup behavior.* Oxford: Basil Blackwell.

Byrne, D. (1971). *The attraction paradigm.* New York: Academic Press.

Byrne, D., & Clore, C. L. (1966). Predicting interpersonal attractions toward strangers presented in three different stimulus modes. *Psychology Science, 4,* 239-240.

Calabrese, R. J. (1975). *The effects of privacy and probability of future interaction on initial interaction patterns.* Unpublished doctoral dissertation, Northwestern University.

Chaikin, A. L., & Derlega, V. J. (1976). Self-disclosure. In J. W. Thibaut, J. T. Spence, & R. C. Carson (Eds.), *Contemporary topics in social psychology.* Morristown, NJ: General Learning Press.

Chaikin, A. L., Derlega, V. J., Harris, M. S., Gregorio, D., & Boone, P. (1973). *Self-disclosure in biracial dyads.* Unpublished manuscript, Old Dominion University.

Clatterbuck, G. W. (1979). Attributional confidence and uncertainty in initial interaction. *Human Communication Research, 5,* 147-157.

Cline, R. J. (1983). The acquaintance process as relational communication. In R. Bostrom (Ed.), *Communication yearbook 7* (pp. 396-413). Beverly Hills, CA: Sage.

Clore, G. L., & Byrne, D. (1974). A reinforcement model of attraction. In T. Hudson (Ed.), *Foundations of interpersonal attraction.* New York: Academic Press.

Condon, J. C. (1984). *With respect to the Japanese: A guide for Americans.* Yarmouth, ME: Intercultural Press.

Douglas, W. (1985). Anticipated interaction and information seeking. *Human Communication Research, 12,* 243-258.

Douglas, W. (1987). Question-asking in same- and opposite-sex initial interactions: The effect of anticipated future interaction. *Human Communication Research, 14,* 230-245.

Duck, S. (1976). Interpersonal communication in developing acquaintance. In G. R. Miller (Ed.), *Explorations in interpersonal communication.* Beverly Hills, CA: Sage.

Eysenck, H. J. (1973). *Eysenck on extraversion.* New York: John Wiley.

Fiske, S. T., & Taylor, S. E. (1984). *Social cognition.* New York: Random House.

Giles, H., & Johnson, P. (1981). The role of language in ethnic group relations. In J. Turner & H. Giles (Eds.), *Intergroup behavior.* Chicago: University of Chicago Press.

Gudykunst, W. B. (1983a). Similarities and dissimilarities in perceptions of initial intracultural and intercultural encounters: An exploratory investigation. *Southern Speech Communication Journal, 49,* 49-65.

Gudykunst, W. B. (1983b). Uncertainty reduction and predictability of behavior in high and low context cultures. *Communication Quarterly, 31,* 49-55.

Gudykunst, W. B. (1985a). The influence of cultural similarity, type of relationship, and self-monitoring on uncertainty reduction processes. *Communication Monographs, 52,* 203-217.

Gudykunst, W. B. (1985b). An exploratory comparison of close intracultural and intercultural friendships. *Communication Quarterly, 33,* 270-283.

Gudykunst, W. B. (1986). Ethnicity, type of relationship, and intraethnic and interethnic uncertainty reduction. In Y. Kim (Ed.), *Interethnic communication.* Beverly Hills, CA: Sage.

Gudykunst, W. B. (1987). *Uncertainty and anxiety.* Paper presented at the Speech Communication Association Convention, Boston.

Gudykunst, W., Chua, E., & Gray, A. (1987a). Cultural dissimilarities and uncertainty reduction processes. In M. McLaughlin (Ed.), *Communication yearbook 10* (pp.456-469). Newbury Park, CA: Sage.

Gudykunst, W. B., & Nishida, T. (1984). Individual and cultural influences on uncertainty reduction. *Communication Monographs, 51,* 23-36.

Gudykunst, W., Nishida, T., & Chua, E. (1987). Perceptions of social penetration in Japanese-North American dyads. *International Journal of Intercultural Relations, 11,* 171-190.

Gudykunst, W., Nishida, T., Koike, H., & Shiino, N. (1986). The influence of language on uncertainty reduction: An exploratory study of Japanese-Japanese and Japanese-North American interactions. In M. McLaughlin (Ed.), *Communication yearbook 9* (pp.555-575). Beverly Hills, CA: Sage.

Gudykunst, W., Sodetani, L., & Sonoda, K. (1987). Uncertainty reduction in Japanese-American/Caucasian relationships in Hawaii. *Western Journal of Speech Communication, 51,* 256-278.

Gudykunst, W., & Ting-Toomey, S. (1988). *Culture and interpersonal communication.* Beverly Hills, CA: Sage.

Gudykunst, W., Yang, S., & Nishida, T. (1985). A cross-cultural test of uncertainty reduction theory: Comparisons of acquaintances, friendships, and dating relationships in Japan, Korea, and the United States. *Human Communication Research, 11,* 407-454.

Hall, E. T. (1976). *Beyond cultures.* Garden City, NY: Doubleday.

Harvey, J. H., Yarkin, K. L., Lightner, J. M., & Town, J. P. (1980). Unsolicited interpretation and recall of interpersonal events. *Journal of Personality and Social Psychology, 38,* 551-568.

Heider, F. (1958). *The psychology of interpersonal relations.* New York: John Wiley.

Hewes, D. E., & Planalp, S. (1982). There is nothing as useful as a good theory . . .: The influence of social knowledge on interpersonal communication. In M. E. Roloff & C. R. Berger (Eds.), *Social cognition and communication.* Beverly Hills, CA: Sage.

Hewstone, M., & Brown, R. J. (1986). *Contact and conflict in intergroup encounters.* Oxford: Basil Blackwell.

Imahori, T. T. (1987). *Intercultural interpersonal epistemology: Behavioral comparisons of intimacy and interrogative strategies between initial intracultural and intercultural interactions.* Paper presented at the Speech Communication Association Annual Convention, Boston.

Jones, S., & Diener, E. (1976). Ethnic preference of college students for their own and other racial groups. *Social Behavior and Personality, 4,* 225-231.

Kang, K. W., & Pearce, W. B. (1983). Reticence: A transcultural analysis. *Communication, 8,* 79-106.

Kellermann, K. (1986). Anticipation of future interaction and information exchange in initial interaction. *Human Communication Research, 13*, 41-75.

Maruyama, F., & Miller, N. (1981). Physical attractiveness and personality. In B. Maher & W. Maher (Eds.), *Progress in experimental personality research* (Vol. 10). New York: Academic Press.

Miller, G. R., & Steinberg, M. (1975). *Between people: A new analysis of interpersonal communication.* Palo Alto, CA: Science Research Associates.

Miller, N., & Brewer, M. B. (1984). *Groups in contact.* Orlando, FL: Academic Press.

Osterkamp, M. B. (1980). Communication during initial interactions: Toward a different model. *Western Journal of Speech Communication, 44*, 198-213.

Parks, M. R. (1978). *Perceived sex differences in friendship development.* Paper presented at the annual convention of the Speech Communication Association, Minneapolis.

Parks, M. R., & Adelman, M. B. (1983). Communication networks and the development of romantic relationships: An expansion of uncertainty reduction theory. *Human Communication Research, 10*, 55-79.

Pettigrew, T. (1986). The intergroup contact hypothesis reconsidered. In M. Hewstone & R. Brown (Eds.), *Contact and conflict in intergroup encounters.* Oxford: Basil Blackwell.

Planalp, S., & Honeycutt, J. (1985). Events that increase uncertainty in interpersonal relationships. *Human Communication Research, 11*, 593-604.

Rose, T. L. (1981). Cognitive and dyadic processes in intergroup contact. In D. L. Hamilton (Ed.), *Cognitive processes in stereotyping and intergroup behavior.* Hillsdale, NJ: Lawrence Erlbaum.

Ruben, B. D., & Kealey, D. J. (1979). Behavioral assessment of communication competency and the prediction of cross-cultural adaptation. *International Journal of Intercultural Relations, 3*, 15-47.

Rubin, R. B. (1977). The role of context in information seeking and impression formation. *Communication Monographs, 44*, 81-90.

Rubin, R. B. (1979). The effect of context on information seeking across the span of initial interactions. *Communication Quarterly, 27*, 13-20.

Schneider, M. J., & Jordan, W. (1981). Perceptions of the communicative performance of Americans and Chinese in intercultural dyads. *International Journal of Intercultural Relations, 5*, 175-191.

Scott, W. A. (1955). Reliability of content analysis: The case of nominal scale coding. *Public Opinion Quarterly, 19*, 321-325.

Shaffer, D. R., & Ogden, J. K. (1986). On sex differences in self-disclosure during the acquaintance process: The role of anticipated future interaction. *Journal of Personality and Social Psychology, 51*, 92-101.

Sherblom, J., & Rheenen, D. (1984). Spoken language indices of uncertainty. *Human Communication Research, 11*, 221-230.

Sherif, M. (1966). *Group conflict and co-operation.* London: Routledge & Kegan Paul.

Shuter, R. (1982). Initial interactions of American Blacks and Whites in interracial and intraracial dyads. *Journal of Social Psychology, 117*, 42-52.

Sillars, A. L. (1982). Attribution and communication: Are people "naive scientists" or just naive? In M. E. Roloff & C. R. Berger (Eds.), *Social cognition and communication.* Beverly Hills, CA: Sage.

Simard, L. M. (1981). Cross-cultural interaction: Potential invisible barriers. *Journal of Social Psychology, 113*, 171-192.

Snyder, M., & Uranowitz, S. W. (1978). Reconstructing the past: Some cognitive consequences of person perception. *Journal of Personality and Social Psychology, 36,* 941-950.

Street, L., Jr., & Giles, H. (1982). Speech accommodation theory: A social cognitive approach to language and speech behavior. In M. E. Roloff & C. R. Berger (Eds.), *Social cognition and communication.* Beverly Hills, CA: Sage.

Sunnafrank, M. J., & Miller, G. R. (1981). The role of initial conversations in determining attraction to similar and dissimilar strangers. *Human Communication Research, 8,* 16-25.

Tedeschi, J. T. (1981). *Impression management theory and social psychological research.* New York: Academic Press.

Ting-Toomey, S. (1981). Ethnic identity and close friendship in Chinese-American college students. *International Journal of Intercultural Relations, 5,* 338-406.

Wilder, D. A. (1981). Perceiving persons as a group: Categorization and intergroup relations. In D. L. Hamilton (Ed.), *Cognitive processes in stereotyping and intergroup behavior.* Hillsdale, NJ: Lawrence Erlbaum.

Word, C. O., Zanna, M. P., & Cooper, J. (1974). The nonverbal mediation of self-fulfilling prophecies in interracial interaction. *Journal of Experimental Social Psychology, 10,* 109-120.

Yum, J. O. (1987). Korean philosophy and communication. In D. L. Kincaid (Ed.), *Communication theory from Eastern and Western perspectives.* New York: Academic Press.

12

Influence of Language and Similarity on Initial Intercultural Attraction

HYUN J. KIM • *Chungnam National University*

This study examines the influence of language and similarity on attraction between intercultural partners involved in initial interaction. Results indicated that the native partner's perception of nonnative partner's host language competence was positively correlated with the native partner's attraction to the nonnative partner, whereas the nonnative partner's perception of the native partner's speech accommodation was not correlated with the nonnative partner's attraction to the native partner. For both native and nonnative partners, on the other hand, the perception of attitudinal similarity was a much stronger correlate of attraction than the perception of cultural similarity. When regression analyses were performed combining the language and similarity variables, perception of attitudinal similarity emerged as a prime predictor of attraction between intercultural partners.

One of the major concerns of communication research has been the role of communication in initiating and developing interpersonal relationships (Berger & Calabrese, 1975; Miller & Steinberg, 1975). To date, however, few empirical studies have examined the role of communication in developing interpersonal relationships in intercultural settings. Because the language barrier has been understood as a factor that makes intercultural interactions more difficult than intracultural interactions, the effect of language differences should be a primary focus of intercultural communication research (Giles & Powesland, 1975; Gudykunst, 1983; Simard, 1981).

Thus language variables of host community members and their non-native partners are the major focus of the current study. These language variables include the nonnative partner's competence in the host language (i.e., English; Kim, 1977; Savignon, 1983) and the native partner's tendency to accommodate his or her speech style to that of the nonnative partner (Giles & Powesland, 1975). These two variables were selected due to their ability to augment or discount the perception of language difference between the native and nonnative partners. As such,

AUTHOR'S NOTE: An earlier version of the manuscript was presented at the annual meeting of the International Communication Association, San Francisco, May 1989.

this study attempts to identify the influence of these variables on attraction between intercultural partners.

Furthermore, though many researchers have addressed the role of similarity in the development of interpersonal relationships (Byrne, 1969; Newcomb, 1961), there remains a question as to whether the same should be true for the relationships among intercultural partners. The fact that intercultural partners are different in terms of their ethnocultural backgrounds may lead one to be concerned about the role of similarity in guiding intercultural relationships.

Although several research endeavors have addressed the similarity issues (Gudykunst, 1985; Gudykunst & Nishida, 1984; Gudykunst, Nishida, Koike, & Shiino, 1986), their results may not be generalizable to the communication behaviors occurring in natural intercultural settings. One typical shortcoming of these studies is their use of the bogus-stranger technique for operationalizing the level of similarity, which does not involve actual interactions between partners. As such, more studies are needed to examine intercultural communication as an interactive phenomenom (Howell, 1979). The current study employs actual interactions between native and nonnative partners.

In particular, the efforts of partners in the initiation stage of relationships will most likely be devoted to various forms of communication to enhance predictability about each other (Berger, 1979). In addition, the information to be used in assessing the possibility of future interaction is obtained during initial information exchange (Sunnafrank & Miller, 1981). The current study focuses on the very beginning stage of intercultural relationships.

FACTORS THAT INFLUENCE INITIAL INTERCULTURAL ATTRACTION

Nonnative Partner's Host Language Competence

Communicative competence has been referred to as an attribute that shapes interpersonal impressions and allows for satisfactory outcomes Spitzberg & Hecht, 1984). Because the nonnative partner's ability to communicate effectively in the host language comprises the major portion of communicative competence in intercultural settings (Kim, 1977; Savignon, 1983), it is considered a crucial communication variable that affects the native partner's impression about the nonnative partner. When nonnative partners speak in the host language, wide variation in their perceived ability to command the host language

(D'Anglejan & Tucker, 1973) should produce variation in the native partner's impression about them.

Borrowing the similarity-attraction theory (Byrne, 1969), it could be that the nonnative partner's language competence leads to the native partner's perception of linguistic similarity, which then increases his or her attraction to the nonnative partner. Thus the perception produced less difference in linguistic behaviors between the intercultural partners and would create more positive interaction outcomes.

Also, gaining interpersonal knowledge about the partner is an important factor in determining initial attraction (Berger & Calabrese, 1975), and the quality of relational development (Altman & Taylor, 1973; Miller & Steinberg, 1975). Conversation with nonnative speakers who are less fluent in the host language would be more restricted in terms of the variety and depth of topics exchanged. In fact, incompetent nonnative speakers were found to avoid uttering certain words, formulating grammatically demanding phrases, and initiating certain topics (Klein, 1986). This impaired conversation would prevent the native partner from gaining as much interpersonal knowledge as he or she would with a more fluent nonnative partner, thus lowering the overall attraction level. Here, what matters more should be the native partner's perception of the nonnative partner's competence in the host language rather than the nonnative partner's actual competence. A hypothesis is formulated accordingly:

> *Hypothesis 1:* The native partner's perception of the nonnative partner's host language competence will be positively correlated with the native partner's attraction to the nonnative partner.

Native Partner's Speech Accommodation

A basic postulate of the speech accommodation theory (Giles & Powesland, 1975) states that people are motivated to adjust their speech style as a way of expressing attitudes and intentions toward others. Though individual variations may exist, people will basically seek to accommodate their speech style as a means of reducing the linguistic differences between them. Evidence for the influence of speech accommodation on attraction is widely available (Giles, Bourhis, & Taylor, 1977; Giles, Taylor, & Bourhis, 1973; Simard, 1981). These studies were concerned with situations in which people from subordinate language communities accommodate their speech to the dominant host language. For example, bilingual French Canadians were more favorably perceived by English Canadians when they spoke in English (i.e., full accommodation) rather than in French (i.e., no accommodation; Giles et al., 1973).

However, the paucity of empirical research on the situations where host community members accommodate their speech to the nonnative partners dictates the need to examine them in their own right. Because nonnative partners in many cases do not have bilingual skills sufficient to freely command their second language, it is often the native partner who has to accommodate his or her speech. Particularly when the nonnative partner's perceived host language competence is low, the motivation to reduce linguistic difference will be reflected as the native partner's tendency to adjust his or her language use according to the presumed competence of the nonnative partner (Clyne, 1984; Ferguson & de Bose, 1977; Gallois, Franklyn-Stokes, Giles, & Coupland, 1988; Snow, Van Eeden, & Muysken, 1981).

The native partner's efforts to accommodate speech will be interpreted favorably by the nonnative partner as a sign of positive attitude, which will lead to increased attraction to the native partner. Conversely, the nonnative partner's perception of the native partner's non-accommodation may be attributed to a lack of goodwill effort rather than to inability thus decreasing the nonnative partner's attraction to the native partner. Therefore, the following two hypotheses are posed:

Hypothesis 2: The degree of the native partner's speech accommodation will be positively correlated with the native partner's perception of the nonnative partner's host language competence.

Hypothesis 3: The nonnative partner's perception of the native partner's speech accommodation will be positively correlated with the nonnative partner's attraction to the native partner.

Perception of Similarity Between Native and Nonnative Partners

The influence of perceived similarity on attraction between intercultural partners can occur on two different dimensions: attitudinal and cultural (Gudykunst, 1985). Research findings in intracultural contexts have suggested that people are more attracted to demographically similar (Newcomb, 1961) and attitudinally similar (Byrne, 1969; Kandel, 1978) partners. However, studies in intercultural settings have often produced inconsistent findings. While several studies have identified the perception of ethnocultural similarity as a stronger correlate of attraction than the perception of attitudinal similarity (Allen, 1976;

Gudykunst & Nishida, 1984; Jones & Diener, 1976; Triandis, 1961), others have suggested the opposite (Byrne & Wong, 1962; Hendrick, Stikes, & Murray, 1972; Simard, 1981). Still others found no effect of perceived cultural similarity on attraction (Gudykunst, 1985).

The inconsistency among these findings can be attributed partly to the different research procedures employed by these studies. The participants in these studies were involved in a setting where the target person was presented through written descriptions, tape recordings, or television. The few studies that posited face-to-face interaction used confederates. Given these limitations, it becomes possible that the noninteractive nature of these studies might have produced different results than studies employing actual interactions.

In fact, Simard (1981), in a study employing interactions among English and French Canadians, found that after an encounter with members of a different ethnic group, people had increasingly positive attitudes about the encounter and perceived their partners as similar to themselves. She argued that the perception of dissimilarity in terms of ethnic affiliation might have been compensated for by increased similarity along a number of other dimensions. Because so much dissimilarity was expected, after the actual encounter, the overall similarity surprised the participants (Simard, 1981, p. 187). Therefore, the current study postulates that the perception of attitudinal similarity will be as important as the perception of ethnocultural similarity in determining attraction. That is, as interactants find themselves attitudinally similar to each other through actual conversation, they will perceive each other to be attractive regardless of their initial perceptions of cultural similarity.

One other goal of this study is to identify how dimensions of perceived similarity, along with the language variables (i.e., the nonnative partner's host language competence and the native partner's speech accommodation), determine the overall level of attraction. Hence the following research questions are advanced.

Research Question 1: How do attitudinal and cultural dimensions of perceived similarity differentially influence the attraction between intercultural partners?

Research Question 2: How do the nonnative partner's host language competence, the native partner's speech accommodation, and the perception of attitudinal and cultural dimensions of similarity contribute to the attraction between intercultural partners?

METHOD

Research Participants

Participants in the study were 122 students attending a large midwestern university in the United States. Half of the participants were international students and half were U.S. students. The average age of the international students was 27 years and their average length of stay in the United States was 2 years and 9 months. The average age of the U.S. students was 22 years. Participants were asked to come to the research session individually, where they were paired to form intercultural dyads. Among the formed dyads, 37 were same sex dyads and 24 were opposite sex dyads. Participants were given extra course credit for their efforts.

Procedures

Each experimental session was composed of an international student (nonnative partner) and a U.S. student (native partner), who were presumed to be strangers to each other. Upon arrival, participants were joined to form a dyad and were given a brief description of the study and their task. The task was to engage in a "get-to-know" conversation for approximately 15 minutes. The topics of conversation were allowed to vary as long as they were considered helpful for participants to understand each other.

Right after the conversation, the participants reported their own host language competence (for international students) or speech accommodation (for U.S. students) and their perception of the partner's host language competence (for U.S. students) or speech accommodation (for international students). They also indicated their perception of cultural and attitudinal similarity. Finally, they responded on a separate questionnaire asking about their attraction to each other. Participants were then fully informed about the nature of the study and thanked for their participation.

Instrumentation

A six-item measure (Wilds, 1975) was used for the perceived host language competence. The measure was concerned with the U.S. students' perception about the international students' English use along such dimensions as nativeness of accent, accuracy of grammar, adequacy of vocabulary, and overall fluency. The same items were used to solicit the international students' self-report of host language competence.

A seven-item measure was developed to assess the international students' perception of the U.S. students' speech accommodation. The measure was constructed based on findings of previous research (Ferguson & de Bose, 1977; Snow et al., 1981). The measure tapped such aspects as phonology, syntax, and vocabulary of the U.S. students' communication with the international students. More specifically, the items asked about slowness of speech rate and the clarity of articulation (phonology); avoidance of compound and complex sentences (syntax); avoidance of idiomatic expressions and use of paraphrases (vocabulary); and attention to comprehension checks. Perception of a greater display of these linguistic behaviors was operationalized as a higher degree of perceived speech accommodation. The same items were used to ask about the U.S. students' own speech accommodation.

From McKroskey, Richmond, and Daly's (1975) homophily measure, four items were adopted to indicate perceived cultural similarity and four items were adopted to indicate perceived attitudinal similarity. A six-item measure was developed to indicate the overall attraction to the partner. The measure was concerned with the participants' satisfaction with the partner (e.g., "talking with this person was pleasant"; "this person would fit into my circle of friends"; "the conversation with this person was interesting") and their desire for extended future relationship with the partner (e.g., "I would like to meet and talk with this person again"; "I want to develop a friendship with this person"; "this person can be a good friend of mine"). All items of this study employed a seven-point semantic-differential-type response format.

RESULTS

Descriptive Statistics

Examination of the structural qualities of the measures preceded tests of the hypotheses. Confirmatory factor analysis (Hunter, 1980) showed a unidimensional factor structure for most of the original measures except for the attraction measure. After deleting one ("this person would fit into my circle of friends") of the original six items of the attraction measure, all measures met the requirements of internal consistency and parallelism. Though the two dimensions of similarity (i.e., attitudinal and cultural) were correlated ($r = .48$, $p < .01$), two clearly distinguished factor structures were detected, and they were treated as two different variables.

Reliability of the measures was assessed by Cronbach's alpha. Measures of perceived language competence (α = .86), self-reported language competence (α = .91), perceived speech accommodation (α = .86), and self-reported speech accommodation (α = .84) were all found to be highly reliable. Measures of attraction (α = .70), perceived cultural similarity (α = .71), and perceived attitudinal similarity (α = .65) also showed fairly acceptable reliabilities.

The average rating of perceived language competence was 5.42 (SD = .90), reflecting that most of the international students sampled in this study were perceived as relatively advanced speakers of English. Furthermore, the international students seemed to have an accurate perception of their own English competence as indicated by a moderate sized correlation between the perceived competence and the self-reported competence (r = .41, p < .01). Perceived speech accommodation averaged 3.89 (SD = 1.37).

The international and U.S. students converged on their perceptions of similarity. The average perceptions of attitudinal similarity were 4.23 (SD = .96) for international students and 4.39 (SD = .74) for U.S. students on a seven-point scale (*paired t* = −1.05, df = 59, p = ns). The perception of cultural similarity averaged 3.65 (SD = 1.18) for international students and 3.42 (SD = 1.06) for U.S. students (*paired t* = 1.30, df = 60, p = ns).

However, U.S. students reported a significantly higher rating of attraction (mean = 5.64, SD = .79) than international students (mean = 5.07, SD = .99; *paired t* = −3.81, df = 60, p < .01). This may be due to different communication energy expenditures by each party (Miller & Steinberg, 1975). That is, because the conversation was in English, U.S. students may have expended less encoding and decoding energy than the international students, who had to speak and listen in their second language.

Tests of the Hypotheses

Following the assessment of the measurement quality, correlations among the variables were obtained to test the hypotheses. Because the hypotheses were formulated separately for native and nonnative partners, two different correlation matrices are provided. Table 12.1 contains the correlations among the language and similarity variables and the native partner's attraction to the nonnative partner. Table 12.2 contains the correlations among the language and similarity variables and the nonnative partner's attraction to the native partner.

TABLE 12.1 Correlations Among the Language and Similarity Variables and the Native Partner's Attraction Toward Nonnative Partner

Variable	1	2	3	4	5
1. Native partner's self-report of speech accommodation	—				
2. Native partner's perception of the nonnative partner's host language competence	−.52**	—			
3. Native partner's perception of cultural similarity to the nonnative partner	−.02	.23*	—		
4. Native partner's perception of attitudinal similarity to the nonnative partner	−.09	.29*	.31*	—	
5. Native partner's attraction toward the nonnative partner	−.42**	.31*	.25*	.44**	—

NOTE: N = 61.
*p < .05; **p < .01.

TABLE 12.2 Correlations Among the Language and Similarity Variables and the Nonnative Partner's Attraction Toward the Native Partner

Variable	1	2	3	4	5
1. Nonnative partner's self-report of host language competence	—				
2. Nonnative partner's perception of the native partner's speech accommodation	−.30*	—			
3. Nonnative partner's perception of cultural similarity to the native partner	.30*	−.21	—		
4. Nonnative partner's perception of attitudinal similarity to the native partner	.24*	−.05	.62**	—	
5. Nonnative partner's attraction toward the native partner	.06	.08	.23*	.46**	—

NOTE: N = 61.
*p < .05; **p < .01.

Hypothesis 1 predicted a positive correlation between the native partner's perception of the nonnative partner's host language competence and the native partner's attraction to the nonnative partner. The data were consistent with the hypothesis. The correlation was moderate, but significantly different from zero ($r = .31, p < .05$). This suggests that nonnative partners who were perceived competent in the host language were more liked by native partners than those who were not perceived as competent in the host language.

As expected, however, the nonnative partner's self-report of host language competence per se was not correlated with the native partner's attraction to the nonnative partner ($r = .06, p = $ ns). Although it was positively correlated with the nonnative partner's perception of cultural similarity to the native partner ($r = .30, p < .05$). Also, quite consistent with the expectation, perceived language competence was positively correlated with the native partner's perception of cultural similarity to the nonnative partner ($r = .23, p < .05$). Thus it can be argued that the correlation between perceived language competence and attraction may be influenced by perception of cultural similarity.

In hypothesis 2, a positive correlation was expected between perceived language competence and the native partner's self-report of speech accommodation. The hypothesis was supported ($r = .52, p < .01$), indicating that the native partners did accommodate their language use according to the perceived competence of the nonnative partners. That is, native partners accommodated their speech more to the nonnative partners who were perceived as less competent in the host language.

Hypothesis 3 expected a positive correlation between the nonnative partner's perception of speech accommodation and the nonnative partner's attraction to the native partner. The data, however, were not consistent with the prediction. The correlation between these variables was .08 ($p = $ ns). Unlike the native partners, the language variable made little difference for the nonnative partner's attraction to the native partner. This suggests that, for nonnative partners, at least for the international students sampled in this study, the way the members of the host community communicated with them appeared unimportant.

Another unexpected finding was a negative correlation between the native partner's self-report of speech accommodation and the native partner's attraction to the nonnative partner ($r = - .42, p < .01$). Though the correlation decreased considerably after controlling for the effect of the perceived language competence on attraction, it remained significant (partial $r = -.25, p < .05$). Thus it could be that the native partners who had to exert special efforts to change their communication style from what they would normally do with their fellow native partners felt decreasing attraction to the nonnative partners.

Finally, a negative correlation ($r = -.30$, $p < .05$) between nonnative partner's self-report of host language competence and perceived speech accommodation merits scrutiny. Given little influence on the two variables from other sources, the finding is indicative of the nonnative partner's reaction to perceive speech accommodation. That is, the more competent nonnative partners considered them in commanding the host language, the less they perceived them as being communicated to by native partners in a way deliberately tuned to the nonfluent nonnative partners.

Research Questions 1 and 2

Regarding the first research question, the correlation between perceived attitudinal similarity and attraction was much stronger than the correlation between perceived cultural similarity and attraction. For the native partners, the correlation between attitudinal similarity and attraction was .44 ($p < .01$) and the correlation between cultural similarity and attraction was .25 ($p < .05$). For the nonnative partners, the correlations were .46 ($p < .01$) and .23 ($p < .05$), respectively. Here, given moderate to strong correlations between perceptions of attitudinal and cultural similarities ($r = .31$, $p < .05$, for the native partners; $r = .62$, $p < .01$, for the nonnative partners), the above findings should be interpreted with some caution. It becomes necessary to examine the effect of each dimension of similarity on attraction after eliminating the influence of each of the others.

For the native partners, the partial correlation between perceived attitudinal similarity and attraction was .39 ($p < .01$) after the effect of perceived cultural similarity was controlled. On the other hand, the zero-order correlation between perceived cultural similarity and attraction ($r = .25$) decreased considerably and became nonsignificant after eliminating the effect of perceived attitudinal similarity (*partial r* = .13, $p =$ ns). For the nonnative partners, the partial correlations were .41 ($p < .01$) and $-.07$ ($p =$ ns), respectively. Thus it would be safe to argue that, for both native and nonnative partners, the perception of cultural similarity by itself did not contribute to attraction unless mediated through the perception of attitudinal similarity.

The second research question concerns how the language variables and perceptions of similarity differentially contribute to determining attraction between intercultural partners. Two separate multiple regression analyses were performed to answer it.

The first regression analysis predicted the native partner's attraction to the nonnative partner. The predictor variables included perceived language competence, native partner's self-report of speech accommodation, perceived cultural similarity, and perceived attitudinal similarity. Because no theoretical reasoning is available about which of these predictors should have priority in terms of entry into the regression equation, all variables were entered simultaneously as a block (Pedhazur, 1982).

Though the four variables accounted for a substantial portion of the variance ($R = .59$, $R^2 = .35$, $p < .01$), only two of them emerged as significant predictors of intercultural attraction. For native partners, perception of attitudinal similarity increased their attraction to nonnative partners (*beta* = .37, $p < .01$), while their self-report of speech accommodation decreased attraction (*beta* = $-.40$, $p < .01$). Two other variables had nonsignificant beta coefficients ($-.03$ for perceived language competence; .13 for perceived cultural similarity). Though these two variables showed moderate correlations with attraction ($r = .31$, $p < .05$, for perceived language competence; $r = .25$, $p < .05$, for perceived cultural similarity), their effects were obscured by a stronger influence of perceived attitudinal similarity and self-reported speech accommodation.

The second regression analysis predicted the nonnative partner's attraction to the native partner. Predictor variables were perceived speech accommodation, native partner's self-report of host language competence, perceived cultural similarity, and perceived attitudinal similarity. Again, the block entry method was used for this analysis due to the lack of theoretical guidance for deciding entry order. Among the four variables, only the nonnative partner's perception of attitudinal similarity was a significant predictor of attraction (*beta* = .50, $p < .01$). All other variables had nonsignificant beta coefficients (.08 for perceived speech accommodation, $-.03$ for self-report of host language competence, and $-.05$ for perceived cultural similarity). In particular, the correlation between perceived cultural similarity and attraction ($r = .23$, $p < .05$) lost its significance when the influence of other variables was considered simultaneously. The multiple R was .46 ($R^2 = .22$, $p < .01$).

In both regression analyses, multicollinearity was not a concern because all predictor variables surpassed the tolerance criteria. Tables 12.3 and 12.4 summarize the results of the regression analyses for the native partner's intercultural attraction and the nonnative partner's intercultural attraction, respectively.

TABLE 12.3 Results of a Regression Analysis to Predict the Native Partner's Attraction Toward the Nonnative Partner

Variable	b (S.E.)	Beta (S.E.)	r	Partial	Tolerance	p
1. Perceived host language competence	−.03 (.12)	−.03 (.13)	.31	−.03	.66	.82
2. Self-reported speech accommodation	−.26 (.08)	−.40 (.13)	−.42	−.39	.73	.00
3. Perceived cultural similarity	.10 (.09)	.13 (.12)	.25	.15	.87	.27
4. Perceived attitudinal similarity	.40 (.13)	.37 (.12)	.44	.39	.85	.00
(constant)	4.45 (.81)					.00

NOTE: Block entry method was used. $R = .595$, $R^2 = .354$, $p < .01$. N = 61.

TABLE 12.4 Results of a Regression Analysis to Predict the Nonnative Partner's Attraction Toward the Native Partner

Variable	b (S.E.)	Beta (S.E.)	r	Partial	Tolerance	p
1. Perceived speech accommodation	.06 (.09)	.08 (.13)	.08	.08	.89	.54
2. Self-reported host language competence	−.03 (.15)	−.03 (.13)	.06	−.03	.85	.82
3. Perceived cultural similarity	−.04 (.13)	−.05 (.16)	.23	−.04	.57	.74
4. Perceived attitudinal similarity	.53 (.17)	.50 (.16)	.46	.40	.59	.00
(constant)	2.96 (.98)					.00

NOTE: Block entry method was used. $R = .465$, $R^2 = .216$, $p < .01$. N = 61.

DISCUSSION

The process leading to intercultural attraction seemed to be different between the native and nonnative partners. That is, the language variable had direct influence on attraction only for native partners, though perceived attitudinal similarity was commonly predictive of attraction for both native and nonnative partners. One noteworthy finding in this regard is that the native partner's perception of the nonnative partner's host language competence did not influence the native partner's attraction. Instead, the native partner's self-report of greater speech accommodation led to the native partner's decreased attraction to the nonnative partner.

Though the simple fact that nonnative partners spoke in the host language already provided enough reason for the native partners to feel a certain degree of similarity and hence attraction (Byrne, 1969), variation of the perception of the nonnative partner's ability to command the host language produced variation in the native partner's degree of speech accommodation, which, in turn, determined attraction. We should also note the finding that the nonnative partner's perception of the native partner's speech accommodation did not influence the nonnative partner's attraction. Several possible explanations for this finding are possible.

First, the nonsignificant correlation between the nonnative partner's perception of speech accommodation and the native partner's self-report on the same items ($r = -.04$) suggests that the measure of speech accommodation contained linguistic cues too subtle to be easily detectable by the naive, nonexpert judgments of the nonnative partners. Second, given the low average of the native partner's self-report of speech accommodation (mean = 2.84), it may be that native partners did not accommodate their speech to a great extent. Third, because the nonnative partners in this study were advanced second-language speakers, they might have interpreted the native partner's accommodations as a sign of social distance and condescension and felt uncomfortable with being communicated to in such a manner (Klein, 1986, p. 45). Thus accommodations might have functioned in a negative way to decrease the attraction level, which otherwise would have been higher.

However, a strong negative correlation between perceived language competence and self-reported speech accommodation ($r - .52, p < .01$) denies the plausibility of the second explanation. The correlation suggests that native partners did accommodate their speech according to the perceived level of the nonnative partner's language competence, as suggested elsewhere (Ferguson & de Bose, 1977; Gallois et al., 1988; Snow et al., 1981). Thus, without further evidence, it would be conservative to retain both the first and the third explanations. Also, it may be possible to speculate a curvilinear relationship between speech accommodation and nonnative partner's attraction. That is, for deficient nonnative speakers, accommodation may have some effect on attraction but not for advanced nonnative speakers.

Another meaningful finding of the current study is that, for both nonnative and native partners, perception of attitudinal similarity was a significant predictor of attraction (beta coefficients were .37 for native partners and .50 for nonnative partners), while perception of cultural similarity had little predictive power. Similar results were reported by other studies (Byrne & Wong, 1962; Gudykunst, 1985; Simard, 1981). As Sunnafrank and Miller (1981) pointed out, initial interaction might be a significant determinant of attraction. That is, the highly visible barrier (i.e., ethnocultural dissimilarity) that intercultural partners experienced during the very beginning stage of interaction might give way to other dimensions of similarity (i.e., attitudinal similarity) as they build up "common ground" through interaction. This finding is also consistent with Miller and Steinberg's (1975) argument that, as partners rely more on psychological than cultural data to make predictions about each other, the relationship becomes more interpersonal.

In sum, the current study was successful in identifying the roles of language and similarity variables in naturally occurring interactive settings. In particular, use of regression analyses enabled an examination of relative contributions of these language and similarity variables in determining attraction between intercultural partners. Though the variables examined in the current study seemed to have heuristic value, other potentially crucial variables were not included in this endeavor. A large portion of variance of intercultural attraction was left unexplained by this study. Future research integrating more conceptually relevant variables, such as relationship expectations, relationship attributions, and relationship commitments, may enhance our understanding of this potentially complex process of developing intercultural relationships.

REFERENCES

Allen, B. P. (1976). Race and physical attractiveness as criteria for White subjects' dating choices. *Social Behavior and Personality, 4,* 289-296.

Altman, I., & Taylor, D. (1973). *Social penetration: The development of interpersonal relationships.* New York: Holt, Rinehart & Winston.

Berger, C. R. (1979). Beyond initial interaction: Uncertainty, understanding, and the development of interpersonal relationships. In H. Giles & R. St. Clair (Eds.), *Language and social psychology* (pp. 122-144). Baltimore: University Park Press.

Berger, C. R., & Calabrese, R. (1975). Some explorations in initial interaction and beyond. *Human Communication Research, 1,* 99-112.

Byrne, D. (1969). Attitudes and attraction. In L. Berkowitz (Ed.), *Advances in experimental social psychology* (Vol. 4). New York: Academic Press.

Byrne, D., & Wong, T. J. (1962). Racial prejudice, interpersonal attraction, and assumed dissimilarity of attitudes. *Journal of Abnormal and Social Psychology, 65,* 246-253.

Clyne, M. G. (1984). *Language and society in the German-speaking countries.* New York: Cambridge University Press.

D'Anglejan, A., & Tucker, G. R. (1973). Communicating across cultures: An empirical investigation. *Journal of Cross-Cultural Psychology, 4,* 121-130.

Ferguson, C., & de Bose, C. E. (1977). Simplified registers, broken language, and pidginization. In A. Valdman (Ed.), *Pidgin and creole linguistics* (pp. 99-125). Bloomington: Indiana University Press.

Gallois, C., Franklyn-Stokes, A., Giles, H., & Coupland, N. (1988). Communication accommodation in intercultural encounters. In Y. Kim & W. Gudykunst (Eds.), *Theories in intercultural communication* (pp. 157-185). Newbury Park, CA: Sage.

Giles, H., Bourhis, R., & Taylor, D. M. (1977). Towards a theory of language in ethnic group relations. In H. Giles (Ed.), *Language, ethnicity, and intergroup relations* (pp. 307-348). London: Academic Press.

Giles, H., & Powesland, P. F. (1975). *Speech style and social evaluation.* London: Academic Press.

Giles, H., Taylor, D. M., & Bourhis, R. (1973). Toward a theory of interpersonal accommodation through language: Some Canadian data. *Language in Society, 2,* 177-192.

Gudykunst, W. B. (1983). Similarities and differences in perceptions of initial intracultural and intercultural encounters. *Southern Speech Communication Journal, 49,* 40-65.

Gudykunst, W. B. (1985). The influence of cultural similarity, type of relationship, and self-monitoring on uncertainty reduction processes. *Communication Monographs, 52,* 203-217.

Gudykunst, W. B., & Nishida, T. (1984). Individual and cultural influences on uncertainty reduction. *Communication Monographs, 51,* 23-36.

Gudykunst, W. B., Nishida, T., Koike, H., & Shiino, N. (1986). The influence of language on uncertainty reduction: An exploratory study of Japanese-Japanese and Japanese-North American interactions. In M. L. McLaughlin (Ed.), *Communication yearbook 9* (pp. 555-575). Beverly Hills, CA: Sage.

Hendrick, C., Stikes, C. S., & Murray, D. J. (1972). Race versus belief similarity as determinants of attraction in a live interaction situation. *Journal of Experimental Research in Personality, 6,* 162-168.

Howell, W. S. (1979). Theoretical directions for intercultural communication. In M. Asante, E. Newmark, & C. Blake (Eds.), *Handbook of intercultural communication* (pp. 23-41). Beverly Hills, CA: Sage.

Hunter, J. E. (1980). Factor analysis. In P. R. Monge & J. N. Cappella (Eds.), *Multivariate techniques in human communication research* (pp. 229-258). New York: Academic Press.

Jones, S., & Diener, E. (1976). Ethnic preference for college students for their own and other racial groups. *Social Behavior and Personality, 4,* 225-231.

Kandel, D. B. (1978). Similarity in real-life adolescent friendship pairs. *Journal of Personality and Social Psychology, 36,* 306-312.

Kim, Y. (1977). Inter-ethnic and intra-ethnic communication: A study of Korean immigrants in Chicago. In N. Jain (Ed.), *International and intercultural communication annual* (Vol. 4, pp. 53-68). Falls Church, VA: Speech Communication Association.

Klein, W. (1986). *Second language acquisition.* Cambridge: Cambridge University Press.

McKroskey, J. M., Richmond, V., & Daly, J. (1975). The development of a measure of perceived homophily in interpersonal communication. *Human Communication Research, 1,* 323-332.

Miller, G. R., & Steinberg, M. (1975). *Between people.* Chicago: Science Research Associates.

Newcomb, T. M. (1961). *The acquaintance process.* New York: Holt, Rinehart & Winston.

Pedhazur, E. J. (1982). *Multiple regression in behavioral research: Explanation and prediction* (2nd ed.). New York: Holt, Rinehart & Winston.

Savignon, S. J. (1983). *Communicative competence: Theory and classroom practice.* Reading, MA: Addison-Wesley.

Simard, L. M. (1981). Cross-cultural interaction: Potential invisible barriers. *Journal of Social Psychology, 113,* 171-192.

Snow, C., Van Eeden, R., & Muysken, P. (1981). The interactional origins of foreigner talk: Municipal employees and foreign workers. *International Journal of the Sociology of Language, 28,* 81-92.

Spitzberg, B., & Hecht, M. L. (1984). A component model of relational competence. *Human Communication Research, 10,* 575-599.

Sunnafrank, M. J., & Miller, G. R. (1981). The role of initial conversations in determining attraction to similar and dissimilar strangers. *Human Communication Research, 8,* 16-25.

Triandis, H. (1961). A note on Rokeach's theory of prejudice. *Journal of Abnormal and Social Psychology, 62,* 184-186.

Wilds, C. P. (1975). The oral interview test. In R. L. Jones & B. Spolsky (Eds.), *Testing language proficiency* (pp. 29-44). Arlington, VA: Center for Applied Linguistics.

13

Themes in Opposite Sex, Japanese-North American Relationships

WILLIAM B. GUDYKUNST • *California State University, Fullerton*

GE GAO • *San Jose State University*

SANDRA SUDWEEKS • *Golden West Community College*

STELLA TING-TOOMEY • *California State University, Fullerton*

TSUKASA NISHIDA • *Nihon University*

The purpose of this study was to extend our earlier study (Sudweeks, Gudykunst, Ting-Toomey, & Nishida, 1990) of relational themes (patterns of discourse that focus on partners' interpretations of their interaction) in same sex intercultural relationships to those in opposite sex relationships. Two research questions were addressed: What themes emerge in opposite sex intercultural relationships? How do specific themes relate to the intercultural relationship development? Partners in 15 acquaintance, friend, and romantic Japanese-North American, male-female dyads were interviewed individually in their native language. An interpretive analysis of the participants' accounts of their relationships revealed four themes: typicality, communication competence, similarity, and involvement. The presence, form, and interconnections among the themes and subthemes varied by type of relationship. The themes isolated in the current study were compared with the themes isolated in our earlier study of same sex relationships.

Relatively little research addressing the specific processes that affect the way relationships are created or the processes that move relationships to different levels of intimacy has been conducted. Theorists agree that the growth of interpersonal relationships is a developmental process, but the explanations posited do not explain the process of relational change. A. Bochner (1978) criticized developmental theorists for their failure to discuss the interpretive process of relationship development. More recently, Duck and Perlman (1985, p. 5) argued that "the

AUTHORS' NOTE: An earlier version of this chapter was presented at the International Conference on Cross-Cultural Communication, San Antonio, Texas, March 1989.

single most important question for research in the future is to discover how 'relationships' are created, both subjectively and objectively, from strings of interaction, and from the changing beliefs that persons have about them." To fully understand personal relationships, it is necessary to examine the participants' interpretations, conceptions, and explanations of their relationships.

Isolating themes in participants' accounts of their relationships is one way to study the subjective aspects of personal relationships (Owen, 1984; Rawlins, 1983). Spradley (1979, p. 186) defines a *theme* as "any cognitive principle, tacit or explicit, recurrent in a number of domains and serving as a relationship among subsystems of . . . meaning." He notes that meaning tends to be expressed around a set of major and minor themes and that themes connect different communication domains. The themes that emerge in the study of personal relationships between individuals from the same culture may not describe developmental processes in all relationships. Unique themes, for example, emerge in intercultural relationships (Sudweeks et al., 1990). There should, however, be extensive overlap with themes observed in intracultural relationships because the underlying process of communication is, to a certain extent, similar (Gudykunst & Kim, 1984). Isolating themes in intercultural relationships and determining which themes are different from those in intracultural relationships can provide new insights into the dynamics of personal relationship development. The purpose of this study, therefore, was to isolate developmental themes in partners' accounts of male-female intercultural relationships.

RELATIONAL THEMES

Accounts—individuals' stories about their patterns of interactions (Harvey, Weber, Galvin, Huszti, & Garnick, 1986)—are important to the study of personal relationships because they are "real people's self representations of their real relationships" (Weber, Harvey, & Stanley, 1987, p. 114). Gergen (1982) argues that individuals' descriptions of events are best understood as their attempt to make sense out of the events in which they are involved and not as "empirical statements." Similarly, Shotter (1985, p. 451) contends that

> *accounts* can be distinguished from theories in the sense that an account of an action or activity is concerned with talking about the action or activity as the activity *is.* It is an aid to *perception,* functioning to instruct one as to how to constitute an otherwise indeterminate flow of activity as a sequence of recognizable events, events of a kind already known about

within a society's way of making sense of things. Rather than being a *report* about a state of affairs which can be evaluated for its falsity, an account works in a quite different way: it *tells* us something, it informs us or instructs us as to how practically to go about seeing what the "is" is, that is, what we ought to see as the "is."

The logic individuals use to reconstruct a sequence of events and the factors on which they focus in their accounts are influenced by their culture and native language. Accounts of personal relationships in one culture, therefore, should be different from accounts of the same type of relationship in another culture. Because both partners' cultures influence how they communicate in intercultural relationships, some aspects of the accounts of intercultural relationships should be different from accounts of intracultural relationships.

Accounts of relationships can be studied by isolating themes. *Themes* are issues or concerns around which interaction is focused (Owen, 1984). Spradley (1979) argues that, while some themes are explicit, most are tacit and taken for granted. In addition, as themes connect different domains of meaning, they are interrelated and overlap. Spradley goes on to point out that thematic analysis allows us to see more than just the parts that make up a system (e.g., a personal relationship). Focusing on themes forces us to look for systems of meaning that can be integrated into larger patterns.

Previous research on themes in personal relationships has revealed patterns of communication that would not have been discovered by other methods (e.g., standard content analyses). Rawlins (1983, p. 258), for example, examined the "practical organization of interactions that sustain close friendships." His analysis of both partners' accounts of their relationships revealed that two dialectical themes are typically present for close friendships to be sustained: the freedom to be independent and the freedom to be dependent. He concluded that the two freedoms are contingent upon both partners' actions and must be negotiated continually (although not necessarily explicitly) throughout a relationship.

In a related study, Owen (1984) isolated themes in five different types of relationships (married couples, dating couples, relatives, live-in friends, and non-live-in friends). He discovered seven themes individuals used to make sense of their relationships: commitment, involvement, work, uniqueness/specialness, fragility, consideration/respect, and manipulation. Owen (1984, p. 285) concluded that "relational participants used themes as episodic, processual, and, most importantly, *interactive* interpretive ways of maintaining or altering an otherwise static state of relationship."

More recently, Sillars, Weisberg, Burggraf, and Wilson (1987) studied content themes in marital conversations. They argued that conversational themes are a type of metacommunication about the relationship, which can be used to identify factors that influence the relationship. Three themes emerged, with each one having subthemes. The communal theme consisted of five subthemes: togetherness, cooperation, communication, romanticism, and interdependence. The individual theme had three subthemes: separateness, personality, and role. The impersonal theme also included three subthemes: organic properties, stoicism, and environmental influences. Sillars and his associates found that the presence of the various subthemes in conversations varied by marital types and the degree of satisfaction with the marriage.

To the best of our knowledge, only two studies of themes vis-à-vis the cultural aspects of communication have been conducted. The first study (Ting-Toomey, 1986a) did not specifically examine themes in intercultural relationships but focused on themes in Japanese patterns of communication from insiders' (Japanese) and outsiders' (sojourners living in Japan) perspectives. She discovered four themes underlying Japanese communication: (a) communication style—concealment versus revealment; (b) communication ritual—obligatory versus voluntary reciprocity; (c) relational placement—complementarity versus symmetricality and (d) relational distance—remoteness versus closeness. All four themes were emphasized repeatedly and forcefully in insiders' and outsiders' interpretive accounts of the Japanese culture.

The only study of themes in intercultural relationships, to our knowledge, is our earlier study (Sudweeks et al., 1990) of nine female-female Japanese-North American relationships (Table 13.1 summarizes the findings of this study for the theme/subthemes across intimacy levels of the relationships). The respondents' accounts suggested that subthemes under communication competence (language/cultural knowledge, empathy, and accommodation) are rare in low-intimacy dyads, present in some moderate-intimacy dyads, and prominent in high-intimacy dyads. A parallel pattern emerged for the similarity theme. There were no background/life-style or attitude/value similarities reported in the accounts of partners in the low-intimacy dyads. Some were observed in the moderate-intimacy dyads, and many similarities were noted in the high-intimacy dyads. Further, lack of cultural similarity that was reported as a problem in low-intimacy dyads was noted only minimally in moderate-intimacy dyads, and was a positive factor in the high-intimacy dyads. The participants in the low-intimacy dyads

TABLE 13.1 Summary of Themes Isolated in Sudweeks et al. Study

Theme/Subtheme	Intimacy of Relationship		
	Low	Moderate	High
Communication competence			
1. language/cultural knowledge	limited language/cultural knowledge was barrier to developing intimacy	limited language/cultural knowledge constrained interaction, but compensatory strategies developed	language/cultural knowledge did not constrain interaction
2. empathy	no empathy expressed	empathy present but not prominent	empathy prominent in relationship
3. accommodation	no accommodation	little or no accommodation	one or both partners accommodated
Similarity			
1. cultural	cultural differences used as explanation for lack of intimacy	noted minimally	cultural differences mentioned without judgment or as positive factor
2. background/life-style	none observed	some similarities observed	many similarities observed
3. attitude/value	none observed	some similarities observed	many similarities observed
Involvement			
1. amount	lack of time to interact viewed as a problem	lack of time to interact viewed as a problem	partners made time to interact
2. intimacy	no attempts to increase intimacy	some attempts to increase intimacy	both partners made attempts to increase intimacy
3. shared networks	no shared networks	only one dyad had shared networks	large overlap in networks
Turning points			
1. relational tests	used in all dyads	used in some but not all dyads	no tests
2. responsiveness	no mutual responsiveness	no mutual responsiveness	mutual responsiveness
3. understanding	increases in understanding changed perception of partner but not intimacy of relationship	increases in understanding changed perception of partner and intimacy of relationships in some but not all dyads	increases in understanding led to increased intimacy of relationship

reported little involvement (amount and intimacy of interaction and shared networks), while partners in high-intimacy dyads characterized their relationships as having high levels of involvement, and the moderate-intimacy dyads fell in between the two extremes. All participants in low-intimacy dyads reported using relational tests, while only some of the partners in moderate-intimacy dyads and none in the high-intimacy dyads tested their relationships. In addition, no mutual responsiveness was reported in low-intimacy dyads. Only a little mutual responsiveness was noted in the moderate-intimacy dyads, while both partners in each of the high-intimacy dyads mentioned mutual responsiveness in their accounts. Finally, episodes that increased understanding of the partner did not change the intimacy of the relationship in the low-intimacy dyads but did in the high.

The themes/subthemes that emerged in our earlier study (Sudweeks et al., 1990) provided several new insights regarding personal relationships between same sex members of different cultures. One area in which new insights emerged is the themes/subthemes that appear to be "unique" to intercultural relationships. The subthemes of language/cultural knowledge, accommodation, and cultural similarity were more prominent in the accounts of the Japanese-North American relationships than would be expected in relationships between members of the same culture. The differences in the subthemes in participants' accounts of low- and high-intimacy relationships appeared to be related to their cultural identities. Partners' cultural identities were a salient factor influencing how they presented themselves and how they interpreted each other's behavior in the low-intimacy relationships. More specifically, when participants first got to know their partner from another culture, there was a need for them to express their cultural identities (Ting-Toomey, 1989a). The accounts suggested that, in low-intimacy relationships, cultural identity was managed as a problematic issue or not recognized as a factor influencing communication. This was expressed through not knowing or using the other person's language, seeing cultural differences as problems, and not accommodating to the other's style of communication. In high-intimacy relationships, in contrast, cultural identity was recognized but not seen as problematic. Partners involved in intimate relationships knew the other person as an individual and accommodated to the partner's personal and cultural communication style.

To further our understanding of intercultural relationship development, the current study was designed to extend our earlier research on same sex dyads to opposite sex dyads. More specifically, the study addressed two general research questions: What themes emerge in opposite sex intercultural relationships? How do the themes that emerge relate to intercultural relationship development? To address these research questions, we conducted a thematic analysis of participants' accounts of their relationships. We used a developmental perspective on personal relationships (e.g., Altman & Taylor, 1973; Berger & Calabrese, 1975) to guide our analysis.

METHODS

Respondents

Respondents were nine female Japanese and six male Japanese and the six female North Americans and nine male North Americans with whom the Japanese had formed an opposite sex interpersonal relationship.[1] All Japanese respondents were Japanese natives who had lived in the United States from one month to three years. All respondents volunteered and were paid $5 for their participation.

Procedures

Japanese respondents were solicited and asked to help find other Japanese who would be willing to participate in the study. Japanese who agreed to participate were asked to name a North American of the opposite sex they knew to take part in the study. The North Americans named were contacted by a member of the research team and asked to participate. The partners were interviewed separately. The Japanese were interviewed in Japanese and the North Americans in English.[2] All interviews were tape-recorded with permission. The open-ended interviews were conducted in a single session and varied from 25 minutes to one hour.

Interviews were conducted with an interview guide rather than with a schedule. Participants were told that the purpose of the study was to gather information about their relationships. Initially, they were asked: "Please describe your relationship with [your partner]. We are interested in how you met and how this relationship developed and changed over time. Please be as specific as possible." The interview guide contained questions on topics such as initial and subsequent interactions, attributions, cultural differences, and relationship perceptions. The North American interviews were transcribed in English. The Japanese interviews were transcribed in Japanese and translated into English from the transcripts. The initial translations were made by a bilingual research assistant. Subsequently, the Japanese co-investigator verified each translation. A "meaning," rather than literal, translation was used for the Japanese interviews. The translated Japanese quotes used to support specific themes were edited into conversational English.

To locate relational themes, the recurring patterns of discourse focusing on an individual's interpretation of relational interaction (Owen, 1984) were examined. We tried to interpret each utterance pattern according to the meaning it had for the participant in the context of the account of the relationship and its development (Geertz, 1973). Our focus was on trying to ascertain what the utterance pattern meant to the respondent (i.e., we looked for the interpretive rather than the surface meaning). Given that the focus of the study was on developmental themes, we looked for the meaning of the utterances vis-à-vis the intimacy of the relationship and its relation to changes in the level of intimacy. The criteria for assessing the presence of a relational theme in the participants' accounts were (a) recurrence—at least two parts of an account had the same thread of meaning despite different wording—and (b) repetition—repeated use of the same key words, phrases, or word patterns (Owen, 1984).

We analyzed the transcripts (which ranged from five to fifteen single-spaced pages) in several stages. Interviews were read in dyadic sets to develop a sense of each relationship. Our initial analysis of the interview data involved an indexing of all relational references within each account. The transcripts then were analyzed to identify relational themes. Individual references to interaction were sorted to isolate themes and subthemes. Each utterance was read separately and placed in a stack with other utterances that had similar meaning. Once the sorting was completed, the utterances within each stack were examined to develop labels for the subthemes. The subthemes were then examined to determine commonalities and develop labels for themes. There was overlap in some categories, as would be expected in any interpretive analysis. As Agar and Hobbs (1982, p. 9) note, "Themes are highly intermixed," with the same utterance expressing several themes, and "these links should reveal something about the relations among their underlying themes." Additional analyses were conducted to isolate Japanese and North American differences in perceptions of the relationships and to assess how themes differed across intimacy levels.

The initial sorting of utterances was conducted by one of the coinvestigators. After initial sorting, the other investigators in the United States examined each utterance, its placement within a specific subtheme, and the overall thematic structure that emerged. Based on this analysis, some subthemes were combined to minimize overlap in subthemes (i.e., to make the subthemes more mutually exclusive). At this point, the

Japanese coinvestigator examined each utterance and the thematic structure.

We classified the intimacy level of each dyad based upon the participants' labels (e.g., acquaintance, friend) and descriptions of the relationship. Each dyad was classified as an acquaintance (five), friend (four), or romantic (six) relationship. Questions regarding relationship labels in the interview were open-ended. When the participants used different labels, the relationship was categorized based on their descriptions of it. One relationship characterized as acquaintance by both partners, for example, was placed in the acquaintance category. Another relationship identified by both partners as a close friendship was placed in the friendship category. Relationships where the partners identified each other as boy/girlfriend, lover, and/or husband/wife were placed in the romantic relationship category.

Although culture could affect the perception of intimacy and relationship labels, it did not appear to be an issue in this study. Cross-cultural research on perceived intimacy of relationship terms (Gudykunst & Nishida, 1986) has revealed that there are differences between Japanese and North American perceptions of intimacy in some relationship terms (e.g., Japanese perceive acquaintances to be more intimate than do North Americans, and North Americans perceive roommates to be more intimate than do Japanese). Within each culture, however, the relative ordering of relationship labels in terms of intimacy is the same (e.g., members of both cultures rate strangers as less intimate than acquaintances, roommates, friends, or close friends).

RESULTS AND DISCUSSION

Four themes emerged from an interpretive analysis of the accounts of the partners in the 15 male-female intercultural dyads. Typicality, communication competence, similarity, and involvement occurred in all three types of relationships (romantic, friend, and acquaintance). Communication competence involved two subthemes: cultural/linguistic knowledge and ability to understand. Two subthemes appeared under similarity: cultural similarity and attitude/interest similarity. And two emerged under involvement: amount and intimacy of communication.

Typicality

Typicality was exemplified in accounts given by the respondents when they reported their partners as "atypical" or "different" from average Japanese or North Americans. This theme was most prominent in the romantic relationships, less prominent in friendships, and the least prominent in the acquaintance relationships.

In the romantic relationships and the friendships, the Japanese respondents viewed their North American partners as atypical of their culture and as possessing some Japanese characteristics. Several comments from Japanese respondents illustrated this theme:

> I think American men who get married with Orientals are very different from other Americans. Average American men do not care about Orientals. They do not pay attention to us and have different attitudes towards Oriental girls. (J-1, F, R)[3]

> He is a person who has been in Japan for two years and become partly Japanese. His way of thinking is quite Japanese. He thinks about the other. I think other Americans tend to think themselves more. We Japanese are more conscious about others; in this point, I can say he is very Japanese. (J-2, F, R)

> He is like Japanese; sometimes more Japanese than Japanese. (J-3, F, R)

> His communication pattern is considerably similar to Japanese. I don't think he can be successful in American society. . . . He doesn't seem to be a typical American. (J-5, F, R)

> He is very similar to Japanese. He has Japanese feelings. He can pick up subtle feelings. (J-6, F, R)

> I don't think of him so much as an American. He is very interested in other cultures. He is very considerate and has very deep insights. I think Americans are very self-centered. They don't think of others so much. (J-7, F, F)

> He is really different, different completely. He is shy, maybe like Japanese. He is very kind as compared to other Americans. (J-9, F, F)

North American respondents made similar comments about their Japanese partners:

> He's independent. He figures that if he has an idea and it's not going to hurt someone else . . . he's going to try it his way. So he's very independent. (NA-4, F, R)

> She seemed not really . . . as reserved as the other Japanese girls. (NA-2, M, R)

> She's a little more open maybe or talkative or not quite as reserved [as other Japanese]. (NA-3, M, R)

> She's very similar to the Japanese girls who come here and live and she's quite different from the ones that spend their entire lives in Japan. (NA-5, M, R)

[She is] probably more independent than other Japanese women that would not come to the United States. She is a little less domestic than them. (NA-10, M, F)

In the acquaintance relationships, the attributions were broad and general. Typicality was not an issue in these accounts:

She is not very different [from other Japanese]. (NA-11, M, A)

He knows the English language pretty well. (NA-14, F, A)

The Japanese respondents were attracted to "atypical" Americans who had adopted some Japanese qualities (or characteristics). While the North Americans saw their Japanese partners as atypical regarding some traits, they also showed interest in Japanese who possessed some of the "typical Japanese" qualities that the North Americans respondents admired. The North American respondents also tended to negatively evaluate some North American traits when they compared them with characteristics of their Japanese partners:

I don't think she was real demanding about how we spent our time in a described way. We didn't have to be going to this activity or a movie or dinner, something like that. We would just sit around and talk about things. (NA-2, M, R)

They [Japanese girls] never make a big deal about what they do for you. (NA-3, M, R)

I like the idea that he makes an effort to know what I'm thinking and feeling. He is very considerate. A lot of American men don't seem to feel as obligatory. (NA-4, F, R)

She does a lot of things for me, very caring. I know that any American girl would be much more demanding in a relationship. (NA-6, M, R)

American women are much more concerned with themselves and what they are going to get out of something. I feel as if I personally have to entertain them and spend a lot of money. I tend to give a lot more to have a relationship with some Japanese. (NA-9, N, F)

American women are generally louder and less concerned [as compared with Japanese]. (NA-10, M, F)

To summarize, the respondents in the friend and romantic relationships perceived their partners as atypical of their culture, while respondents in acquaintance relationships did not. Although the current findings do not duplicate those of previous studies, they are compatible with speculation about communication with atypical members of other groups. Perceiving a member of another group to be atypical, for example, can be argued to lead to individuation of that group. "Individuation of the outgroup shatters the assumption of outgroup homogeneity and similarity" (Wilder, 1986, p. 317). Gudykunst and Hammer (1988) also point out that, when a member of another group is perceived as atypical, the interpersonal salience of the relationship increases and the intergroup salience decreases.

Communication Competence

Communication competence was identified as a recurrent theme in all three types of relationships. Communication competence was defined through two subthemes: cultural/linguistic knowledge and ability to understand.

Cultural/linguistic knowledge. The cultural/linguistic knowledge subtheme emerged as an issue in almost all initial interactions reported in the respondents' accounts. The North Americans' knowledge of and insight into Japanese language, culture, literature, history, and religion seemed to be the focus of conversations in the initial stages of the relationships. References to the North Americans' knowledge and interest are recurrent throughout the Japanese partners' accounts. The North Americans' knowledge of and interest in Japan appeared to be strongest in the romantic and friend relationships:

> He asked about Japan. . . . He is very interested in the Japanese culture. (J-1, F, R)

> He is very interested in Japan and he studies about Japan. (J-3, F, R)

> His father often goes to Japan on business and he knows Japan very well. (J-6, F, R)

> She was doing an exchange study with a Japanese. She knows quite a few Japanese. When we first met, she was taking Japanese and she was asking about living in Japan. (J-8, M, F)

> He lived in Tokyo so we often talk about Tokyo. His Japanese is very good. He lived in Japan for six years. He asked about the last six months in Japan. (J-9, F, F)

The North Americans in the acquaintance relationships also expressed an interest in Japan, but their level of knowledge appeared to be less than those involved in friend and/or romantic relationships:

> She talked about her trip to Japan and she said that her boyfriend was in Japan. (J-13, M, A)

> He was also interested in Japan. He asked me many questions about Japanese customs and culture. His girlfriend had studied in Japan. (J-15, F, A)

Some of the North American respondents explicitly stated their interest in and knowledge of the Japanese culture and used them as explanations of why they initiated conversations with their Japanese partners:

> I was curious about Japan in general. (NA-6, M, R)

> We were both helping teach a beginning Japanese class. I'd like to translate. I'd like to teach English as a second language. (NA-4, F, R)

> I told him I spent a year in Japan. I don't speak Japanese very well. (NA-8, F, F)

> We talked mostly about Japan. I told him I had been there. (NA-13, F, A)

> I was interested in Japan. I asked her where she was from in Japan. (NA-15, M, A)

> I told him that I went to Japan once and that was how I met my husband. (NA-14, F, A)

> I studied some things about the Japanese culture. I have an interest [in Japan]. (NA-7, M, F)

Lack of linguistic knowledge was one of the major reasons for a low level of intimacy in the acquaintance relationships. Some of the Japanese and North American respondents attributed a lack of close relationships to the language barrier (not being able to understand or speak the other language fluently):

> There's a language problem and I think it takes a bit longer [to develop the relationship]. (NA-12, F, A)

> [We haven't become close friends] because of the language barrier. (J-15, F, A)

> There's a real language barrier there. It's just really hard to communicate something that's so deep through the language barrier. There are times when she nods and smiles and doesn't understand a word I'm saying and that's terrible. (NA-15, M, A)

> First is the language difference. I feel I'm hindered sometimes because I cannot speak English well. I cannot talk about details. (J-13, M, A)

The North Americans' acceptance of the Japanese partners' inability to speak English well and/or the North American offering help to the Japanese partner in improving his or her English appears to be one of the major factors in allowing relationships to move past the acquaintance stage. Many of the Japanese respondents in the friend and romantic relationships commented on their partners' acceptance and/or help with respect to their English:

> He was patient with my English. For instance, if I meet someone at a bar, or in other places, he/she tends to stop talking to me after finding out that I do not speak natural English. . . . But he was different. Whenever I asked him, he always answered me and explained things to me. And also he taught me some correct English expressions. (J-10, F, F)

> With other Americans, I feel I have to speak complete (correct) English, but he understands what others would not. (J-3, F, R)

> He seldom speaks Japanese [the NA is fluent in Japanese]. Or should I say, he tends not to speak Japanese for me, to help me in my study of English. (J-9, F, F)

> He taught me many things. (J-3, F, R)

> We were doing homework together. She checked my homework [for English] and I checked her Japanese. If I'm with her I learn something. (J-4, M, R)

> He teaches me a lot. He has taught me about the American culture, the ways to socialize in the society and how to talk with others. (J-6, F, R)

In addition to the Japanese commenting on the North Americans' acceptance and/or help, some of the North Americans in the friend and romantic relationships recognized that they made allowances for their Japanese partners' English ability:

> I think I've developed a way of talking to people who do not speak English as a first language. (NA-7, M, F)

> I was in a position to help her become very well accustomed to the U.S. She was insecure and not so confident [in speaking English]. (NA-6, M, R)

The findings for the cultural/linguistic knowledge are consistent with previous research on knowledge of other cultures and second-language competence. Miller and Sunnafrank (1982, p. 226-227), for example, argued that

> knowledge about another person's culture—its language, dominant values, beliefs, and prevailing ideology—often permits predictions of the person's probable response to certain messages. . . . Upon first encountering . . . [people from another culture], cultural information provides the only grounds for communicative predictions.

Cultural/linguistic knowledge has been shown to be related not only to making communicative predictions but also to adjustment to other cultural environments (e.g., cultural knowledge: S. Bochner, 1972; Fiedler, Mitchell, & Triandis, 1971; Guthrie, 1975; linguistic knowledge or second-language competence: Berry, 1980; Kim, 1977; Morris, 1960; Naiman, Frohlich, Stern, & Todesco, 1978).

Before moving on, it should be noted that the North American partners' knowledge of and/or interest in the Japanese culture appears to have been emphasized in the respondents' accounts because it was one of the major factors the Japanese respondents used to explain why they had formed relationships with those specific North Americans and not other North Americans. As would be expected from past research, however, the respondents' accounts also suggested that the Japanese partners' knowledge of the United States and ability to use English influenced their adjustment to being in the United States and their ability to develop interpersonal relationships with the North Americans (e.g., low ability in English inhibited relationship development).

Ability to understand. The ability to understand each other played an important role in the development of the respondents' relationships. The ability to understand was the most salient factor in the romantic relationships, less salient in the friendships, and the least salient in the acquaintance relationships.

In the romantic relationships, partners appeared to have acquired a deep understanding of the nonverbal nuances and emotional aspects of each other's behavior. The respondents obtained information from their partners' nonverbal behaviors that increased their understanding of their partners:

> We can understand each other quite well by just watching each other's face. I can also differentiate his feeling behind the same sentence depending on the way he speaks. . . . Both of us have strong facial expressions and we can understand quite well whether the other person is interested or not. (J-2, F, R)

> I can tell what she wants and her needs without even talking to her. I can tell by the way she looks. (NA-1, M, R)

I can feel what she's thinking. She understands me without words. She understands from facial expressions whether I'm angry or not. (J-4, M, R)

We certainly get across the point if we're unhappy or something bothers us very clearly; but we don't always say something. (NA-4, F, R)

She can read them [frowns] on my face. (NA-5, M, R)

The romantic partners also emphasized verbal understanding in their accounts:

I can even talk about my stupidity with him; but I can't show my stupidity to Japanese friends even if they're very close to me. (J-6, F, R)

He knows me well and understands me. I don't feel uncomfortable at all. (J-1, F, R)

He understands what others would not understand. (J-3, F, R)

He's become aware of not superficial but deep love, I think. He is a person who tells me directly how he feels or thinks and I have confidence in him. We are at the same level and can exchange opinions. (J-5, F, R)

Although the ability to understand was essential in the romantic relationships, areas in which lack of understanding existed were also mentioned by the respondents:

I feel average Japanese men can understand my perspective more deeply. I personally feel more comfortable with Japanese friends. They show me more interest and try to understand. They are better listeners. (J-2, F, R)

If she were a Japanese she would understand Japanese expressions including jokes. (J-4, M, R)

Nonverbal aspects of communication were not mentioned in the partners' accounts in the friendship or acquaintance relationships. Respondents involved in those relationships, however, reported their partners understood them when they had difficulties, with more understanding occurring with friends than with acquaintances:

When I'm in trouble, he tends to understand me. He could understand nuances. (J-9, F, F)

He was patient with my English. He always answered me and explained things to me. (J-10, F, F)

He tried hard to make me understand some difficult English words without showing any fatigue. (J-15, F, A)

Similarity

Similarity emerged as a recurrent theme in relationship development. It was defined through two subthemes: cultural similarity and attitude/interest similarity.

Cultural similarity. Dissimilarity—in terms of cultural customs, characteristics, equality, and communication style—was mentioned frequently in the respondents' accounts. The Japanese respondents were more aware of the cultural dissimilarities existing in the intercultural interactions than were their North American counterparts. Respondents involved in romantic relationships tended to positively evaluate the cultural differences they observed. The evaluations appeared to strengthen the relationships:

> Our customs are different. For example, they open doors for females; they defend girls and escort them. In that sense I like [the way he behaves]. (J-1, F, R)

> Japanese tend to think of others' feelings first and then propose what they think. He usually says directly what he thinks and then sees the reaction of others and reacts to it. (J-2, F, R)

> She is very independent. I like that quality of her. I think we should respect that quality. (J-4, M, R)

> I don't think I'm equal with my Japanese male friends. [He] and I are at the same level and we can exchange opinions. When I'm associating with my Japanese friends, I have to sense how they feel or think because I can't ask them directly. [He] is a person who tells me directly how he feels or thinks, so I have confidence in his honesty. (J-5, F, R)

> Japanese guys behave as if they were rulers of girls and they make girls do everything for them. He does a lot for me. (J-6, F, R)

In the friendships, only general comments were made regarding the influence of cultural dissimilarities on the respondents' relationships:

> I have acquired an awareness that maybe she's sensitive to certain things that Americans would not be (NA-7, M, F)

> I can get whether he enjoys seeing me or not because he tells me directly. (J-9, F, F)

> As Americans, we are very direct about things. If we're speaking English, I can be very direct. (NA-9, M, F)

Only one comment on cultural dissimilarities appeared in the accounts of the respondents in an acquaintance relationship:

> He's very polite. He laughs when he's shy or embarrassed. That's how Japanese people are because they have to cover themselves up like that. (NA-14, F, A)

It is interesting to note that cultural dissimilarities were not mentioned frequently as affecting the relationship in respondents' accounts in the acquaintance relationships. General observations of cultural differences in the relationships were reported in the friendships; while evaluated positively, cultural differences were noted as important in the romantic relationships. This specific pattern has not been reported in any previous research. The difference between the acquaintance and friend relationships, however, are compatible with earlier work. Gudykunst and Kim (1984), for example, point out that people involved in intercultural relationships at low levels of intimacy (e.g., acquaintance) generally are not aware of cultural differences that affect their relationships, while individuals involved in intimate relationships (e.g., friendship) are aware of the differences and take them into account in the relationships.

Attitude/interest similarity. Sharing common attitudes and interests contributed to the development of the respondents' relationships. The common attitudes and interests were more prevalent in the romantic relationships than in the friendships:

> We both like the Beatles, so we talked about their music. We talked about our hobbies such as going to the mountains. (J-1, F, R)

> We talked about Japanese literature. He is interested in Zen as I am. He and I are aiming for the same goal spiritually, I mean a peaceful mind. His attitude and mine are the same in this regard. (J-5, F, R)

> We have similar interests in language and literature. We just get along quite well. We have a lot in common. (NA-5, M, R)

> Our viewpoints are quite similar. I mean both of us have Buddhist viewpoints. He is a Buddhist. (J-6, F, R)

> Our characters are similar and that has nothing to do with our nationalities. (J-3, F, R)

> We have the same emotional needs. (NA-5, M, R)

> Our interests are similar. (J-9, F, F)

> We are close friends because of similar interests and experiences. We are both interested in music so we listen to jazz. (NA-9, M, F)

No common attitudes and/or interests were mentioned in the accounts of the acquaintance relationships. As in intracultural relationships, this lack of common interests may explain why some of the relationships stayed at low levels of intimacy.

The findings for the attitude/interest similarity subtheme appear to be compatible with previous work in this area. Research on attitude similarity (e.g., Byrne, 1971) consistently reveals that similar attitudes are necessary for the development of intimate relationships between people of the same culture. Recent research (e.g., Gudykunst, 1985) also suggests that these findings are generalizable to intercultural relationships.

Involvement

Involvement also was identified as a recurrent theme in all three types of relationships. Involvement was manifested in two subthemes: amount and intimacy of communication.

Amount of communication. The amount of time the partners spent together was one of the critical factors in their relationship development. Respondents in the acquaintance relationships indicated that they would get to know the other person better and develop intimate relationships if they could spend more time with the person:

> There are very few occasions that I see him. (J-11, F, A)

> I don't see her often. If I had more time, I would be glad to know her better. (NA-11, M, A)

> We need more time. (J-12, M, A)

> Maybe if there were more time [we would become friends]. . . . Sometimes it takes a bit longer to warm up to [Japanese] because they're reserved. (NA-12, F, A)

> I haven't seen her that often. (J-13, M, A)

> Not enough time. (NA-13, F, A)

> I haven't seen him that many times. (NA-14, F, A)

> It is hard for me to suspect what he is thinking since I have known him only for a short period of time. (J-15, F, A)

The friends and romantic partners, in contrast, spent a considerable amount of time together:

I saw her every day, five days a week. (NA-4, F, R)

We went out a lot. (J-3, F, R)

We say each other once a week. (J-7, F, F)

The patterns that emerged regarding the amount of communication are consistent with most of the work on interpersonal relationship development. Most theorists (e.g., Hinde, 1981; Kelley et al., 1983) include frequency of interaction as a major component necessary for relationship development. Rose and Serafica (1986) also found that proximity and frequent interactions are the major prerequisites for the maintenance of casual friendships.

Intimacy of communication. Self-disclosing personal information and spending time alone with the partner promoted intimate interpersonal relationships. In the romantic and friend relationships, as compared with the acquaintance relationships, the level of self-disclosure was much higher, and partners spent more time alone. Examples of comments from romantic partners included the following:

When I broke up with this other guy, I even talked to him about it. His attitude toward me changed overnight. Apparently he liked me enough to consider me a girlfriend. (NA-4, F, R)

We did things mostly alone (e.g., picnics, movies, dancing, dinner). (NA-15, M, R)

I can be open with him, but I would be careful when I'm talking with Japanese friends. (J-6, F, R)

We can discuss a lot about various subjects. We don't feel bored when we talk. (J-2, F, R)

Intimate topics also were discussed in the friend relationships:

I talk about things with her that I do not talk about with others. (J-8, M, F)

I can talk about myself and my family. (J-9, F, F)

Representative comments from respondents in acquaintance relationships include the following:

We rarely meet alone. We have never gone to some place alone. I often go out with other friends and talk about personal things. (J-11, F, A)

There's more politeness there because I don't know her very well. (NA-11, M, A)

I have always seen her with other friends. I have not talked with her about anything personal. (J-12, M, A)

It was always through the school, with the group and most of the class. (NA-13, F, A)

She does not come into my personal life so we are not so close. (J-14, M, A)

The findings for the intimacy of communication subtheme are consistent with much of the previous research on personal relationships. The discussion of intimated topics in the friend and romantic relationships, but not in the acquaintance relationships, would be expected from a social penetration perspective (e.g., Altman & Taylor, 1973), for example. To illustrate, Altman and Taylor argue that there is little self-disclosure at the orientation (e.g., strangers) or exploratory affective exchange (e.g., acquaintances) stages of relationship development. Partners in relationships at the stable exchange stage (e.g., friendships and romantic relationships), in contrast, engage in self-disclosure on intimate topics. Argyle and Henderson (1984) also found that one of the few rules for friendship to be consistently endorsed across cultures is that partners must confide in one another.

SUMMARY AND CONCLUSION

To summarize, Table 13.2 presents the themes that emerged in the current analysis. For the typicality theme, no subthemes were observed. Partners in acquaintance relationships were viewed as relatively typical of their cultures, while partners in friend and romantic relationships were seen as somewhat atypical members of their cultures.

Two subthemes emerged under communication competence: cultural/linguistic knowledge and ability to understand. In the acquaintance relationships, the partners had an interest in each other's culture, but linguistic knowledge inhibited them from getting to know each other. In the friend and romantic relationships, the partners had an interest in and knowledge of each other's culture, and there were few linguistic barriers to communication. There was only minimal understanding of the partner in the acquaintance relationships, while there was moderate understanding at the verbal level in the friend relationships. Only the romantic partners reported deep understanding at both the verbal and the nonverbal levels.

There also were two subthemes for similarity: cultural similarity and attitude/interest similarity. There was a relatively low level of awareness of cultural differences in the acquaintances; there was some awareness

TABLE 13.2 Summary of Themes by Type of Relationship

Theme/Subtheme	Type of Relationship		
	Acquaintance	Friend	Romantic
Typicality	partner seen as typical of his/her culture	partner seen as atypical of his/her culture	partner seen as atypical of his/her culture
Communication competence			
1. cultural/linguistic knowledge	interest in partner's culture, but language problems inhibit partners getting to know each other	knowledge of partner's culture; no apparent language problem	knowledge of partner's culture; no apparent language problem
2. ability to understand	some understanding of partner	moderate levels of understanding between partners at verbal level	deep understanding of partner at verbal and nonverbal levels
Similarity			
1. cultural similarity	low awareness of cultural differences	some awareness of general cultural differences	cultural differences were noticed and evaluated positively
2. attitude/interest similarity	no common attitudes or interests mentioned	some common attitudes or interests observed	many common attitudes and interests observed
Involvement			
1. amount of communication	lack of time spent together limited relationship	sufficient time spent together to develop relationship	sufficient time spent together to develop relationship
2. intimacy of communication	little self-disclosure on intimate information	some self-disclosure of intimate information	high levels of self-disclosure of intimate information

of general cultural differences in the friendships; and cultural differences were noticed and evaluated positively in the romantic relationships. No attitude/interest similarity was recognized in the acquaintance relationships, but many similarities were recognized in the friend and romantic relationships.

Two subthemes also emerged for involvement: amount and intimacy of communication. The small amount of time spent together limited the development of the acquaintance relationships. There was, in contrast, sufficient time spent together for the relationship to develop in the friend and romantic relationships. Finally, there was little self-disclosure of intimate information in the acquaintance relationships, but there was some in the friendships, and there were high levels in the romantic relationships.

There are several similarities and differences in the themes/subthemes that emerged in this analysis and those isolated in our earlier study (Sudweeks et al., 1990) of same sex relationships. Three of the four themes in the opposite sex dyads also emerged in the same sex dyads: communication competence, similarity, and involvement. One theme, typicality, was isolated in the opposite sex but not in the same sex relationships, and one theme, turning points, emerged in the same sex but not in the opposite sex relationships. In addition to these themes being different, some of the subthemes under the major themes also were different. Under communication competence, ability to understand appeared as a subtheme in opposite sex but not same sex dyads, while empathy and accommodation emerged as subthemes in same sex but not opposite sex dyads. For similarity, a subtheme of background/life-style similarity was isolated in the same sex but not the opposite sex relationships. Finally, under involvement, shared networks appeared as a subtheme for same sex but not opposite sex relationships. The differences in the themes that emerged in the two studies deserve brief discussion.

As indicated above, typicality emerged as a theme in the opposite sex relationships but not in the same sex relationships. Given that the findings for typicality have not been observed in previous research, we can only speculate about why typicality emerged as a theme in opposite sex and not same sex relationships. One plausible explanation for the findings involves the differences between the two types of relationships. Parlee (1979), for example, found that opposite sex relationships differ from same sex relationships because of sexual tension and social discouragement, and there is relatively less commonality in opposite sex relationships than in same sex relationships. The last difference is consistent with findings for the subthemes in the two studies; that is, background/life-style similarity was a subtheme in the same sex but not in the opposite sex relationships. It is possible that if background/life-style similarity is not present in intercultural relationships, it may be necessary to "compensate" for cultural differences by forming relationships with members of other cultures perceived to be atypical of their culture (e.g., more similar to the respondents' culture).

In addition to typicality, there also was a difference in the turning-point theme in the two studies (i.e., turning points was a theme in Sudweeks et al.'s study of same sex dyads but was not in this study of opposite sex relationships). There appear to be two plausible explanations for the differences in the two studies. First, turning points may be more predominant in same sex relationships than in opposite sex relationships because of increased uncertainty events. Planalp, Rutherford, and Honeycutt (1988), for example, found that events that increased uncertainty are reported more frequently in same sex friendships than in opposite sex friendships or romantic relationships.

An alternative explanation for the findings on turning points can be posited based on the nature of opposite sex relationships examined in this study. Baxter's (1987) analysis of opposite sex relationship growth trajectory schemas suggests that romantic relationships that begin as romantic relationships are different than romantic relationships that begin as friendships, with turning points being reported more in those beginning as friendships. The majority of the opposite sex "friendships" included in the current study had romantic overtones (e.g., the partners had dated but did not consider their partner as a "boyfriend," or "lover" yet). Given that the display of physical affection (Wilmont & Baxter, 1984) and the first "date" (Bullis & Baxter, 1986) are the most salient factors that appear to transform opposite sex relationships from platonic to romantic, several of the friendships in this study have romantic overtones. The lack of a turning-point theme, therefore, may be due to the opposite sex relationships in the current study having begun as romantic relationships and not friendships. Because this study did not focus on turning points as a specific issue, future research is needed to examine the role of turning points in opposite sex intercultural relationships (Ting-Toomey, 1989b).

There was one additional difference between the accounts of these opposite sex dyads and the same sex dyads in our earlier study (Sudweeks et al., 1990). The Japanese respondents in this study consistently commented on the display of emotions in their accounts, but display of emotions was not mentioned by the respondents in the earlier study of same sex relationships. While the display of emotions recurred throughout the current interviews, no specific pattern emerged.

In many cases, the North Americans appeared to accommodate to their Japanese partners with respect to the display of emotions (i.e., little display of emotions):

> We usually do not have any touching. He is an American but he has experienced living in Japan. He is a little different from ordinary Americans. (J-2, F, R)

> He's not as expressive as most Americans. He doesn't use a lot of gestures. He touches comparatively less than others. We don't sit so close. (J-5, F, R)

> He shows his feelings through his facial expressions, but he doesn't hug. (J-7, F, F)

> I don't look at his eyes when I talk to him. I don't touch him. We sit rather far apart. (J-11, F, A)

> She does not touch me. (J-12, M, A)

There were reports of the Japanese accommodating to their North American partners, however:

> I often use facial expressions. I look at his eyes for a long time and I usually sit next to him. (J-3, F, R)

> Compared with Japanese couples we touch more often. (J-6, F, R)

There were also comments suggesting that the partners worked out a compromise:

> He hugs me a lot because he is an American. In my view he does not touch me as often as other Americans. (J-10, F, F)

It is important to note that virtually all comments on the display of emotions came from the Japanese respondents. This is consistent with Barnlund's (1975) research. He found that people in the United States engage in approximately twice the amount of touching in opposite sex relationships as do people in Japan. It, therefore, would be expected that, because the Japanese are used to less contact than the North Americans, they would comment on it when it occurred. Barnlund also discovered that there is little difference in touching behavior in same sex relationships in Japan and the United States. This finding may explain why display of emotions did not emerge in the earlier study of same sex dyads.

To conclude, this thematic analysis provided data in supporting the interplay between the context of discovery and the context of verification (Kaplan, 1964). In the context of verification, several themes emerged in the current data that are compatible with previous studies of intercultural relationships (see Gudykunst, 1989, for a summary of this research). In the context of discovery, this analysis not only provided specifics regarding the themes observed in previous interpersonal relationship research (e.g., the content of the themes and how they differ across relationships), the study also uncovered new interpretive themes/subthemes not observed in previous cross-cultural interpersonal relationship studies.

NOTES

1. The respondents for the current study were part of a larger study (Gudykunst, Nishida, & Chua, 1986, 1987; Sodetani & Gudykunst, 1987; Sudweeks et al., 1990). The data base, however, was different. Data for three of the earlier papers were self-report responses to questionnaires, while data for this chapter (and Sudweeks et al., 1990) are from extensive open-ended interviews.

2. The interviews were conducted by Sarah Hall and Hiroko Koike. Toyoko Yoshiyama and Chieko Nabetani assisted in the transcription and translation of the Japanese interviews.

3. The culture from which the respondent comes (e.g., J = Japanese), the dyad number (e.g., 3), sex (e.g., F = female), and type of relationship (e.g., F = friend) are given for each quote.

REFERENCES

Agar, M., & Hobbs, J. R. (1982). Interpreting discourse: Coherence and the analysis of ethnographic interviews. *Discourse Processes, 5,* 1-32.

Altman, I., & Taylor, D. (1973). *Social penetration.* New York: Holt, Rinehart & Winston.

Anataki, C. (1987). Performed and unperformable: A guide to accounts of relationships. In R. Burnett, P. McGhee, & D. Clarke (Eds.), *Accounting for relationships.* London: Methuen.

Argyle, M., & Henderson, M. (1984). The rules of friendship. *Journal of Social and Personal Relationships, 1,* 211-237.

Barnlund, D. (1975). *The public and private self in Japan and the United States.* Tokyo: Simul.

Baxter, L. A. (1987). Cognition and communication in the relationship process. In R. Burnett, R. McGhee, & D. Clarke (Eds.), *Accounting for relationships.* London: Methuen.

Baxter, L. A., & Bullis, C. (1986). Turning points in developing romantic relationships. *Human Communication Research, 12,* 469-493.

Baxter, L. A., & Wilmot, W. W. (1984). "Secret tests": Social strategies for acquiring information about the state of the relationship. *Human Communication Research, 11,* 171-201.

Berger, C. R., & Calabrese, R. (1975). Some explorations in initial interactions and beyond: Toward a developmental theory of interpersonal communication. *Human Communication Research, 1,* 99-112.

Berry, J. W. (1980). Acculturation as varieties of adaptation. In A. Padilla (Ed.), *Acculturation: Theory, models, and new findings.* Boulder, CO: Westview.

Bochner, A. (1978). On taking ourselves seriously: An analysis of some persistent problems and promising directions in interpersonal research. *Human Communication Research, 4,* 179-191.

Bochner, S. (1972). Problems in culture learning. In S. Bochner & P. Wicks (Eds.), *Overseas students in Australia.* Randwick: New South Wales University Press.

Bullis, C., & Baxter, L. A. (1986, February). *A functional typology of turning point events in the development of romantic relationships.* Paper presented at the Western Speech Communication Association Convention.

Burnett, R., McGhee, P., & Clarke,d D. (Eds.). (1987). *Accounting for relationships.* London: Methuen.

Byrne, D. (1971). *The attraction paradigm.* New York: Academic Press.

Duck, S. W. (1977). *The study of acquaintance.* Westmead, England: Saxon House.

Duck, S. W., & Perlman, D. (1985). The thousand islands of personal relationships: A prescriptive analysis for future explorations. In S. Duck & D. Perlman (Eds.), *Understanding personal relationships.* London: Sage.

Fiedler, F. E., Mitchell, T., & Triandis, H. C. (1971). The culture assimilator: An approach to cross-cultural training. *Journal of Applied Psychology, 55,* 95-102.

Geertz, C. (1973). *The interpretation of cultures.* New York: Basic Books.

Gergen, K. J. (1982). *Towards transformation in social knowledge.* New York: Springer-Verlag.

Gudykunst, W. B. (1985). An exploratory comparison between close intracultural and intercultural friendships. *Communication Quarterly, 33,* 270-283.

Gudykunst, W. B. (1989). Culture and the development of interpersonal relationships. In J. Anderson (Ed.), *Communication yearbook 12* (pp. 315-354). Newbury Park, CA: Sage.

Gudykunst, W. B., Chua, E., & Gray, A. (1987). Cultural dissimilarities and uncertainty reduction processes. In M. McLaughlin (Ed.), *Communication yearbook 11.* Newbury Park, CA: Sage.

Gudykunst, W. B., & Hammer, M. R. (1988). The influence of social identity and intimacy of interethnic relationships on uncertainty reduction processes. *Human Communication Research, 14,* 569-601.

Gudykunst, W. B., & Kim, Y. Y. (1984). *Communicating with strangers.* Reading, MA: Addison-Wesley.

Gudykunst, W. B., & Nishida, T. (1986). The influence of cultural variability on perceptions of communication behavior associated with relationship terms. *Human Communication Research, 13,* 147-166.

Gudykunst, W. B., Nishida, T., & Chua, E. (1986). Uncertainty reduction in Japanese-North American dyads. *Communication Research Reports, 3,* 39-46.

Gudykunst, W. B., Nishida, T., & Chua, E. (1987). Perceptions of social penetration in Japanese-North American dyads. *International Journal of Intercultural Relations, 11,* 171-189.

Guthrie, G. M. (1975). A behavioral analysis of culture learning. In R. Brislin, S. Bochner, & W. Lonner (Eds.), *Cross-cultural perspectives on learning.* New York: John Wiley.

Harvey, J. H., Weber, A. L., Galvin, K. S., Huszti, H. C., & Garnick, N. N. (1986). Attribution and the termination of close relationships: A special focus on the account. In R. Gilmour & S. Duck (Eds.), *The emerging field of personal relationships.* Hillsdale, NJ: Lawrence Erlbaum.

Hinde, R. A. (1981). The bases of a science of interpersonal relationships. In S. Duck & R. Gilmour (Eds.), *Personal relationships I: Studying personal relationships.* London: Academic Press.

Kaplan, A. (1964). *The conduct of inquiry.* San Francisco: Chandler.

Kelley, H. H., Berscheid, E., Christensen, A., Hawey, J., Huston, T., Levinger, G., McClintock, E., Peplau, L., & Peterson, D. (1983). *Close relationships.* San Francisco: Freeman.

Kim, Y. Y. (1977). Communication patterns of foreign immigrants in the process of acculturation. *Human Communication Research, 41,* 66-76.

Miell, D. (1987). Remembering relationship development. In R. Burnett, P. McGhee, & D. Clarke (Eds.), *Accounting for relationships.* London: Methuen.

Mikula, G. (1984). Personal relationships: Remarks on the current state of research. *European Journal of Social Psychology, 14,* 339-352.

Miles, M. B. (1983). Qualitative data as attractive nuisance: The problem of analysis. In J. Van Maanen (Ed.), *Qualitative methodology.* Beverly Hills, CA: Sage.

Miller, G. R., & Sunnafrank, M. J. (1982). All is for one but one is not for all. In F. Dance (Ed.), *Human communication theory.* New York: Harper & Row.

Morris, R. T. (1960). *The two way mirror: National status in foreign students' adjustment.* Minneapolis: University of Minnesota Press.

Naiman, N., Frohlich, M., Stern, H., & Todesco, A. (1978). *The good language learner.* Toronto: Ontario Institute for Studies in Education.

Owen, W. F. (1984). Interpretive themes in relational communication. *Quarterly Journal of Speech, 70,* 274-287.

Parlee, M. B. (1979, October). The friendship bond. *Psychology Today,* pp. 42-54.

Planalp, S., Rutherford, D., & Honeycutt, J. (1988). Events that increase uncertainty in personal relationships II. *Human Communication Research, 14,* 516-547.

Rawlins, W. K. (1983). Negotiating close friendship: The dialectic of conjunctive freedoms. *Human Communication Research, 9,* 255-266.

Rose, S., & Serafica, F. (1986). Keeping and ending casual, close, and best friendships. *Journal of Social and Personal Relationships, 3,* 275-288.

Shotter, J. (1985). Accounting for place and space. *Environment and Planning D: Society and Space, 3,* 447-460.

Sillars, A., Weisberg, J., Burggraf, C., & Wilson, E. (1987). Content themes in marital conversations. *Human Communication Research, 13,* 495-528.

Sodetani, L. L., & Gudykunst, W. B. (1987). The effects of surprising events on intercultural relationships. *Communication Research Reports, 4*(2), 1-6.

Spradley, J. P. (1979). *The ethnographic interview.* New York: Holt, Rinehart & Winston.

Sudweeks, S., Gudykunst, W. B., Ting-Toomey, S., & Nishida, T. (1990). Developmental themes in Japanese-North American interpersonal relationships. *International Journal of Intercultural Relations, 14,* 207-233.

Ting-Toomey, S. (1986a). Japanese communication patterns: Insider versus the outsider perspective. *World Communication, 15,* 113-126.

Ting-Toomey, S. (1986b). Interpersonal ties in intergroup communication. In W. Gudykunst (Ed.), *Intergroup communication.* London: Edward Arnold.

Ting-Toomey, S. (1989a). Identity and interpersonal bonding. In M. Asante & W. Gudykunst (Eds.), *Handbook of international and intercultural communication.* Newbury Park, CA: Sage.

Ting-Toomey, S. (1989b). Culture and interpersonal relationship development: Some conceptual issues. In J. Anderson (Ed.), *Communication yearbook 12* (pp. 371-382). Newbury Park, CA: Sage.

Weber, A. L., Harvey, J. H., & Stanley, M. A. (1987). The nature and motivations of accounts for failed relationships. In R. Burnett, P. McGhee, & D. Clarke (Eds.), *Accounting for relationships.* London: Methuen.

Wilder, D. A. (1986). Social categorization. In L. Berkowitz (Ed.), *Advances in experimental social psychology* (Vol. 19). New York: Academic Press.

Wilmot, W., & Baxter, L. A. (1984, February). *Defining relationships: The interplay of cognitive schemata and communication.* Paper presented at the Western Speech Communication Association Convention.

14

Intercultural Communication Competence

A Systems-Theoretic View

YOUNG YUN KIM • *University of Oklahoma*

Individuals in intercultural encounters must meet the challenges of divergent and unfamiliar cultural habits and identities to achieve successful communication outcomes. This chapter explores the concept of intercultural communication competence, defined as the overall internal capability of an individual to manage key challenging features of intercultural communication: namely, cultural differences and unfamiliarity, intergroup posture, and the accompanying experience of stress. Grounded in systems-theoretic principles, intercultural communication competence is explained not as communication competence in dealing with a specific culture but as the cognitive, affective, and operational adaptability of an individual's internal system in all intercultural communication contexts.

In today's world of unprecedented movement and contact across the boundaries of human communities, intercultural encounters come in many forms and circumstances. Individuals with differing cultural backgrounds come together in varying degrees of formality, involvement, and intimacy. From encounters of national leaders, business men and women, students on college campuses, to immigrants and refugees, each intercultural encounter presents the interactants with a unique set of constraints. As no two cultures and no two individuals are quite alike, the cultural difference and incompatibility that the interactants bring to specific encounters add complexity to their communication experiences.

Correspondingly, academic attention among social scientists continues to give prominence to issues of cultural differences and intercultural communication. The age-old phenomena of intercultural interface of individuals continue to present researchers with special challenges and promises in their individual and collective pursuits to explain

AUTHOR'S NOTE: A preliminary discussion of some of the ideas presented in this chapter appeared in a paper that was coauthored with Brent D. Ruben and presented at the annual conference of the Speech Communication Association (San Francisco, November 1989). I gratefully acknowledge the important insights that Ruben provided in the initial development of her thinking on this topic.

human behavior beyond their own cultural milieu. Many studies have been carried out in various parts of the world exploring and comparing a variety of cultural institutions, values, worldviews, ideologies, languages, cognitions, and verbal and nonverbal behaviors (see Gudykunst & Ting-Toomey, 1989; Munroe & Munroe, 1980; Segall, Dasen, Berry, & Poortinga, 1990).

Identifying cultural differences, indeed, has been the focal research interest among many intercultural communication researchers, closely following the research traditions of cultural anthropology, cross-cultural psychology, and sociolinguistics. The majority of the concepts presented in this volume demonstrate the predominant attention to cultural and cross-cultural analyses of patterns of uncertainty reduction, self-disclosure, nicknaming practices, relational stability, and relational conflict. Ultimately, cultural and cross-cultural studies of communication-related phenomena such as these would serve the ends of providing systematic insights into the interfaces of specific cultural elements and of suggesting ways to help maximize successful communication across cultures.

More directly relevant to these research goals is the investigation of the phenomenon of *intercultural communication competence* (or, similarly, *intercultural effectiveness, intercultural skills,* or *cultural competence*). Intercultural communication competence (ICC) has been extensively investigated with an implicit or explicit goal of improving the quality of face-to-face communication between cultural strangers. This line of research continues to gain prominence, as manifested in the number of relevant publications during the past two decades, including the recent issue of the *International Journal of Intercultural Relations* (Martin, 1989) that was exclusively devoted to the topic.

By far the most frequent goal of ICC research has been the identification of variables that could be used as "predictors" of effective intercultural performance. For example, a widely cited study of Hammer, Gudykunst, and Wiseman (1978) attempted to explain intercultural adjustment of sojourners from a pool of variables derived from reviewing prior studies, which were then rated by interculturally experienced subjects on the importance of the variables in facilitating effective functioning in the cultures to which they had been exposed. Factor-analytic methods were used to identify three interpretable factors: (a) the ability to deal with psychological stress, (b) the ability to communicate effectively, and (c) the ability to establish interpersonal relationships. Of the three factors, the ability to communicate effectively (which corresponds to this discussion of ICC) included the abilities to interact with a stranger, to deal with communication misunderstandings between oneself and others, and to deal effectively with different communication styles.

Other models of ICC have been presented based on inductive, database approaches similar to the approach employed by Hammer and his colleagues (e.g., Dinges & Lieberman, 1989). Such efforts have produced a variety of models of ICC in which lists of specific abilities or attributes of the communicator are included as variables that correspond with, contribute to, and constitute the domain of ICC. Across the existing models, a considerable amount of divergence and inconsistency exists, as repeatedly pointed out by reviewers including Dinges (1983), Hammer (1989), Kealey and Ruben (1983), Ruben (1989), and Spitzberg (1989). Although few disagreements exist among researchers on the potential theoretic and pragmatic significance of ICC, disagreements persist as to what it means, where to look for it, how to explain it theoretically, and how to assess it empirically. In many cases, researchers use the same terms to refer to different phenomena and, sometimes, different terms for the same phenomena. When researchers do agree on both the phenomenon and the term representing the phenomenon, they operationalize the terms differently—adding to the confusion. As Spitzberg (1989) observes, the scholarly effort in this area has shown tendencies not to be cumulative and to lack efforts to integrate research and theory across studies and perspectives.

In this regard, this chapter is an attempt to help clarify some of the ambiguities and inconsistencies observed in the current approaches to conceptualizing ICC. Based on a systems-theoretic perspective, it lays the groundwork for developing an alternative approach to ICC that allows consolidation of some of the divergent views. Systems theory—specifically general systems theory—is unique in its characteristic values in relation to the current discussion of ICC in that it is domain free (or content free). It is useful for investigating the isomorphy of concepts, laws, and models in various fields, minimizing the duplication of theoretical efforts in different fields, and aiding communication activities among scientists with specialized interests (see Bertalanffy, 1975; Ruben, 1975). Because the theory is not tied to a specific physical or social phenomenon, it best serves as a metatheory, or a perspective, based on which domain-specific theories may be developed. As such, the current application of the systems-theoretic perspective to ICC does not seek to develop a single theory designed to replace all existing models but seeks to ground the concept in its most basic and general level.

CONCEPTUAL GROUNDING

The systems perspective emphasizes the dynamic, interactive nature of the communication process between two or more individuals. The relationship between the individual communication system and the multiperson (including two-person) communication system is multidirectional and multilateral in causality. Like the relationship of the mind and the reality it experiences, the relationship between the person and the environment is viewed as mutually affecting and being affected by the other. Everything involved in a given encounter, including the conditions of the social context in which the encounter takes place, codetermines the communication outcomes. This means that no one element in a multiperson communication system can be singled out as being solely responsible for the outcomes. Each person has a reality of his or her own, with its own tokens of significance with which the individual comes to organize new experiences.

Competence Versus Successful Outcome

From this systems principle of multilateral causality, the commonly accepted views that regard ICC as identical or exchangeable in meaning with successful interaction outcome (such as effectiveness and appropriateness) presents a possible problem of conceptual validity (e.g., Imahori & Lanigan, 1989). Addressing this issue is crucial to any attempt to solidify the concept of ICC, particularly in light of the fact that implicit assumptions in equating competence with successful interaction outcome have not been closely examined in the past.

One of the most elaborate presentations of the correspondence between competence and successful interaction outcome has been made by Spitzberg and Cupach (1984) and Spitzberg (1988, 1989). In this view, *communication competence* means "evaluative impression of communication quality," or judgments of the decoder's communication competence on the bases of perceived effectiveness and appropriateness. This outcome-oriented conceptualization of communication competence, however, does not take into account the fact that different decoders may assess the same person's competence differently and that the same person may be evaluated differently by a same decoder in different situations. As noted earlier, a given individual's performance is affected not only by his or her own communicative abilities but also by many external factors operating in a given communication context—such as the biases in the decoder's perception that are likely to be influenced by the level of his or her own level of competence. The decoder's perception should be further affected by the nature of the relationship and the interaction goal as well as the degree of incompatibility of normative cultural expectations about what is effective and appropriate communication behavior.

Accordingly, conceptualizing ICC as identical to or exchangeable with performance outcomes—subjective or objective—tends to blur the principle of multilateral causality in the interpersonal communication system. Although a given individual's competence should clearly facilitate successful outcomes, it cannot necessarily produce them. To equate ICC with successful interaction outcome—whichever indicators may be employed—allows the conceptual domain of ICC to "float" and be confounded by contextual and relational conditions, which, therefore, cannot contribute to developing a definition of ICC that is consistent across varied types and situations of intercultural encounter.

Comparatively, the current systems-theoretic view suggests that ICC must be conceptually separated from communication outcomes. It emphasizes that ICC should be located *within* a person as his or her overall *capacity* or *capability* to facilitate the communication process between people from differing cultural backgrounds and to contribute to successful interaction outcomes. Here, ICC is considered a necessary, but not sufficient, condition for achieving success in intercultural encounters—just as a highly competent driver may not always be able to prevent accidents due to factors external to the driver (such as hazardous road conditions or serious mistakes made by other incompetent drivers).

Cultural Versus Intercultural Communication Competence

Another source of divergence observed in current approaches to ICC is the "mixing" of cultural (or culture-specific) communication competence (CCC) in conceptualizing ICC. Many ICC models have been derived from the empirical data obtained from a specific cultural context for the purpose of predicting "overseas success' of temporary sojourners such as Peace Corps volunteers, navy personnel, and technical advisers (see Furnham & Bochner, 1986; Kealey & Ruben, 1983). Such studies and the resultant conceptualizations of ICC parallel those in the culture-specific approaches common in cultural anthropology, cross-cultural psychology, and sociolinguistics. Field studies in these areas have provided extensive knowledge of the cultural patterns characteristic of different societies. Notably, cultural anthropological studies have provided ample ethnographic insights into implicit communication patterns in varied cultures. Hall (1976), for example, derived an analytic concept, "contexting," on which he compared various cultural communication systems along a continuum of high context and low context. Similarly, sociolinguistic ethnographers have described how people use the linguistic means specific to their speech community to communicate (see Knapp & Knapp-Potthoff, 1987). Among cross-cultural psychologists, Triandis (1972) has provided extensive data on various "subjective cultures" and has presented an analytic framework that identifies the "essentials" of cultural elements, including patterns of dress, child rearing, decision making, language, philosophy, and aesthetics (Triandis, 1983).

The knowledge generated from the cultural studies provides useful insights into improving communication competence in dealing with specific cultural groups. To enhance the chances of successful communication and functioning in the United States, for example, college students from China must equip themselves with abilities to communicate with individuals in the United States. To be successful in the Japanese market, U.S. business men and women must equip themselves with abilities to communicate with their Japanese counterparts. Based on such culture-specific goals of individuals, training programs have been developed to enhance the individual's cultural communication competence, utilizing such culture-specific methods as "intercultural sensitizer" or "culture assimilator" (see Albert, 1983; Triandis, 1973).

What is important for this exploration of ICC, however, is that intercultural competence and cultural competence must be clearly distinguished as separate conceptual domains, even though both operate together in any given intercultural encounter. While the content of ICC clearly varies from culture to culture, the content of ICC should remain constant across all intercultural situations regardless of the specific cultures involved.

From this viewpoint, some of the variables included in the existing lists of ICC indicators (or factors) are questionable in their conceptual validity. We may, for instance, question the validity of "self-disclosure" as a crucial element of ICC that is universally applicable in all intercultural encounters. Research has shown that high-context and low-context cultures do differ in self-disclosure behavior (and related information seeking behavior) in initial interactions and that, even within a cultural group, individuals vary their self-disclosure behavior depending on whether their interaction partners are from within or outside their own culture (e.g., Gudykunst, 1986; Hall, 1976). Other ICC-related concepts such as "expressiveness" (e.g., Hammer, 1989) may also be subject to a similar evaluation, based on the fact that many of the "high-context" cultures emphasize formalized and stylized interaction rituals and discourage unnecessary verbal expressiveness, particularly during initial encounters between strangers.

Similar questions can be raised about the very notion that communication competence is exchangeable with interactants' evaluation of each other's performance (e.g., Spitzberg, 1989; Spitzberg & Cupach, 1984). This assumption may reflect the humanistic-democratic-individualistic value prevalent in the North American and Western European academic subcultures, in which a competent communicator is expected to behave in a way that is satisfactory to all parties involved. This normative interpersonal value may not be a significant factor in intercultural encounters that involve people from cultures where uneven distribution of power and "undemocratic" communication practices may be more readily accepted by individual communicators. Even within the humanistic cultural group, competent interpersonal communication does not always lead to mutual satisfaction, as in the case of parents having to "punish" and discipline their children.

In the current systems perspective, then, ICC must be conceptually distinguished from successful interaction outcomes and from culture-specific communication competence. Instead, ICC must be anchored *within* a person as his or her capacity to manage the varied contexts of the intercultural encounter regardless of the specific cultures involved.

TOWARD A GENERAL THEORY

As we begin to solidify the meaning of ICC by distinguishing it from the commonly accepted definitions, we are able to "ground" the concept in its most basic, generic, and value-neutral level. Having proposed distinctions between what is and what is not within the domain of ICC, an attempt is made next to explore the key dimensions of ICC itself. Specifically, the nature of ICC is viewed in terms of the key challenges that individuals must manage in all intercultural encounters in varying degrees: namely, cultural difference/unfamiliarity, intergroup posture, and the accompanying stress.

Key Challenges of Intercultural Encounters

By definition, intercultural communication presents a significant amount of differences between interactants' cultural backgrounds. Relatedly, cultural differences that enter into a given encounter introduce a high degree of *unfamiliarity* with each other's messages and meanings. Such cultural difference and unfamiliarity between culturally dissimilar interactants bring the experiences of anxiety or lack of "attributional confidence" to the interactants (see Gudykunst, 1988c; Lalljee, 1987; Lee & Boster, in this volume). The gap between respective experiential backgrounds limits the interactant's ability to encode and decode messages with fidelity. In cybernetic terms, "The limitations of man's [woman's] communication are determined by the capacity of his [her] intrapersonal network, the selectivity of his [her] receivers, and the skill of his [her] effector organs" (Ruesch, 1951/1968, p. 17). As such, the number of incoming and outgoing message signals, as well as the signals that can be transmitted within each person's intrapersonal system, is limited in many intercultural encounters.

An assumption here, of course, is that individuals who have been socialized within the same culture are more similar and familiar with each other's system of meaning and behavior. Although no two individuals within a culture are alike, they are likely to share many common characteristics that will help them encode and decode the messages. They may differ or even argue about individual preferences, but, by and large, they do understand each other satisfactorily. Comparatively, individuals from different cultures frequently are faced with a potentially greater problem of understanding each other. Recognition of verbal and nonverbal codes and behaviors and interpretation of the hidden assumptions underlying those behaviors are likely to be more difficult.

In addition, intercultural communication is viewed as distinct from (intra)cultural communication in that the psychological posture the interactants take is based on each other's cultural identity (see Collier, 1989; Collier & Thomas, 1988). As articulated extensively in studies of social identity theory, intercultural interactants tend to see themselves, as well as their interaction partners, in light of the respective cultural group membership (see Brewer & Miller, 1984; Gudykunst, 1988a, 1988b; Kim, 1986, 1989b; Ross, 1988; Tajfel, 1974; Turner & Giles, 1981). The differing cultural identities of the interactants psychologically position them into "intergroup" (as compared with "interpersonal") relational orientations, which, in turn, encourages them to perceive each other as a group representative rather than as a unique person.

The interfacing of group identities and intergroup postures creates a "psychological distance" that places each interactant apart from the other. Such intergroup postures often are accompanied by "in-group loyalties" and "out-group discrimination" (see Brewer & Miller, 1984; Brown & Turner, 1981). The "we-they" intergroup orientation influences the intercultural context to be less personalized (or individualized) and more impersonal. Empirical studies have reported the tendencies of intercultural interactants to shy away from requesting intimate information about each other and to accentuate mutual differences in perceiving each other's attributes (e.g., Lee & Boster, in this volume). Ross (1977) and Pettigrew (1979), for example, have labeled such psychological tendencies of intergroup posture as "attribution errors," which is closely related to "ethnocentrism" and other similar concepts such as "prejudice" (see Brewer & Miller, 1984; Milner, 1981).

Intergroup posturing tendencies have been observed to be particularly acute when the interactants come from groups that have a history of dominance/subjugation or a significant discrepancy in the current power status or prestige of the respective groups (see Kim, 1989b), as in the case of encounters between a person from the West Indies and one from Great Britain or between an Anglo American and an American Indian. The actual and perceived power discrepancy between the interactants' group memberships tends to be further accentuated when physically observable cultural differences, or cultural (or ethnic) "markers" (such as dress, physical features, and behavioral idiosyncracy), are strongly present in intercultural encounters.

The above intercultural challenges—cultural difference and intergroup posture—lead to stress. Stress experiences, no matter how minimal, are inherent in the very nature of the intercultural communication context, because stress is a generic process of a human system, which is experienced whenever the capabilities of the system are not adequately equipped to manage the demands of an environment (including an interaction partner). Stress, indeed, is considered to be inherent in intercultural encounters, disturbing the internal equilibrium of the individual system. Accordingly, to be interculturally competent means to be able to manage such stress, regain internal balance, and carry out the communication process in such a way that contributes to successful interaction outcomes. In fact, management of stressful experiences is a precondition for managing the challenges of cultural difference and unfamiliarity as well as intergroup posture. The importance of the ability to manage stress in intercultural encounters is clearly demonstrated in the numerous studies that have examined such stress-related phenomena as "intergroup anxiety" (Barna, 1983; Gudykunst, 1988c; Stephan & Stephan, 1985) and "culture shock" (see Furham & Bochner, 1986; Kim, 1988, 1989a).

Intercultural stress, along with cultural difference and intergroup posture, varies in different encounters. Yet they serve as key challenges to intercultural communication, suggesting that the domain of ICC must refer to that capacity of an individual to manage the challenges. In other words, individuals who hope to carry out effective intercultural inter-actions must be equipped with a set of abilities to be able to understand and deal with the dynamics of cultural difference, intergroup posture, and the inevitable stress experiences.

Adaptability and Intercultural Communication Competence

In this systems perspective, the capacity of an individual to manage intercultural challenges is referred to as *adaptability*-the capability of an individual's internal psychic system to alter its existing attributes and structures to accommodate the demands of the environment. In this view, each person is an "open system" with a fundamental goal of adapting to its environment through its inherent homeostatic drive to maintain an equilibrium, both internally and in relation to the environ-ment (including the other person). When the system is challenged by the environment, its internal equilibrium is temporarily disturbed as the person-environment symmetry is broken. Under such conditions, a person experiences stress and begins the process of regaining internal equilibrium by adapting (acting upon), or adapting to (accommodating), the environmental challenges.

As such, stress and adaptation of a person's internal system are inseparably linked, jointly and interactively facilitating the process of new learning and of developing new capabilities to deal with new challenges (see Burns & Farina, 1984; Kim, 1988). This adaptive, "self-organizing" (Jantsch, 1980) characteristic enables human thought to generate more adaptive alternatives than lower animals are capable of generating. More meanings can be attributed to objects and ideas, and a greater number of connections between meanings arise, achiev-ing a greater complexity and thus a greater number of alternative, cre-ative outcomes for humans to use to manage themselves vis-à-vis the environment.

In intercultural encounters, therefore, adaptability means the indi-vidual's capacity to suspend or modify some of the old cultural ways, to learn and accommodate some of the new cultural ways, and to creatively find ways to manage the dynamics of cultural difference/unfamiliarity, intergroup posture, and the accompanying stress. In-deed, this adaptability—the self-altering and creative capacity—can be placed at the heart of ICC as metacompetence. A person equipped with greater adaptability is likely to be more open to learning different cultural patterns with less intergroup posturing—less ethnocentrism and discrimination toward the other person based on his or her cultural identity. Such an interculturally competent person is likely to be less defensive and rigid in the face of differences, unfamiliarity with differences, and the intergroup posturing of cultural identities.

Further, the individual's adaptability is synonymous with his or her capacity to stretch beyond the internalized cultural parameters and to absorb the attendant psychological "pain" in the process. As Jourard (1974, p. 426), stated, "Temporary disorganization, or even shattering, of one way to experience the world, is brought on by new disclosure." In this regard, facing intercultural challenges is a significant way to achieve psychic growth beyond the conditions that are already known, familiar, and comfortable into those that are unknown, strange, and unsettling.

A variety of specific concepts exist in the psychological and communication literature that are directly or indirectly related to the systems-theoretic concept of adaptability. Such specific concepts, particularly the ones identified below, show promise as indicators of ICC as defined in terms of adaptability. Essentially, these concepts range from cognitive to affective to operational (or behavioral) realms of the individual's internal information processing (see Goss, 1989; Kim, 1988).

The *cognitive dimension* refers to the "sense-making" activities for ascertaining the meaning of the various verbal and nonverbal codes one receives. In this dimension, psychological concepts—such as "cognitive simplicity/complexity" (Applegate & Sypher, 1988; Burleson, 1987; Schroder, Driver, & Streufert, 1975), "narrow/broad category width" (Detweiler, 1986), "cognitive rigidity/flexibility" (Kim, 1988), and "perspective taking" (Pearce & Stamm, 1973)—correspond in meaning to the adaptability of an individual's internal system in intercultural encounters.

The *affective dimension* focuses on the emotional and aesthetic tendencies of an individual's internal system. In psychological terms, it refers to motivational and attitudinal predisposition in responding to external stimuli. In intercultural encounters, in particular, the affective dimension of competence means "readiness" to accommodate intercultural challenges. Existing concepts that are related to this dimension include "adaptive motivation" (Kim, 1988), "affirmative self/other attitude" (Kim, 1988), "ambiguity tolerance" (Ruben & Kealey, 1979), "empathy" (Ruben & Kealey, 1979), "empathic motivation" (Burleson, 1983), and "psychological distance" (Amir, 1969) as well as "intergroup anxiety" (Gudykunst, 1986; Stephan & Stephan, 1985), "ethnocentrism" (Brewer & Campbell, 1976), and "prejudice" (Tajfel, 1974; Weigel & Howes, 1985).

In the *operational* (or behavioral) dimension, an individual's adaptive capacity is defined as his or her abilities to be flexible and resourceful in actually carrying out what he or she is capable of in the cognitive and affective dimensions. Here, concepts such as "behavioral complexity" (Applegate & Sypher, 1988), "behavioral flexibility" (Samter, Burleson & Basden-Murphy, 1989), "communication accommodation" (Gallois, Franklyn-Stokes, Giles, & Coupland, 1988), "message complexity" (Applegate & Sypher, 1988), "person-centered communication" (Applegate & Delia, 1980), "interpersonal management" (Applegate & Leichty, 1984), and "interaction involvement" (Cegala, Savage, Brunner, & Conrad, 1982) are potentially relevant to the current conceptualization of the behavioral dimension of ICC. Additional concepts of possible relevance to the behavioral dimension of ICC include "non-judgmental interaction posture," "self-oriented role behavior," and "interaction management" (Olebe & Koester, 1989; Ruben & Kealey, 1979).

Collectively, the cognitive, affective, and behavioral dimensions of adaptive capacity are viewed as constituting the present conceptual domain of ICC. Each of these dimensions refers to a process that is generic to each person's internal communication system, promoting the individual capacity to manage environmental challenges. These dimensions, and the specific manifestations thereof, need to be thoroughly articulated and integrated into a comprehensive theory of ICC that is applicable to all intercultural interfaces.

CONCLUSION

The main objectives of this chapter have been to argue for integrating the divergent approaches to investigating the phenomena of ICC and to propose an alternative, systems-theoretic conceptualization that enables us to view ICC at its most generic, fundamental level. The key ideas discussed so far can be summarized as follows:

(1) The system-theoretic principles of personal and interpersonal communication serve as the metatheoretical ground for investigating the nature of ICC in its most basic and generic realm.

(2) ICC must not be equated with interaction outcomes such as actual or perceived success, effectiveness, or appropriateness. Instead, ICC must be viewed as located within the person as his or her capability to communicate with individuals from other cultures.

(3) ICC must not be equated with cultural (or culture-specific) communication competence. Instead, ICC and CCC must be viewed as two concepts that are separate in meaning but that operate simultaneously in a given intercultural encounter, contributing to its successful outcome.

(4) The prerequisite to theorizing ICC that is generic to all intercultural situations is an identification of those challenges that are characteristically intercultural (and not cultural).

(5) Key intercultural challenges can be identified as cultural differences/unfamiliarities, intergroup posture, and the accompanying stress experience.

(6) The interculturalness of different intercultural encounters varies in degree based on the magnitude of cultural differences/unfamiliarity, intergroup posture, and stress operating in the respective contexts.

(7) The adaptability of an individual's internal system is viewed as the core of ICC, which is manifested in specific cognitive, affective, and operational abilities of the person.

On the whole, this view emphasizes that individuals differ in their internal adaptive capacity to deal with challenging intercultural situations and that the concept of ICC should refer to that internal capacity and not to the consequences of interaction. In this view, *adaptive capacity* means the capacity to self-reorganize by being open, flexible, resilient, and creative—and not being closed, rigid, intolerant, and habitual. This capacity, together with culture-specific knowledge and skills, should enable a person to approach each intercultural encounter with the psychological posture of an interested learner and a talented negotiator of divergent identities and to strive for the communication outcomes that are as effective as possible under a given set of relational and situational constraints.

In reality, there are those who have achieved impressive intercultural adaptability as well as those who seriously lack this internal capacity. In the end, the critical difference between these two groups may well be the willingness (or lack of willingness) to *go through* the challenges and to creatively restructure oneself as situations demand. After all, "successful communication with self and with others implies correction by others as well as self-correction" (Ruesch, 1951/1968, p. 18).

REFERENCES

Albert, R. (1983). The intercultural sensitizer or culture assimilator: A cognitive approach. In D. Landis & R. Brislin (Eds.), *Handbook of intercultural training: Vol. 2. Issues in training methodology* (pp. 186-217). New York: Pergamon.

Amir, Y. (1969). Contact hypothesis in ethnic relations. *Psychological Bulletin, 7*(5), 319-342.

Applegate, J., & Delia, J. (1980). Person-centered speech, psychological development, and the contexts of language usage. In R. St. Clair & H. Giles (Eds.), *The social and psychological contexts of language* (pp. 245-282). Hillsdale, NJ: Lawrence Erlbaum.

Applegate, J., & Leichty, G. (1984). Managing interpersonal relationships: Social cognitive and strategic determinants of competence. In R. Bostrom (Ed.), *Competence in communication: A multidisciplinary approach* (pp. 33-55). Beverly Hills, CA: Sage.

Applegate, J., & Sypher, H. (1988). A constructivist theory of communication and culture. In Y. Kim & W. Gudykunst (Eds.), *Theories in intercultural communication* (pp. 41-65). Newbury Park, CA: Sage.

Barna, L. (1983). The stress factor in intercultural relations. In D. Landis & R. Brislin (Eds.), *Handbook of intercultural training: Vol. 2. Issues in training methodology* (pp. 19-49). New York: Pergamon.

Bertalanffy, L. (1975). General system theory. In B. Ruben & J. Kim (Ed.), *General systems theory and human communication* (pp. 6-20). Rochelle Park, NJ: Hayden.

Brewer, M., & Campbell, D. (1976). *Ethnocentrism and intergroup attitudes.* New York: John Wiley.

Brewer, M., & Miller, N. (1984). Beyond the contact hypothesis: Theoretical perspectives on desegregation. In N. Miller & M. Brewer (Eds.), *Groups in contact: The psychology of desegregation* (pp. 281-302). New York: Academic Press.

Brown, R., & Turner, J. (1981). Interpersonal and intergroup behavior. In J. Turner & H. Giles (Eds.), *Intergroup behavior* (pp. 33-65). Chicago: University of Chicago Press.

Burleson, B. (1983). Social cognition, empathic motivation, and adults' comforting strategies. *Human Communication Research, 10,* 295-304.

Burleson, B. (1987). Cognitive complexity. In J. McCroskey & J. Delia (Eds.), *Personal and interpersonal communication* (pp. 305-349). Beverly Hills, CA: Sage.

Burns, G., & Farina, A. (1984). Social competence and adjustment. *Journal of Social and Personal Relationships, 1,* 99-113.

Cegala, D., Savage, G., Brunner, C., & Conrad, A. (1982). An elaboration of the meaning of interaction involvement: Toward the development of a theoretical concept. *Communication Monographs, 49,* 229-248.

Collier, M. (1989). Cultural and intercultural communication competence: Current approaches and directions for future research. *International Journal of Intercultural Relations, 13*(3), 287-302.

Collier, M., & Thomas, M. (1988). Cultural identity: An interpretive perspective. In Y. Kim & W. Gudykunst (Eds.), *Theories in intercultural communication* (pp. 99-120). Newbury Park, CA: Sage.

Detweiler, R. (1986). Categorization, attribution and intergroup communication. In W. Gudykunst (Ed.), *Intergroup communication* (pp. 62-73). London: Edward Arnold.

Dinges, N. (1983). Intercultural competence. In D. Landis & R. Brislin (Eds.), *Handbook of intercultural training: Vol. 1. Issues in theory and design* (pp. 176-202). New York: Pergamon.

Dinges, N., & Lieberman, D. (1989). Intercultural communication competence: Coping with stressful work situations. *International Journal of Intercultural Relations, 13*(3), 371-386.

Furnham, A., & Bochner, S. (1986). *Culture shock: Psychological reactions to unfamiliar environments.* London: Methuen.

Gallois, C., Franklyn-Stokes, A., Giles, H., & Coupland, N. (1988). Communication accommodation in intercultural communication. In Y. Kim & W. Gudykunst (Eds.), *Theories in intercultural communication* (pp. 157-185). Newbury Park, CA: Sage.

Goss, B. (1989). *The psychology of human communication.* Prospect Heights, IL: Waveland.

Gudykunst, W. (1986). Ethnicity, types of relationship, and intraethnic and interethnic uncertainty reduction. In Y. Kim (Ed.), *Interethnic communication* (pp. 201-224). Newbury Park, CA: Sage.

Gudykunst, W. (Ed.). (1988a). *Language and ethnic identity.* Clevedon, England: Multilingual Matters.

Gudykunst, W. (Eds.). (1988b). *Intergroup communication* London: Edward Arnold.

Gudykunst, W. (1988c). Uncertainty and anxiety. In Y. Kim & W. Gudykunst (Eds.), *Theories in intercultural communication* (pp. 123-156). Newbury Park, CA: Sage.

Gudykunst, W., & Ting-Toomey, S. (1989). *Culture and interpersonal communication.* Newbury Park, CA: Sage.

Hall, E. (1976). *Beyond culture.* Garden City, NY: Anchor/Doubleday.

Hammer, M. (1989). Intercultural communication competence. In M. Asante & W. Gudykunst (Eds.), *Handbook of international and intercultural communication* (2nd ed., pp. 247-260). Newbury Park, CA: Sage.

Hammer, M., Gudykunst, W., & Wiseman, R. (1978). Dimensions of intercultural effectiveness: An exploratory study. *International Journal of Intercultural Relationships, 2,* 382-392.

Imahori, T., & Lanigan, M. (1989). Relational model of intercultural communication competence. *International Journal of Intercultural Relations, 13*(3), 269-286.

Jantsch, E. (1980). *The self-organizing universe: Scientific and human implications of the emerging paradigm of evolution.* New York: Pergamon.

Jourard, S. (1974). Growing awareness and the awareness of growth. In B. Patton & K. Griffin (Eds.), *Interpersonal communication* (pp. 456-465). New York: Harper & Row.

Kealey, D., & Ruben, B. (1983). Cross-cultural personnel selection criteria, issues, and methods. In D. Landis & R. Brislin (Eds.), *Handbook of intercultural training: Vol. 1. Issues in theory and design* (pp. 155-175). New York: Pergamon.

Kim, Y. (1986). (Ed.). *Interethnic communication.* Newbury Park, CA: Sage.

Kim, Y. (1988). *Communication and cross-cultural adaptation: An integrative theory.* Clevedon, England: Multilingual Matters.

Kim, Y. (1989a). Intercultural adaptation. In M. Asante & W. Gudykunst (Eds.), *Handbook of international and intercultural communication* (pp. 275-299). Newbury Park, CA: Sage.

Kim, Y. (1989b). Explaining interethnic conflict. In J. Gittler (Ed.), *The annual review of conflict knowledge and conflict resolution* (Vol. 1, pp. 101-125). New York: Garland.

Knapp, K., & Knapp-Potthoff, A. (1987). Instead of an introduction: Conceptual issues in analyzing intercultural communication. In K. Knapp, W. Enninger, & A. Knapp-Potthoff (Eds.), *Analyzing intercultural communication* (pp. 1-13). New York: Mouton de Gruyter.

Lalljee, M. (1987). Attribution theory and intercultural communication. In K. Knapp, W. Enninger, & A. Knapp-Potthoff (Eds.), *Analyzing intercultural communication* (pp. 37-49). New York: Mouton de Gruyter.

Martin, J. (Ed.). (1989). Intercultural communication competence [Special issue]. *International Journal of Intercultural Relations, 13*(3).

Martin, J., & Hammer, M. (1989). Behavioral categories of intercultural communication competence: Everyday communicators' perceptions. *International Journal of Intercultural Relations, 13*(3), 303-332.

Miller, N., & Brewer, M. (1984). The social psychology of desegregation: An introduction. In N. Miller & M. Brewer (Eds.), *Groups in contact: The psychology of desegregation* (pp. 1-27). New York: Academic Press.

Milner, D. (1981). Racial prejudice. In J. Turner & H. Giles (Eds.), *Intergroup behavior* (pp. 102-143). Chicago: University of Chicago Press.

Munroe, R., & Munroe, R. (1980). Perspectives suggested by anthropological data. In H. Triandis & W. Lambert (Eds.), *Handook of cross-cultural psychology* (pp. 253-317). Boston: Allyn & Bacon.

Olebe, M., & Koester, J. (1989). Exploring the cross-cultural equivalence of the behavioral assessment scale for intercultural communication. *International Journal of Intercultural Relations, 12,* 233-246.

Pearce, B., & Stamm, K. (1973). Communication behavior and coorientation relation. In P. Clarke (Ed.), *New models for mass communication research* (pp. 177-203). Beverly Hills, CA: Sage.

Pettigrew, T. (1979). The ultimate attribution error: Extending Allport's cognitive analysis of prejudice. *Personality and Social Psychology Bulletin, 5,* 461-476.

Ross, E. (1977). The intuitive psychologist and his shortcomings: Distortions in the attribution process. In L. Berkowitz (Ed.), *Advances in experimental social psychology* (Vol. 10). New York: Academic Press.

Ross, E. (1988). *Interethnic communication.* Athens: University of Georgia Press.

Ruben, B. (1975). Intrapersonal, interpersonal, and mass communication processes in individual and multi-person systems. In B. Ruben & J. Kim (Eds.), *General systems theory and human communication* (pp. 164-190). Rochelle Park, NJ: Hayden.

Ruben, B. (1989). The study of cross-cultural competence: Traditions and contemporary issues. *International Journal of Intercultural Relations, 13*(3), 229-240.

Ruben, B., & Kealey, D. (1979). Behavioral assessment of communication competency and the prediction of cross-cultural adaptation. *International Journal of Intercultural Relations, 3,* 15-48.

Ruesch, J. (1968). Values, communication, and culture: An introduction. In J. Ruesch & G. Bateson, *Communication: The social matrix of psychiatry* (pp. 1-20). New York: Norton. (Original work published 1951)

Samter, W., Burleson, B., & Basden-Murphy, L. (1989). Behavioral complexity is in the eye of the beholder: Effects of cognitive complexity and message complexity on impressions of the source of comforting message. *Human Communication Research, 15*(4), 612-629.

Schroder, H., Driver, M., & Streufert, S. (1975). Intrapersonal organization. In B. Ruben & J. Kim (Eds.), *General systems theory and human communication* (pp. 96-113). Rochelle Park, NJ: Hayden.

Segall, M., Dasen, P., Berry, J., & Poortinga, Y. (1990). *Human behavior in global perspective.* New York: Pergamon.

Spitzberg, B. (1988). Communication competence: Measures of perceived effectiveness. In C. Tardy (Ed.), *A handbook for the study of human communication* (pp. 67-105). Norwood, NJ: Ablex.

Spitzberg, B. (1989). Issues in the development of a theory of interpersonal competence in the intercultural context. *International Journal of Intercultural Relations, 13*(3), 241-269.

Spitzberg, B., & Cupach, W. (1984). *Interpersonal communication competence.* Beverly Hills, CA: Sage.

Stephan, W., & Stephan, C. (1985). Intergroup anxiety. *Journal of Social Issues, 41*(3), 157-175.

Tajfel, H. (1974). Social identity and intergroup behavior. *Social Science Information, 13,* 65-93.

Triandis, H. (1972). *The analysis of subjective culture.* New York: John Wiley.

Triandis, H. (1973). Culture training, cognitive complexity, and interpersonal attitudes. In D. Hoopes (Ed.), *Readings in intercultural communication (Vol. 2, pp. 55-67). Pittsburgh: Regional Council for International Education.*

Triandis, H. (1983). Essentials of studying cultures. In D. Landis & R. Brislin (Eds.), *Handbook of intercultural training: Vol. 1. Issues in theory and design* (pp. 203-223). New York: Pergamon.

Turner, J., & Giles, H. (1981). *Intergroup behavior.* Chicago: University of Chicago Press.

Weigel, R., & Howes, P. (1985). Conceptions of racial prejudice: Symbolic racism reconsidered. *Journal of Social Issues, 4*(3), 117-138.

Index

About the Editors

FELIPE KORZENNY is Professor of Communication and Coordinator of Graduate Studies, San Francisco State University. He has served as Chairperson of the Intercultural and Development Communication Division of the International Communication Association. His publications have appeared in many major communication journals. His current work includes a book on Mexican Americans and the mass media as well as research articles and projects on communication discrimination, communication, and drug use across cultures and effects of international news. His most recent book is *Communicating for Peace: Diplomacy and Negotiation Across Cultures* (coedited with Stella Ting-Toomey; Sage, 1989).

STELLA TING-TOOMEY is Associate Professor of Speech Communication at California State University, Fullerton. Her research focuses on identity negotiation, face work, and conflict styles across cultures. Her most recent books include *Culture and Interpersonal Communication* (with W. Gudykunst; Sage, 1988) and *Language, Communication, and Culture: Current Directions* and *Communicating for Peace: Diplomacy and Negotiation Across Cultures* (both coedited with F. Korzenny; Sage, 1988, 1989). Her work has appeared in *American Behavioral Scientist, Communication Monographs, Human Communication Research,* and *International Journal of Intercultural Relations,* among others. She has served as the Chairperson of the Speech Communication Association's International and Intercultural Communication Division. She is currently working on a textbook in intercultural communication patterns.

About the Authors

JOHN ADAMOPOULOS was awarded the Ph.D. degree in social psychology from the University of Illinois and is now Associate Professor of Psychology at Indiana University at South Bend. He was born in Greece but received most of his education in the United States. His research has focused on the structure and evolution of interpersonal behavior across cultures and historical periods. He was recently appointed editor of the *Cross-Cultural Psychology Bulletin.*

ANNA BANKS received her Ph.D. in 1989 from the University of Southern California and is currently Assistant Professor of Communication at the University of Idaho. Her research focuses on cultural and cross-cultural issues in visual communication. She is currently examining the impact of culture on the editing of news photographs in media from Latin America, Europe, and the United States.

STEPHEN P. BANKS received his Ph.D. in 1987 from the University of Southern California and is currently Assistant Professor of Communication at the University of Idaho. His research pursues issues in ethnolinguistic identity, the relation of discourse and social structure in work organizations, and discourse and conversational analysis. He recently coedited *Foundations of Organizational Communication: A Reader.*

SHOSHANA BLUM-KULKA is Associate Professor in the Departments of Communication and Education at Hebrew University. She holds a Ph.D. in linguistics from Hebrew University. She has published extensively in the areas of cross-cultural pragmatics, interlanguage pragmatics, and translation theory. Her most recent publication is *Cross-Cultural Pragmatics: Requests and Apologies* (with members of the Speech Act Realization Project, coedited with Juliane House and Gabriele Kasper; Ablex, 1989). Currently, she is engaged in a cross-cultural study of family discourse focusing on Israeli, American, and American Israeli immigrants' interactional styles at the dinner table.

FRANKLIN J. BOSTER received his Ph.D. at Michigan State University in 1978 and is currently Associate Professor in the Department of Communication at Michigan State University. His research interests center on social influence and group dynamics.

HUI-CHING CHANG received her Bachelor of Law at National Taiwan University and a master's degree at the University of Illinois. She was a doctoral candidate at the Department of Speech Communication, University of Illinois at Urbana-Champaign and is currently at the University of Louisville. Her research interests include cross-cultural interpersonal communication, comparative philosophy, ethnography, and critical studies in anthropology. Her work on Chinese philosophy and Western communication has appeared in the *International and Intercultural Communication Annual*.

MARY JANE COLLIER is Associate Professor of Speech Communication at Oregon State University. Her research focuses on issues in communication theory and cultural and ethnic identity and on the study of conduct and competence between and among ethnic and culture groups. Her work has appeared in *Communication Yearbook, International Journal of Intercultural Relations, Communication Quarterly,* and *Howard Journal of Communications*. Currently, she is collaborating on a book about African American ethnic identity.

GE GAO is Assistant Professor of Communication Studies at San Jose State University. Her research interests are in cross-cultural interpersonal relationship development and intercultural adaptation and communication. Her publications have appeared in the *International Journal of Intercultural Relations, Journal of Cross-Cultural Psychology, Communication Research Reports,* and *World Communication,* among others.

WILLIAM B. GUDYKUNST is Professor of Speech Communication at California State University, Fullerton. Currently, he is generating a theory to explain interpersonal and intergroup communication that will be included in *Strangeness and Similarity: A Theory of Interpersonal and Intergroup Communication* (Sage Publications, forthcoming). He applied the theory in *Bridging Differences: Communicating Effectively with Strangers* (Sage, 1991). He recently coedited *Theories in Intercultural Communication* (with Young Yun Kim; Sage, 1988) and the *Handbook of International and Intercultural Communication* (with Molefi Kete Asante; Sage, 1989) and coauthored *Culture and Interpersonal Communication* (with Stella Ting-Toomey; Sage, 1988).

G. RICHARD HOLT received his Ph.D. in the Department of Speech Communication, University of Illinois at Urbana-Champaign. He is Assistant Professor in the Department of Communication, University of Louisville. His research interests include comparative philosophy, Chinese philosophy, ethnography, organizational/small group communication, and critical studies in anthropology. His work has appeared in the *International and Intercultural Communication Annual, Western Journal of Speech Communication,* and *Mediation Quarterly.*

TAMAR KATRIEL is Senior Lecturer at the School of Education, University of Haifa. She is the author of *Talking Straight: "Dugri" Speech in Israeli Sabra Culture* (Cambridge University Press, 1986) and *Communal Webs: Communication and Culture in Contemporary Israel* (State University of New York Press, forthcoming). She has published in the areas of sociolinguistics, communication, and cultural studies in such journals as *Communication Monographs, The Quarterly Journal of Speech, Language in Society, Anthropological Linguistics,* and others.

HYUN J. KIM received his Ph.D. at Michigan State University in 1989 and is currently Assistant Professor in the Department of Communication at the Chungnam National University, South Korea. He has presented papers on such topics as interpersonal communication and relational development, intercultural communication, and social networks. In 1989, he received the "Top Student Paper" award from the Intercultural Division of the International Communication Association and the "Top Four Papers" award from the Interpersonal Communication and Small Group Interaction Division of the Speech Communication Association.

YOUNG YUN KIM is Professor of Communication at the University of Oklahoma, Norman. She has written *Communicating with Strangers* (with W. Gudykunst; McGraw-Hill) and *Communication and Cross-Cultural Adaptation* (Multilingual Matters). Among her edited books are *Interethnic Communication* (Sage, 1986), *Cross-Cultural Adaptation* (with W. Gudykunst; Sage), and *Theories in Intercultural Communication* (with W. Gudykunst; Sage). She is currently investigating the dynamics of communication within and across domestic ethnic/subcultural groups and the role of an individual's communication competence in generating successful outcomes in such intergroup encounters.

HYUN O. LEE received his Ph.D. at Michigan State University in 1989 and is currently Assistant Professor of Speech Communication at Wake Forest University. He has conducted many cross-cultural comparison studies in various contexts. His recent research project concerns the development of communicative competence in intercultural negotiation and conflict management behaviors.

S. IRENE MATZ received her M.A. at California State University, Fullerton. She is presently the Academic Advisor and Retention Coordinator for the School of Communications at California State University, Fullerton. She also teaches various courses in the Department of Speech Communication at the university. Her travel to Ghana, West Africa, led to researching uncertainty reduction and coauthoring three convention papers. Her research interests focus on intercultural and organizational communication.

JOAN G. MILLER received her Ph.D. in Human Development from the University of Chicago. She is Associate Professor of Developmental Psychology at Yale University. Her research program focuses on cultural influences on the development of moral reasoning and social attribution. She contributed a chapter to *The Cross-Cultural Challenge to Social Psychology* (M. H. Bond, editor; Sage, 1988). Her articles have appeared in *Developmental Psychology, Journal of Personality and Social Psychology,* and *Social Cognition,* among others.

TSUKASA NISHIDA is Associate Professor of Intercultural Relations at Nihon University, Japan. His research interests involve explaining differences and similarities in human relations in Japan and the United States. His recent work in Japan includes *A Study of Intercultural Behavior* (Kobundo, 1986) and *A Manual for International Businessmen* (Segensa, 1989). His research has also appeared in *Human Communication Research, Communication Monographs, Communication Yearbook, International Journal of Intercultural Relations,* and *Journal of Cross-Cultural Psychology.*

JUDITH A. SANDERS received her J.D. at Loyola Law School. She is currently Assistant Professor in the Department of Communication at California State Polytechnic University, Pomona. Her research interests include effectiveness in intercultural communication, instructional communication, and argumentation. In 1990, she received "Top Three" awards from the Instructional Division of the International Communication Association and the Forensics Division of the Western States Communication Association.

SANDRA SUDWEEKS is Instructor at Golden West Community College. She received her M.A. in Intercultural Communication in 1988 at Arizona State University. Her previous experience includes public health programs in Mexico and advising and administering programs for international students. Her current research interests include instructional issues in the multicultural classroom environment.

RICHARD L. WISEMAN received his Ph.D. from the University of Minnesota. He is currently Professor of Speech Communication at California State University, Fullerton. His research interests include intercultural communication effectiveness, interpersonal persuasion, and nonverbal communication. His work has appeared in *Communication Monographs, International Journal of Intercultural Relations,* and *Communication Yearbook,* among others.

MYONG JIN WON-DOORNINK is Research Associate in the Department of Rural Sociology at Washington State University. She has published articles about reciprocity of self-disclosure and television viewing and its effect upon the acculturation of Korean immigrants in the United States. More recently, she has conducted research and published in the area of business negotiation, intercultural communication, and international trade in Pacific Rim nations.

NOTES

NOTES

NOTES

NOTES

NOTES